EPIC STORIES
OF THE
SECOND WORLD WAR

EPIC STORIES
OF THE
SECOND
WORLD WAR

★

WITH A PREFACE BY
GUY RAMSEY

ODHAMS PRESS LIMITED
LONG ACRE, LONDON

First published 1957
Reprinted 1961
Reprinted 1962
Reprinted 1964

Made and printed by offset in The Netherlands by
'Jan de Lange' n.v., Deventer
T.557.RA.

CONTENTS

CONTENTS

PREFACE

IN THE house of heroism there are many mansions. From Sir Philip Sidney and the Unknown Soldier on Zutphen field to that very gallant gentleman, Captain Oates, whose tragically sterile self-sacrifice has become a criterion of courage; from St. Lawrence on his grid to the heart-rending courtesy of St. Francis faced with the cautery of his eyes; from More, jesting with the headsman, to Latimer's unquenchable candle, the history of Man is shot with the stars of fortitude and valour.

There is the courage of action and the courage of endurance. No schoolboy, I suppose, but has been required to pen, laboriously, with examples, an essay comparing and contrasting the merits of "Courage and Fortitude"—invoking, inevitably, the charge of Rupert or the Light Brigade and the irresistible jog-trot advance of the Ironsides or the grim attrition of Flanders. But heroism, like peace, is indivisible; courage and fortitude are but obverse and reverse of the selfsame medal, struck from identical bronze and bearing the legend: For Valour.

In compiling this Anthology of the Heroic I have tried, within the compass of some 100,000 words, to cover as wide a canvas as possible: geographical, historical, and even occupational and temperamental. The *panache* of a Bader, flamboyant and irrepressible, is balanced by the deliberate understatement of a Young; the gregarious gaiety of the Royal Air Force by the isolated agony of a single Agent in the hands of the enemy, broken in body but unbroken in soul; the suffocating terror of undersea war with the icy nerve which can probe the very entrails of a secret weapon.

So many war-books have poured from the presses since 1939 that the task has been less one of selection than, too often, of rejection. None but can criticize the ultimate choice, which must of necessity, exclude something that every reader would himself have regarded as essential.

But Space, no less than Time, must have a stop.

The test I have applied has been threefold. First, catholicity of field; second, universality of type; but, not far behind, has come the actual quality of the record.

> Brave men were living before Agamemnon,
>> And since, exceeding valorous and sage;
> A good deal like him, too, but quite the same none—
>> But then they shone not on the poet's page

wrote Byron a hundred and fifty years ago.

For the very title of the book has imposed upon me its own criterion; this is an anthology of the *epic* —and an epic does not, and cannot, exist until it has been cast in epic form. The poet— even if, as here, he write in prose—is indispensable.

A mere catalogue of citation would, I fear, make for dull reading, blurring with *cliché* and repetition the splendour of action and achievement and turning the heroism of the heroes from an inspiration to a bore. So I have been guided partly by the deed, partly by the doer, partly by the recorder. Only when all three have, as it were, coalesced to produce that epic quality which is at once indefinable but unmistakable and which, transcending the epitome, must achieve the incarnation of the heroic.

This is not to claim that this handful of authors have all written great literature, or even great journalism. The Homeric, the Shakespearian is not only out of fashion—the purple patch is, to-day, an automatic target for the blue pencil!—but it is not to be found. All I can legitimately claim is this: that these are the best examples I have been able to find of modern epic writing.

Those who, like myself, have lived through two world wars, and who, also like myself, regard war as intrinsically evil, may question the wisdom, or even the justification, of compiling a book which, however realistic, tends to glorify war.

In the first place, I would claim, the deeds recorded in this book glorify not war but warriors; however base the setting, the jewels of courage are of the purest water. But, at a deeper level, I would justify such a volume as this on graver grounds. For fifty years, this swift-changing, shifting modern world of ours has been dominated, philosophically, by the doctrine of Relativity, In contradistinction to that prevailing trend, the epic is an Absolute.

The old Absolutes, which were so binding upon our fathers— the Good, the Pure, the Beautiful—we are prone to shrug aside, as Pilate, with a few drops of water, dismissed, in cynicism, despair, or cowardice, the supreme Absolute of Truth. But in our modern, moral quicksand, heroism remains an Absolute which still exerts its appeal and commands its adherence; one which few will controvert. Valour has a validity of its own, transcending its own immediate occasion or existence. When Man defies those dreary gods who are always said to be on the side of the big battalions, a nerve which sceptics and agnostics believe to be useless and obsolete vibrates into sudden and urgent life. For that reason I hold that this record—for all its inevitable emphasis on brutality and destruction, on the slime and grime of modern total war, on the savages and ravages of humanity— is justified.

A professional man of letters is, of all creatures, the most prone to fall into the two perils of *ennui* and disillusion. When, for a national newspaper, I wrote for five years a regular weekly column of literary criticism, I was wont to survey the weekly selection of books with a jaded eye.

Another volume dealing with the barbed-wire fever of the prisoners-of-war? Another record of secret service agents living anonymously in a world of shadows? Another story of frigid Himalayan heights or steamy Amazonian swamps? Another— oh, surely not another—distillation of the stale tea-leaves of R.A.F. slang, Army reticence, Naval meiosis. Partly, of course, my dismay was professional: what could the hapless critic find

9

to say that he had not said a dozen times before? What, indeed, had this new volume to contribute that a hundred predecessors had not already given?

Yet, while collecting and collating this present book, though I found myself sickened by the suffering and outraged by the positive, bestial evil of the elemental environment, I found myself succumbing, as I did as a boy, to the ancient and wholly beneficent spell of the heroic. Each of these heroes seemed, as it were, frozen in the very moment of his most urgent mobility, like the Apollo Belvedere. The men had become gods.

Normally, to a writer, editing is something of a chore. But contrary to my own expectation, the production of this book has been no chore but rather a labour, if not of love, at least of exhilaration and, at times, of exaltation.

As it has brought to me, the editor, who touches so much of life at second-hand, a lifting of the spirit which is the essence of eternal youth, I dare to hope that it may bring something of the same quickening to you, the reader.

Perhaps it is primarily through the heroic that we can touch the immortal.

GUY RAMSEY.

The Last Enemy

by RICHARD HILLARY

Richard Hillary stands revealed in The Last Enemy *as the epitome of the 1930 generation: sceptical, intelligent, individualist, exasperating, charming. He styled himself one of the "long-haired boys"—the cynical, cavalier undergraduates who joined the R.A.F.V.R. while still at the University, not primarily out of political idealism or Christian conscience, but because fighting in the air held more dignity, more adventure, more individuality than combat in any other arm.*

Hillary baled out from a blazing plane into the sea, where he lay for half a day; his skin peeling from him in strips. For some time he was blind—his eyelids had been burned off. The Last Enemy *is—although he would have been appallingly embarrassed had it been said—the record of a Pilgrim's Progress in search of his soul.*

He found it, in an air-raid: wherein heroism, although perhaps not of so exalted a type as Hillary's, was almost universal. This is, I believe, an epic less of the body than the spirit.

. . . **K**EN MACDONALD, Don's brother who had been with "A" Flight at Dyce, had been killed. He had been seen about to bale out of his blazing machine at 1,000 feet; but as he was over a thickly populated area he had climbed in again and crashed the machine in the Thames. . . .

★ ★ ★

Tony Tollemache had crashed in March, night flying. Coming in to land, his Blenheim had turned over and caught fire, throwing him free. His passenger was also thrown free and killed; but under the impression that he was still inside, Tony climbed in again and wandered up and down the flaming machine, looking for him. He had been badly burned on his face, hands, and, above all, legs. For this action he got the Empire Gallantry Medal and nearly a year in hospital. . . .

★   ★   ★

Liverpool Street Station was a dull-grey blur of noise and movement. I managed somehow to get hold of a taxi and make a start across London, but my driver seemed doubtful whether we should be able to go very far. Some machine dropped a flare, and in the sudden brightness before it was put out I saw that the street was empty. What cars there were, were parked along the kerb and deserted.

"I'm afraid we'll be stopped soon, sir," said the taxi-driver. At that moment there was a heavy crump unpleasantly close and glass flew across the street.

"See if you can find a pub and we'll stop there," I shouted.

A few yards farther on he drew in to the kerb and we got out and ran to a door under a dimly-lit sign of "The George and Dragon". Inside there was a welcoming glow of bright lights and beery breaths, and we soon had our faces deep in a couple of mugs of mild and bitter.

In one corner on a circular bench that ran round a stained wooden table sat a private in battle-dress and a girl, the girl drinking Scotch. She had light-brown hair and quite good features. I suppose if one had taken her outside and washed her face under a pump she would have had a rather mousy look, but she would still have been pretty. She was pretty now in spite of the efforts that she had made to improve on nature, had made and continued to make, for every few minutes she would take out a vanity case, pull a face into the mirror, lick her lower lip and dash her lipstick in a petulant streak of scarlet across her mouth. She was also talking very loud and laughing immoderately. I caught the barmaid's eye. She gave me a conspiratorial wink and shook her head knowingly; ah yes, we understood, we two.

But she was wrong: the girl was not drunk, she was very, very frightened, and, I thought, with good reason. For though at the Masonic I had dozed off regularly to the lullaby of the German night offensive, I had never before heard anything like this. The volume of noise shut out all thought, there was no lull, no second in which to breathe and follow carefully the note of an oncoming bomber. It was an orchestra of madmen playing in a cupboard. I thought, "God! what a stupid waste if I were to die now." I wished with all my heart that I was down in a shelter.

"We'd be better off underground to-night, sir, and no mistake." It was my taxi-driver speaking.

"Nonsense," I said. "We couldn't be drinking this down there," and I took a long pull at my beer.

I was pushing the glass across the counter for a refill when we heard it coming. The girl in the corner was still laughing and for the first time I heard her soldier speak. "Shut up!" he said, and the laugh was cut off like the sound track in a movie. Then everyone was diving for the floor. The barmaid (she was of considerable bulk) sank from view with a desperate slowness behind the counter and I flung myself tight up against the other side, my taxi-driver beside me. He still had his glass in his hand and the beer shot across the floor, making a dark stain and setting the sawdust afloat. The soldier too had made for the bar counter and wedged the girl on his inside. One of her shoes had nearly come off. It was an inch from my nose: she had a ladder in her stocking.

My hands were tight-pressed over my ears but the detonation deafened me. The floor rose up and smashed against my face, the swing-door tore off its hinges and crashed over a table, glass splinters flew across the room, and behind the bar every bottle in the place seemed to be breaking. The lights went out but there was no darkness. An orange glow from across the street shone through the wall and threw everything into a strong relief.

I scrambled unsteadily to my feet and was leaning over the

bar to see what had happened to the unfortunate barmaid when a voice said "Anyone hurt?", and there was an A.F.S. man shining a torch. At that everyone began to move, but slowly and reluctantly as though coming out of a dream. The girl stood white and shaken in a corner, her arm about her companion, but she was unhurt and had stopped talking. Only the barmaid failed to get up.

"I think there is someone hurt behind the bar," I said. The fireman nodded and went out, to return almost immediately with two stretcher-bearers who made a cursory inspection and discovered that she had escaped with no more than a severe cut on the head. They got her on to the stretcher and disappeared.

Together with the man in the A.F.S., the taxi-driver and I found our way out into the street. He turned to us almost apologetically. "If you have nothing very urgent on hand," he said, "I wonder if you'd help here for a bit. You see it was the house next to you that was hit and there's someone buried in there."

I turned and looked on a heap of bricks and mortar, wooden beams and doors, and one framed picture, unbroken. It was the first time that I had seen a building newly blasted. Often had I left the flat in the morning and walked up Piccadilly, aware vaguely of the ominously tidy gap between two houses, but further my mind had not gone.

We dug, or rather we pushed, pulled, heaved, and strained, I somewhat ineffectually because of my hands[1]; I don't know for how long, but I suppose for a short enough while. And yet it seemed endless. From time to time I was aware of figures round me: an A.R.P. warden, his face expressionless under a steel helmet; once a soldier swearing savagely in a quiet monotone; and the taxi-driver, his face pouring sweat.

[1]Hillary's hands had been seared in his crash virtually to the bone.

And so we came to the woman. It was her feet that we saw first, and whereas before we had worked doggedly, now we worked with a sort of frenzy, like prospectors at the first glint of gold. She was not quite buried, and through the gap between two beams we could see that she was still alive. We got the child out first. It was passed back carefully and with an odd sort of reverence by the warden, but it was dead. She must have been holding it to her in the bed when the bomb came.

Finally we made a gap wide enough for the bed to be drawn out. The woman who lay there looked middle-aged. She lay on her back and her eyes were closed. Her face, through the dirt and streaked blood, was the face of a thousand working women; her body under the cotton nightdress was heavy. The nightdress was drawn up to her knees and one leg was twisted under her. There was no dignity about that figure.

Around me I heard voices. "Where's the ambulance?" "For Christ's sake don't move her!" "Let her have some air!"

I was at the head of the bed, and looking down into that tired, blood-streaked, work-worn face I had a sense of complete unreality. I took the brandy flask from my hip pocket and held it to her lips. Most of it ran down her chin but a little flowed between those clenched teeth. She opened her eyes and reached out her arms instinctively for the child. Then she started to weep. Quite soundlessly, and with no sobbing, the tears were running down her cheeks when she lifted her eyes to mine.

"Thank you, sir," she said, and took my hand in hers. And then, looking at me again, she said after a pause, "I see they got you too."

Very carefully I screwed the top on to the brandy flask, unscrewed it once and screwed it on again, for I had caught it on the wrong thread. I put the flask into my hip pocket and did up the button. I pulled across the buckle on my great-coat and noticed that I was dripping with sweat. I pulled the cap down over my eyes and walked out into the street.

Someone caught me by the arm, I think it was the soldier

with the girl, and said: "You'd better take some of that brandy yourself. You don't look too good"; but I shook him off. With difficulty I kept my pace to a walk, forcing myself not to run. For I wanted to run, to run anywhere away from that scene, from myself, from the terror that was inside me, the terror of something that was about to happen and which I had not the power to stop.

It started small, small but insistent deep inside of me, sharp as a needle, then welling up uncontrollable, spurting, flowing over, choking me. I was drowning, helpless in a rage that caught and twisted and hurled me on, mouthing in a blind unthinking frenzy. I heard myself cursing, the words pouring out, shrill, meaningless, and as my mind cleared a little I knew that it was the woman I cursed. Yes, the woman that I reviled, hating her that she should die like that for me to see, loathing that silly bloody twisted face that had said those words: "I see they got you too." That she should have spoken to me, why, oh Christ, to me? Could she not have died the next night, ten minutes later, or in the next street? Could she not have died without speaking, without raising those cow eyes to mine?

"I see they got you too." All humanity had been in those few words, and I had cursed her. Slowly the frenzy died in me, the rage oozed out of me, leaving me cold, shivering, and bitterly ashamed. I had cursed her, cursed her, I realized as I grew calmer, for she had been the one thing that my rage surging uncontrollably had had to fasten on, the one thing to which my mind, overwhelmed by the sense of something so huge and beyond the range of thought, could cling. Her death was unjust, a crime, an outrage, a sin against mankind—weak inadequate words which even as they passed through my mind mocked me with their futility.

That that woman should so die was an enormity so great that it was terrifying in its implications, in its lifting of the veil on possibilities of thought so far beyond the grasp of the human mind. It was not just the German bombs, or the German Air

Force, or even the German mentality, but a feeling of the very essence of anti-life that no words could convey. This was what I had been cursing—in part, for I had recognized in that moment what it was that Peter[2] and the others had instantly recognized as evil and to be destroyed utterly. I saw now that it was not crime; it was Evil itself—something of which until then I had not even sensed the existence. And it was in the end, at bottom, myself against which I had raged, myself I had cursed. With awful clarity I saw myself suddenly as I was. Great God, that I could have been so arrogant!

How long I had been walking I don't know, but the drone of aircraft had ceased, so the All Clear must have sounded. I had a horror of thinking, of allowing my mind to look back armed with this new consciousness, but memories of faces, scenes, conversations flooded in, each a shock greater than the last. I was again in the train with Peter, on the way to Edinburgh, sitting forward on the seat, ridiculing his beliefs with glib, patronizing assurance. Once again I was drawing from him his hopes and fears, his aspirations for a better life, extracting them painfully one by one, and then triumphant, holding them up to the light, turning them this way and that, playing with them for a moment only to puncture them with ridicule and, delighted with my own wit, to throw them carelessly aside. Once again Peter was sitting opposite me, unruffled and tolerant, saying that I was not quite unfeeling, predicting that some shock of anger or of pity would serve to shake me from the complacency of my ivory tower; Peter quoting Tolstoi to me:

Man, man, you cannot live entirely without pity! words which I had taken it upon myself to dismiss as the sentimental gub of an old man in his dotage.

Oh, God, that memory might be blotted out; but it was

[2]Peter Pease, a brother officer and Hillary's greatest friend, whose death in action occurred while Hillary was in hospital. Pease was a profound Christian and argued interminably with Hillary, the arch-individualist. In hospital Hillary had a psychic pre-knowledge of his friend's death.

remorseless. Peter's death lived by me all its vivid intensity, offering me yet again the full life by all its implications, but rejected by me later to Denise.[3] Rejected brutally, "Let the dead bury their dead," close the door on the past, be grateful for the experience, use it, but understand that there is no communication, no message, no spiritual guidance, no bridge between life and death. Go on, do not look back, there is nothing there, nothing; it is all over. Denise, who had not been angry, who was now working day and night with Peter beside her, who had shown me the way, who with patience and understanding had let me look into her heart that I might learn. And I who, having looked, closed my eyes and turned away not wishing to believe, turned away irritated. Something there to be absorbed perhaps, an experience which might be useful; very interesting emotionally, of course, but nothing more. No, decidedly not. Dangerous morbid introspection; must get away.

Noel,[4] Peter Howes,[5] Bubble,[6] and the others—their deaths. Not felt quite as fully as one had expected perhaps, but then there was a war on, people dying every minute, one must harden one's heart. They were gone; good friends all of them, but there it was, nothing there for me, no responsibility, no answering to them for my actions before or after.

And the hospital. I saw myself again that first day in Sussex, standing in the doorway and looking down Ward Three. Once again I saw Joan[7] in the bed by the saline bath, saw her hairless head, her thin emaciated face, and heard that voice like a child of seven's whimpering, saw myself register it vaguely and pass on to look with interest at the others. The blind man learning Braille, utterly dependent on his wife; bad that, should be help-

[3]Denise—Peter Pease's fiancée—who met Hillary in hospital; a mystic who still, to Hillary's devoted exasperation, felt communion with her dead lover.

[4]Noel Agazarian—an Oxford friend and brother officer killed in action.

[5]Peter Howes, another friend and brother pilot killed in the Battle of Britain.

[6]"Bubble" Waterston, still another.

[7]A fellow patient in one of the hospitals where Hillary was treated.

ing himself. Joseph the Czech[8] and his nose growing from his forehead; his hands messy stumps and his eyes stupidly trusting. The one with practically no face at all, just a pair of eyes; unable to talk of course, but interesting, oh yes, particularly interesting: Yorkey Law[9] the bombardier, later to be invalided out, but quite fascinating with all those bacon strips off his legs gradually forming a face. And the others; one after another I remembered them until finally Edmonds—Edmonds[10] and his year of pain and disfigurement and my nice comfortable little theory on his will to live.

I remembered them all, remembering how at first they had interested me in their different ways, and then how they had irritated me with their dumb acceptance of the hospital conditions, their gratitude for what was being done for them, and above all their silent, uncomplaining endurance. It had baffled me. I had felt their suffering a little, had seen it, but through a glass darkly. They were too close to me, too much a part of my own suffering for me to focus it like this thing to-night.

To-night. Had it really been such a short time ago, had it been to-day that I had talked to David Rutter?[11]

Again memory dragged me back. It had been I this very day who had sat back smoking cigarettes while David had poured out his heart, while his wife had watched me, taut, hoping. But I had failed. I had been disturbed a little, yes, but when he was finished I had said nothing, given no sign, offered no assurance that he was now right. I saw it so clearly.

"Do you think I should join up?" On my answer had depended many things, his self-respect, his confidence for the future, his final goodbye to the past. And I had said nothing, shying away from the question, even then not seeing. In the train I had

[8]A fellow patient.

[9]Another of the same.

[10]Yet another.

[11]A convinced Pacifist, an Oxford friend; at this time tormented by doubts of pacifism which he discussed with Hillary.

crossed my legs and sat back, amused, God help me, by the irony of it all. They had given so much and were dead. I had given so little and was alive. Ah, well!

I was very grateful for the night and my solitude. I who had always repeated the maxim "Know thyself" was seeing now what it meant to live by that maxim. "*Le sentiment d'être tout et l'évidence de n'être rien.*" That was me. The feeling that I was everything and the evidence that I was nothing.

So Peter had been right. It was impossible to look only to oneself, to take from life and not to give except by accident, deliberately to look at humanity and then pass by on the other side. No longer could one say "The world's my oyster and the hell with the rest". What was it Denise had said? "Yes, you can realize yourself, but not by leading the egocentric life. By feeling deeply the deaths of the others you are conferring value on life."

For a moment I had had it, had that feeling, but I had let it go, had encouraged it to go, distrusting it, and now, and now . . . was it, then, too late?

I stopped and looked up into the night. They were there somewhere, all of them around me; dead perhaps, but not gone. Through Peter they had spoken to me, not once but often. I had heard and shrugged my shoulders; I had gone my way unheeding, not bitter, either on their account or mine, but in some curious way suspended, blind, lifeless, as they could never be.

Not so the others. Not so the Berrys,[12] the Stapletons,[13] the Carburys.[14] Again instinct had served. They hadn't had even the need of a Peter. They had felt their universe, not rationalized it. Each time they climbed into their machines and took off into combat, they were paying instinctive tribute to their comrades who were dead. Not so those men in hospital. They too knew, knew that no price was too dear to achieve this victory, knew that their discomforts, their suffering, were as nothing if they could but get back, and should they never get back they knew that silence was their rôle.

[12], [13], [14]Fellow officers.

But I! What had I done? What could I do now?

I wanted to seize a gun and fire it, hit somebody, break a window, anything. I saw the months ahead of me, hospital, hospital, hospital, operation after operation, and I was in despair. Somehow I got myself home, undressed, and into bed and fell into a troubled sleep. But I did not rest; when I awoke the problem was still within me. Surely there must be something.

Then after a while it came to me.

I could write. Later there would be other things, but now I could write. I had talked about it long enough, I was to be a writer, just like that. I was to be a writer, but in a vacuum. Well, here was my chance. To write I needed two things, a subject and a public. Now I knew well enough my subject. I would write of these men, of Peter and of the others. I would write for them and would write with them. They would at my side. And to whom would I address this book, to whom would I be speaking when I spoke of these men? And that, too, I knew. To Humanity, for Humanity must be the public of any book. Yes, that despised Humanity which I had so scorned and ridiculed to Peter.

If I could do this thing, could tell a little of the lives of these men, I would have justified, at least in some measure, my right to fellowship with my dead, and to the friendship of those with courage and steadfastness who were still living and who would go on fighting until the ideals for which their comrades had died were stamped for ever on the future of civilization.

The White Rabbit

by BRUCE MARSHALL

Wing-Commander Yeo-Thomas, known variously as "Shelley", "Dod-kin" and "The White Rabbit", was one of the agents who co-ordinated the work of the French Resistance and the Allies.

Before the war he was manager of the Molyneux dress-salon in Paris; he joined the R.A.F. in the ranks; but, when commissioned after the Fall of France, he was seconded to the Special Services.

After a spectacularly successful tour of duty in France, he returned to Britain and had an audience with Sir (then Mr.) Winston Churchill; he returned to France, was captured by the Gestapo, tortured and sent to Buchenwald, from which he was rescued (unbelievably) alive—to take up again his position in the antithesis of his war service, la haute couture.

As SOON as Yeo-Thomas[1] had been handcuffed two of the Gestapo men set about pushing back the excited crowd: they forbade access to the station and threatened to shoot anybody attempting to approach their prisoner. For a few minutes Tommy, tightly gripped by his captors, stood in a small arena of steps, hemmed in by a throng twenty yards above him and twenty yards below him, and reading on the spectators' faces fear or pity or the shamefaced loathing with which men contemplate misfortunes which they try to believe can never happen to themselves. This tableau, however, was of brief duration: he was quickly hustled up the steps, through the crowd and propelled into a Citroën with a uniformed driver which had been waiting at the corner of the Boulevard Delessert. He was made to sit in the back with two policemen on either side of him. As soon as

[1]Wing-Commander F. F. E. Yeo-Thomas, G.C., M.C.

the car started these two men began to take it in turn to punch him in the face. "Shelley,"[2] they cried, "*Wir haben Shelley. Englischer Offizier. Terrorist. Schweinhund. Scheisskerl.*"

This horrible little litany of imprecation continued until they reached the Gestapo Headquarters in the rue des Saussaies, and so did the cruel blows. Tommy's head felt twice its normal size and the blood from his lacerated face was pouring down over his shirt and suit. He says that he was surprised to find himself "thinking in a completely impersonal manner just as though it were another person being beaten up and it was a very extraordinary feeling". It must have been. What was even more extraordinary was that during this painful passage to prison he was able to wonder whether the attempt to rescue Bollaert[3] and Brossolette[3] would still be made and to think out what he was going to say when he was interrogated.

It was clear that the Dodkin[4] story would no longer serve in its entirety; the fact that the Gestapo men had greeted him as Shelley seemed to indicate that Antonin[5] had talked. (He learned later that the *agent-de-liaison* had been arrested while carrying in his pocket, contrary to all regulations, a piece of paper marked: SHELLEY PASSY II.) It was obvious, therefore, that the Germans would know that the otherwise unimpeachable identity papers in the name of Gaonach[6] which he was carrying were false. The Gestapo knew and had long known that Shelley was a British officer, but they did *not* know the name of the British officer. If they discovered his real identity and failed by normal methods to make him speak they would certainly arrest his father[7] and torture the old man in his presence. Dodkin then he would have to be and not a baled-out Dodkin: the absence

[2]"Shelley": Yeo-Thomas's pseudonym.

[3]Agents.

[4]Another "cover" alias of Yeo-Thomas.

[5]A colleague recently arrested.

[6]Yet another "cover" false identity.

[7]Yeo-Thomas lived in Paris before the war.

of the identity discs stamped with this name and hidden beneath the floorboards of Suni Sandoe's flat would perhaps add to rather than detract from the credibility of the tale, as a British officer would be unlikely to carry such compromising property on his person while actually engaged in the field. All this he thought out while his face was being battered in the car.

When they reached their destination he was yanked violently out of the car and, with a pistol pointed at his back, was propelled into the lift. His abrupt arrival in an office on the third floor astonished the three men sitting. *"Wir haben Shelley"*, the leading policeman shouted as Tommy was pushed into the room. At this the three men rose from their chairs and began to punch him and kick him, knocking him against desks and cupboards and walls. They stopped only when he had been beaten into semi-insensibility. Then they locked the door, stripped him naked and made him stand on a telephone directory. Enraged by the discovery of his tear-gas pen and revolver in a special holster strapped to his thigh they started in on him again. *"Schweinhund. Scheisskerl,"* the thugs shouted as they slapped his face and kicked him in his bare groin with their heavy boots. They tore from his neck the small brown canvas sachet which the Countess Grabbe[8] had given him at the beginning of the war and laid it on a desk beside the other objects which they had removed from his pockets: among these were his identity papers, the keys of four of his apartments of which he had been intending to return three to the owners before he left for Rennes, and two monocles which he had worn to disguise himself. The discovery of the last particularly infuriated his tormentors, for they flung them on the floor and trampled on them. The spectacle was so ridiculous that Tommy laughed aloud in spite of his pain; this earned him another beating up.

This new battering was scientifically administered to him as he stood heels together, arms handcuffed behind his back, naked on the telephone directory: as a blow made him sway sideways,

[8]A Russian living in Paris; a pre-war friend of Yeo-Thomas.

a punch on the jaw, the nose, or the ear or a kick in the stomach restored his equilibrium. "I don't know how long I was kept in this position," Yeo-Thomas says. "To me it seemed hours, but in all probability it was only an hour and a half." Although so dazed that the room was swimming before his eyes, he was still able to think fairly clearly. Two desires were in his mind: to avoid betraying his friends and to escape from his agony. He could do both if only he could get at the signet ring containing the poison tablet which the thugs had omitted to remove from his left hand. Sooner or later, he felt, they would be bound to unhandcuff him and then he could slide open the top of the ring, swallow the tablet and put himself beyond treachery and pain.

He was still standing on the telephone directory when a tall, broad-shouldered man with cold steel-grey eyes and a cruel mouth entered the room. Tommy's tormentors stood sharply to attention, extended their arms in the Nazi salute and said "Heil Hitler".

"Heil Hitler!" said the newcomer, returning the salute and stopping in front of Yeo-Thomas, who even on his perch was a head shorter. Looking down at the prisoner, the tall man spat in his face and gave him a crashing slap on the cheek which sent him careering against the wall. Unable to use his hands, Tommy collapsed on the floor, where the tall man kicked him every time he tried to get up. Tommy let his body go limp to minimize the effect of the kicks. "*Schweinhund, salaud, terroriste,*" the brute cried in bilingual rage, as he bent down, pulled Yeo-Thomas to his feet and flung him into a chair .

Very deliberately the new thug drew up another chair and sat down in front of Tommy, staring at him with his expressionless icy eyes. Tommy describes the man's eyes as being like "twin daggers, trying to pierce his brain". Knowing that the man's purpose was to make him lower his own eyes Yeo-Thomas looked him full in the face. Once again the heavy fist crashed on to his lips and nose, drawing streams of blood. "*Tu as compris, ordure?*" the man asked in correct but guttural French,

25

"Now you know where you stand, you bloody swine." Tommy did not answer.

At a word of command from the new thug two of the other men pounced on Yeo-Thomas and dragged him out of the chair; one stood in front of him with his arms on his shoulders and the other, going behind him, began to unfasten his handcuffs. The moment he had been waiting for seemed to have arrived. But just as his handcuffs were removed the big man noticed the ring. "*Dummkopf,*" he roared at the assistants, himself grabbed Tommy's hand, removed the ring and slipped it into his pocket. Yeo-Thomas was ordered to put on his clothes again. He dressed slowly and painfully, angry and frightened because he had been prevented from escaping from the very much more unpleasant attentions which he knew were in store for him.

As he dressed he made quick calculations: he had been arrested at five minutes past eleven; it must now be about three o'clock. Maud,[9] with whom he had had an appointment at one o'clock, would now be aware that something was wrong. When also he failed to turn up at the Avenue Victor Hugo for his emergency rendezvous at six o'clock she would know for certain that he had been arrested. Within twelve hours all his letter boxes would have been closed down, his meeting places changed and his contacts warned not to keep their appointments. In the meantime, to protect his network, he must, as was the rule for captured agents, hold out for at least forty-eight hours; to do this meant postponing unbearable pain by telling the Gestapo plausible lies and setting them hunting on a false scent.

As soon as he was dressed the big man made a sign to his companions and sat down behind a desk. Tommy was dragged from the chair into which he had deliberately slumped, propelled to the desk and dumped down again in the chair which had been brought up behind him. On the desk were laid out the objects which had been removed from his pockets and from his person: from them his gold fountain pen, his wrist-watch and bank-

[9]Another agent.

26

notes of higher denomination were already missing; but his pistol was still there, with the barrel pointing towards him and nearer to him than to his inquisitor. Intending to shoot the big man and then himself, he lifted his manacled hands and laid them on the edge of the desk. Nobody seemed to notice this gesture.

"*Vous avez joué et vous avez perdu,*" the big man began. "You've had your flutter and you've lost. But nothing will happen to you if you're reasonable and listen to sense. But if you don't. . . ."

Tommy did not answer; it was always a few seconds gained.

"Well, are you going to talk?"

Once again he did not answer.

"*Ordure,*" the big man shouted as one of his assistants slapped Yeo-Thomas across his puffed and bleeding face. "Are you going to speak? Yes or no?"

Again Yeo-Thomas did not reply.

The big man sprang up and crashed his fist on to Tommy's mouth. "*Salaud, crapule, saboteur, espion, tu parleras!* I'll make you speak all right." With the help of his two assistants he started hitting the prisoner again. They did not desist until, his mouth full of blood, his eyes so swollen that he could scarcely see, Yeo-Thomas crumpled up under their onslaught. The big man went back behind his desk and rang a bell.

Pretending not to have completely recovered consciousness, Tommy leaned forward in his chair and slowly slid his hand across the desk towards the pistol: but the big man saw the gesture, laughed, picked up the pistol and put it in a drawer.

"So you thought you'd use it, *cochon*?" was all that he said.

A young, fair, good-looking German with blue eyes and a pink complexion answered the bell. The big man, ordering him to go out and bring back a typewriter, called him "Ernst", and the young man called the big man "Rudi", Tommy made a mental note of the names. (He was later to learn that his tormentor was the famous Rudi von Merode, known in his trade as the Prince

27

de Merode.) When Ernst had fetched a typewriter he sat down at a corner of the desk, inserted a form, a carbon and a blank sheet into the machine and waited in silence.

"Name?" Rudi rapped at Yeo-Thomas.

"Shelley." That at least it was no good denying.

"Fool. Your real name."

"Kenneth Dodkin." This answer seemed to be accepted, for Rudi went on to ask:

"Your serial number?"

"47,685."

"Rank?"

"Squadron Leader."

"Branch of the Service?"

"Royal Air Force."

"Address?"

"I do not require to reply to that question."

"You will reply all the same."

"I shall not." If he were to convince the Gestapo that he was indeed Kenneth Dodkin it seemed to him essential that he should not protest too much by giving them even false information on points about which they were not entitled to ask questions.

Rudi got up, walked round the desk, and using both his hands began to slap Tommy's face from one side to the other, cutting the already bruised cheeks with his heavy signet ring. His ears crushed, dizzy with pain, Yeo-Thomas swayed in his chair: the two assistants propped him up so that Rudi could go on hitting him.

At last Rudi stopped and sat down behind the desk again.

"Listen," he said, suddenly changing to a friendly tone. "It's no good being obstinate. You've had your flutter and you've lost." Tommy wondered to how many others Rudi had used this phrase which seemed to come so readily to his lips. "We know all about you, but we'll treat you as an officer if only you'll be sensible. You're a prisoner; you've done your duty; nobody can say a thing against you. Now I'm going to ask you a few questions; all you've got to do is to answer and it'll be all finished with. I say, what about a cigarette?" He took a cigarette from a gold case, stuck it between Tommy's bruised lips, lit it with a gold lighter. "That's better, isn't it?" he said as he watched Yeo-Thomas take a couple of puffs. "You see, we're not such brutes after all. If you're reasonable you've got nothing to fear. And when you've answered we'll give you some food and something nice to drink."

Tommy did not reply, nor did he make any sign; he went on puffing at his cigarette. Ernst sat expectantly at his typewriter.

"I may as well tell you that it's no use telling us any lies," Rudi went on. "Your *agent-de-liaison* has made a clean breast of everything. We know all you've been doing here since the beginning of the year. We know that you know all about the arms dumps. You've only got to tell us where they are and we'll leave you alone."

Behind his sore face, Yeo-Thomas almost smiled. Rudi had been too clever; if Rudi had been as well informed as he pretended to be he would have known that his prisoner had not been in France at the beginning of the year; and Antonin, who had been working for Tommy only for a week, could not have given him much information. Rudi was bluffing; to gain time Yeo-Thomas decided to bluff, too.

"Then he's talked?" he asked.

"Naturally."

Tommy pretended to be shocked and distressed.

"So you know about my appointments?"

"Of course. You see it's no use your making a martyr of yourself. You've had your flutter and you've lost."

"Did he tell you I had an appointment for this afternoon?"

"We know everything, I tell you."

"In that case it won't do much good my talking, will it?"

This unexpected piece of logic made Rudi's face harder again.

"This is no time for joking," he said. "We know that you have an appointment this afternoon. All I want to know is with whom and where."

"What time is it now?" Tommy asked.

"Half-past four."

"In that case it's too late because my appointment is for a quarter to five."

"Where?"

"At the Porte Maillot."

"Whereabouts exactly?"

"In front of the *ceinture*[10] railway station."

"With whom?"

"With a woman who's bringing me a message."

Rudi picked up the telephone and ordered a car to stand by immediately. One of the guards was sent to fetch another two thugs in civilian clothes, to whom instructions were given by Rudi in German too rapid for Yeo-Thomas to understand. "Heil Hitler!" said the thugs and ran from the room; removing Tommy's revolver from the drawer and pocketing it, Rudi prepared to follow them.

"What's this woman like?" Rudi asked.

Yeo-Thomas gave him a fantastic description of an imaginary woman who, he said, would be carrying a bouquet of flowers in one hand and a newspaper in the other.

"If you're lying you'll pay for it," Rudi shouted as he rushed after the other two men.

Yeo-Thomas knew only too well that he would soon pay dearly for having sent Rudi on a wild-goose chase; but he had gained time and so far he had not talked. Although his whole head was aching he tried to think out how when Rudi came back again he might gain still more time. His two guards watched him stolidly out of their square unimaginative, unpitying faces. Ernst moved from his typewriter to Rudi's chair and began

[10]The Paris "belt" railway—the underground Métro.

examining the property which had been removed from Tommy's person.

"Whose telephone number is this?" Ernst suddenly asked, peering closely at a banknote.

"What telephone number? I don't understand."

"The telephone number you've written on this bank-note."

"I've written no telephone number on any banknote."

"Liar!"

"I am not a liar."

"Yes, you are: look at this." Ernst came over and showed him a ten-franc note on which a telephone number had been scrawled in pencil.

"I didn't write it," Yeo-Thomas said. "It must have been there when I got the note."

This was true, but Ernst didn't believe him and showed his scepticism by punching him heavily in the face.

"Now will you tell me whose number this is?"

"I don't know, I tell you."

"Well, we shall soon find out." Picking up the telephone Ernst gave an order, of which the only part Tommy understood was the repetition in German of the numbers on the ten-franc note. "You'd have done much better to tell me straight away, *salaud*," Ernst said, as he laid down the receiver.

Within a few minutes the telephone rang. Ernst listened eagerly. "*Danke*," he said, asked for an internal number and gave elaborate instructions. "I now know the name of your friend and his address; you'll be seeing him soon," he told Tommy. "The German police are very powerful, you know, and you're very foolish to try to pull the wool over our eyes." After some insulting epithets he continued his examination of the objects on the desk. "What's inside this?" he asked, holding up the little brown canvas sachet.

"I haven't the faintest idea."

"*Liar, pourriture, Scheisskerl.*" With a string of filthy words

Ernst unconsciously proved Talleyrand's contention that swearing is the means by which the inarticulate give themselves the impression of eloquence. "It's no good your coming the innocent with us: we're not bloody fools."

Taking out a penknife, Ernst slit open the sachet: inside was a small slip of paper folded in two and covered with small Russian characters. It was the first time Yeo-Thomas had seen this document which Ernst examined with a scowl.

"Ha, ha," Ernst said. "So you work for the Russians, do you? It's your code, isn't it, *Scheisskerl?*"

"I tell you I don't know what it is."

"You're a liar."

"I am not."

"*Scheisskerl!*" Once again Ernst came round from behind the desk and began to beat up his victim. Tommy went limp; it was his only protection. Tiring at length of his sport, Ernst left off and went back to continue his examination of the objects on the desk.

Through the slits which were all he now had for eyes Tommy tried to examine his possessions, too. There was only one, he thought, which was really dangerous: the bunch of keys, of which one belonged to the flat in the rue de la Tourelle, the address on his identity card. Of his use of this flat only two people knew: Brossolette, who was in prison, and Maud, who, when he failed to turn up for his six o'clock appointment, would give the place a wide berth. He must avoid answering any questions about the keys until after six o'clock, when, if the persistence of his tormentors became too painful, he would tell them which was the key of the flat in the rue de la Tourelle. The Germans would then rush round to the flat and, when they found nobody there, bait a trap which would immobilize a couple of their men for a few days. About the keys of the other flats he would have to lie continuously if their owners were not to get into serious trouble. He was still thinking all this out when Rudi burst into the room livid with rage.

As Rudi promised, Yeo-Thomas paid for having lied: battered again on his puffed and swollen face, he was knocked down on the floor, picked up and knocked down again. He ached all over; his head throbbed; all his teeth felt loose; his nose was squashed and his lips were split, his jacket and his shirt were soaked with blood. Eventually he was picked up for the last time and thrown back on to his chair; Rudi resumed his seat at the desk.

"You've made me lose my time, *salaud*."

"I told you you'd be late," Tommy said. "She can't have waited. It's not my fault."

"Liar."

"It's not my fault if you won't believe me."

Rudi glared at him; he glared ever more fiercely when Ernst had shown him the folded slip of paper.

"Russian? So you're a Communist as well?"

"It may be Russian; I don't know. But I am not a Communist."

"You never know anything, do you, you dirty liar? But I'll show you. I'll have this paper examined by our experts. They'll decipher it all right and then you'll see how much you'll pay for your lying." He telephoned, handed the slip of paper to a small rat-faced man with gold-rimmed spectacles who came in answer to his summons, and then turned to Yeo-Thomas again. "Where are the arms dumps you know of?"

"I know of none."

"Are you going to talk: yes or no?"

"I don't know anything, I tell you."

"We'll see if you know nothing." Rudi signed to the two guards who grabbed Tommy's arms and jerked him to his feet. Taking from a drawer a long chain and an ox-gut whip with a flexible steel rod inside it, Rudi swished the latter threateningly in the air. Tommy was propelled out of the room, up steps and along a narrow passage lined on one side with small circular windows which looked like portholes; he guessed that he was being taken to a torture chamber.

He had a rough journey: every time he stumbled from weakness he was jerked up by the handcuffs which bit deeply into his flesh. At the end of the passage a door opened and he was flung on to the tiled floor of a bathroom, through the open window of which blew in a freezing draught. He was dragged to his feet and two men pulled off his trousers and underpants; his hands were unmanacled while his jacket and shirt were torn off and then handcuffed again behind his back. While Rudi bent and twisted the chain tightly round his ankles Ernst opened the cold-water tap and filled the bath. At an order from Rudi one of the guards left the room and came back accompanied by a crowd of German girls in uniform, who crammed the doorway and laughed and mocked at Yeo-Thomas as he stood naked and shivering in the icy draught.

"Where are the arms dumps?" Rudi asked.

"I don't know."

The ox-gut whip came slashing down on Tommy's chest, searing it and raising a weal; Yeo-Thomas gritted his teeth.

"So you're going to be pig-headed, are you?"

Aching in every joint, Tommy remained silent. He was forced to sit on the edge of the bath. Rudi bent down again, caught hold of the chain around his ankle and gave it a twist and a tug; drawn into the bath on to his feet, Yeo-Thomas stood in the freezing water, facing the grinning, jeering girls. One of the men scooped water up in the palm of his hand and splashed him with it.

"Where are the arms dumps?" Rudi asked again.

"I don't know."

Rudi crashed his big fist into Tommy's jaw and, as he staggered, pushed him headlong into the bath, so that his face was under the water, while his legs stuck up in the air. With his hands manacled behind his back Yeo-Thomas was helpless.

Panicking, he tried to kick, but his legs were caught and held in a powerful grip. His eyes were open and he could see faces distorted by the water wavering above him. His mouth came open and he swallowed water. His lungs felt as though they were bursting. He made another attempt to kick himself out of the bath but the vice-like grip still held him. He tried to lift himself up with his handcuffed arms and failed. Swallowing more water, he became limp; the strength went out of him and he began to lose consciousness; he was drowning and he knew it.

He came to feeling an agonizing pain in his chest. Water was gushing out of his mouth and there was a big wavering black shadow in front of his eyes. The shadow slowly dissolved into lighter filmy circles which shimmered like hot air on a summer's day. As the circles became faces Tommy realized that he was lying on the tiled floor of the bathroom and looking up into Rudi's sadistic eyes. The German girls were crowding round the door, chattering and laughing. Feeling half dead, weak and sick, he closed his eyes so as not to see them. He could breathe only in gasps and his heart, in his own phrase, was "thumping like bellows in a forge". He had been pulled out of the water just as he had been about to drown and given artificial respiration.

He was lifted to his feet.

"Where are the arms dumps?"

"I . . . don't . . . know."

Thrown brutally back into the bath, his head hit the edge. Once more the water engulfed him. Once more he tried in vain to kick and to push himself up with his handcuffed arms. Once more he swallowed water. Once more he felt himself drowning. His mouth opened and the water poured in. There were rushing noises in his ears.

As before he was hauled from the bath just as he was about to drown and was artificially revived. As his consciousness returned he saw the same shimmering visions which slowly took the form of Rudi, his assistants and the laughing girls. Again he was pulled to his feet, but this time he was so weak that he had to be held up. His ears were still buzzing when he heard a voice coming from far away:

"Where are the arms dumps?"

And he heard another voice, which he presumed to be his own, answering faintly:

"I . . . don't . . . know."

He was thrown back into the bath several times. Kicking and swallowing water, oblivion succeeding consciousness and consciousness oblivion, he lost count of his torments and soon was unable to trace their sequence. As soon as he saw the distorted faces of Rudi and Ernst he lost sight of them again. The sound of the girls' laughter was absorbed by the pain in his lungs. He no longer had the strength or the desire to kick. He was brought round for the last time by a kick from a heavy boot and knew from the agony that he was still alive. He was lying on the bathroom floor, with walls, bath and faces swirling around his head. Abominably sick and with his stomach as large as a barrel, water came gushing out of his mouth on to his chest. He saw with surprise that the girls were no longer in the doorway. Numb with cold, he was dragged to his feet, on which he could no longer stand as the chain had stopped the circulation. As he tottered he was struck heavily over the head with a rubber cosh and again collapsed.

When he had recovered from the sickening effects of this blow he was hustled, still naked and dripping with water, along passages and corridors lined with mocking, laughing girls in uniform and female secretaries. Back in Rudi's office, the chain was removed from his feet and he was pushed into a chair while his underpants and trousers were slipped on. His handcuffs were loosened, but fastened again as soon as he had been thrust into his shirt and jacket. Once again Rudi sat at his desk facing him.

"Where are the arms dumps?"

"I don't know."

"Haven't you had enough, *ordure*? Well, we'll see."

At a sign from Rudi the two guards produced rubber coshes with which they began to beat him. He was beaten on the head, arms, leg, body and testicles. He did not cry out. Still less did he speak.

"Where are the arms dumps?"

"I don't know."

Each time that he said this the beating up started all over again. He saw flashes before his eyes; the furniture and Rudi's face began to float in circles. In the end he lost consciousness. . . .

When he came to he was in atrocious agony; the circulation in his arms had been stopped by his handcuffs which had been tightened by the pull on them, and his shoulders had been dislocated. He felt that he had reached breaking point and was afraid that if they tortured him again he would speak and tell them all about the arms dumps and the Secret Army and the Maquis. He knew that his tormentors were fully aware of the extent of his knowledge and would recoil before no brutality in order to make him talk. . . .

He had to spend the night chained by his arms and legs to the settee. Hungry and thirsty, he was refused food, but was eventually given a mug of water. The only time he managed to sleep was during the short period when his guards were snoring; otherwise as soon as he dozed off he was shaken awake by the mean-looking N.C.O. who roared at him: "*Nicht schlaffen.*" He thought of Barbara[11] and longed like a child for the comfort of her arms. He thought of Brossolette and wondered if he would still be rescued. (He did not know that Brossolette, whose identity had been discovered, was already dead; brought from Rennes to Paris for interrogation, Brossolette, who had previously discarded his poison tablet, had either thrown himself or been thrown by the Germans out of a window, and, with his cranium fractured and his arms and legs broken, had died in the *Hospital de la Pitié.*)

[11]Mrs. Yeo-Thomas, who served with the W.A.A.F.

When dawn came the giant went out and brought back bread and sausage and a steaming jug of hot coffee for himself and his companion. The sight and the smell of the warm food made Tommy feel hungry and cold and he asked hopefully for a drink: he was given another mug of water.

"*Mich friert,*"[12] he said, but the only answer he was vouchsafed was "*Englisches Schwein*" and he was left to freeze.

Nor was it only with cold that he was freezing; he was freezing also with fear. As the morning grew lighter he knew that the moment was fast approaching when he would again writhe under the torments of his captors. He was at the end of his tether: he felt that if they did anything too painful to him this time he was bound to break down and speak. He wished for death because it was only in death that he could be sure of not speaking. Terror tore through his bowels when his chains were undone and he was pulled to his feet. Behind his swollen lips this modern saint who did not admire sanctity[13] prayed that the cup might pass from him. "Ah yes, for there are times when all pray," his friend and hero, Mr. Churchill, had said.

But his resolution returned as he thought of Barbara, of his friends who trusted in him, of Dismore,[14] of Thackthwaite,[14] of Johnson,[14] of Whitehead,[14] of Passy,[14] and of Brossolette. Brossolette would never have betrayed the cause and he would not be false to Brossolette. In another office on the fourth floor, with lacerated face, swollen eyelids, tousled hair, collarless and in crumpled clothes covered with coagulated blood, and with the giant seated behind him, he faced a new, sinister and menacing interrogator:

"Are you still going to be pig-headed? Or are you going to talk?"

"I have nothing to say."

"I can see quite clearly that you are a liar. But we have

[12]I am cold.
[13]Yeo-Thomas was not a religious man.
[14]Fellow Agents.

methods of making even liars talk, methods you don't know yet."

Yeo-Thomas made a quick calculation: already he had held out for almost forty-six hours; in another two hours he would have accomplished the statutory forty-eight, and then, perhaps, he could afford to let slip a few unimportant details. In the meantime he must still strive to gain time. . . .

Seated within three feet of a window, Tommy gathered all his strength for a desperate leap across an intervening table: provided that he got through the window quickly enough there was every chance, as the office was on the fourth floor, that he would kill himself or at least hurt himself so badly that he would not recover; and even if he didn't die the Germans would have to put him in hospital where they might forget about him and leave him to be freed by the Allies when they arrived in about three months' time.

"Where are the arms dumps? You have suffered, I know, but I promise you that you shall suffer much more if you do not answer my question."

He sprang and, taking his captors by surprise, jumped clean over the table. His head hit the glass pane and smashed it and his shoulders passed through. But the giant was too quick for him: seizing Tommy by the ankles, he pulled him back into the room and sat him back on his chair, to which he was now securely fastened by chains hurriedly brought by a soldier.

"So you are frightened, are you?" the interrogator said with a leer. "Well, now it's time to speak. If you don't it'll be very unpleasant for you indeed. We'll use new methods and you'll suffer. Make up your mind and be quick about it because I can't afford to waste my time."

Tommy did not answer: he knew that if he spoke it would be to beg for mercy. The faces of those whose lives depended upon his safety passed before his blurred vision in a silent, pleading procession. He could not keep what the militarists and muscular clergymen used to call a stiff upper lip because his upper lip was smashed, but he obstinately held to the only loyalty he knew: he said nothing and by doing so proved himself to be that rarity in a world of mean shifts and compromise: a man of integrity. . . .

Reach for the Sky

by PAUL BRICKHILL

Reach for the Sky *is Paul Brickhill's biography of Douglas Bader, D.S.O., D.F.C.*

Bader was one of the crack stunt pilots of the R.A.F. in the early 'thirties, flying and aerobat-ing in formation in the air pageants of those days. A streak of headstrong recklessness induced him, on a challenge, to flout R.A.F. rules and stunt at too low an altitude. His plane crashed, and both his legs were broken, and amputated.

I have chosen from this remarkable, and remarkably-written, book, not the sections which deal with Bader, the leader of the famous "Dogsbody" Wing which played an appreciable part in the later stages of the Battle of Britain, but two passages dealing with the man shortly after his crash; and two showing the spirit which inspired him after he was shot down and made a prisoner of war.

WALKER[1] and Tulitt[1] took each arm round their shoulders and hauled him to his feet for the first time. As his weight came on both, especially the right stump, it was the worst shock he ever had. He felt absolutely hellish, wildly unbalanced and strange. His right stump was utterly helpless and uncomfortable to the point of hurting and the harness itself seemed to cripple him.

In stung despair he burst out: "Good lord, this is absolutely impossible."

"That's what they all say the first time," Dessoutter said. "You get used to it. Don't forget your right stump has done no work for nearly six months."

[1]Assistants to the Dessoutter brothers at Roehampton Hospital.

Bader said grimly: "I thought I'd be able to walk out of here and start playing games and things."

"Look," Dessoutter said gently. "I think you ought to face it that you'll never walk again without a stick."

Bader looked at him with tense dismay, and then as the challenge stirred him he said pugnaciously: "Damn that! I'll never, *never* walk *with* a stick!"

In his stubborn anger he meant it.

"Try a step or two," Dessoutter[2] suggested.

Feeling he would be more secure staying on the left leg he tried to swing his right leg forward, but it did not move.

"How the hell do I get it to move?" he demanded.

"Try kicking the stump forward," Dessoutter said. "The right knee will bend automatically. Then when it's forward, kick the stump downwards and it'll straighten out on the heel. It's like cracking a whip."

He kicked the stump forward and the metal knee bent as the leg went forward. He jerked the stump down and the knee straightened as the heel hit the mat.

"That's better," Dessoutter said. "Now come forward."

Bader suddenly felt paralysed, unable to move. It was like having a chair back stuck under a door handle.

"How the devil *do* I?" he asked irritably. "I *can't* move."

"That's the big lesson you've just learned," Dessoutter said. "You haven't got any toe or ankle muscles now to spring you forward as you used to. That's the secret of it. Or the catch. That right leg is a firm barrier that you have to push yourself over, on top of, by leaning forward and by your momentum when you're moving."

Bader said to Tulitt and Walker: "Pull me forward over this damn' leg."

They heaved him forward till he was precariously balanced on the weak right stump. Having his own knee, he was able

[2]Robert Dessoutter.

quite easily to swing the left leg forward and then he stuck again, unable to push forward with toe and ankle.

"Pull me, for God's sake," he said.

They pulled and he flicked his right stump forward again, and they pulled him on to it and he got his left leg forward once more; so it went on in clumsy, stiff, jerky movements as they pulled him the length of the room. There was no natural automatic movement at all; he had to think each step out in advance and then signal his mind to make the move. Whenever they eased the forward tug he felt that the stiff leg out in front would push him over backwards. At the end he lowered himself on to another stool and uttered with grim feeling: "This is—awful".

"It always is the first time," Dessoutter said. "Don't be too depressed. The first steps always feel like that. It's learning to walk all over again with an entirely new system and you can only learn it by practice, like playing the piano. Don't worry. You'll do it, but it might take you six months."

Bader looked at him with a humourless grin. "Don't be silly. There's a girl I want to see in a couple of days and I want to be walking on these things then."

Dessoutter broke a slightly appalled silence: "You'll find a stick useful in pushing yourself over the leg in front."

Bader stuck his jaw out aggressively. "Not me! Come on, you two. Let's have another go."

They hauled him to his feet again and this time they took his elbows instead of having his arms round their shoulders. "Try taking very short steps," [3] Walker said. "It'll be easier to lean forward over a short step."

He tried that and the improvement was immediate. They still had to pull him forward, but he did not get quite the feeling of coming to a dead stop whenever he put a leg forward, especially the right leg. They went up and down the room several more times and slowly, subconsciously, he began to get the hang of

[3] This is one of the real secrets at the beginning.

it, leaning the top of his body well forward so that his unbalanced weight tended to carry him on to the leg placed just in front.

Dessoutter said after a while, "Let's try taking half an inch off that right leg. Might make it a bit easier."

Bader sat down and unstrapped it. Walker and Tulitt took it away for half an hour and lowered the thigh about half an inch into the knee socket. Bader put it on again and without so much height to overcome found that he could transfer his weight with a little less trouble. It was not so much that it was easier but just a little less impossible, still wildly clumsy and unnerving. They helped him up and down the room several more times and then he said: "All right, now let me go." They were too cautious to do so, so he shrugged his elbows to push them away and took his first steps alone, three or four jerky stumbles that ended with him just grabbing the parallel bars before he fell over. He hung on to them, grinning all over his face where the sweat was shining again. Turning to Dessoutter, he said: "There you are. You can keep your damn' sticks now."

Dessoutter was laughing in genuine delight. "I've never even seen a chap with *one* leg do that before first time," he said. Walker and Tulitt were openly surprised, obviously not pretending.

"I think you've done enough for to-day," Dessoutter said; "you must be feeling pretty tired. . . ."

★   ★   ★

In the morning as he woke he remembered with satisfaction that he was mobile and, after the previous night's lesson, lay a while planning procedure. Was it worth putting on his legs to walk to the bath, taking them off and putting them on again afterwards? No. He went to the bathroom on his rump and put his legs on afterwards. Clutching the banister rail he dot-and-carried alone down the stairs to breakfast and after that teetered out into the garden, where he got another shock as he stepped on to a patch of grass and instantly felt as dismayingly insecure as the first time he had stood on the legs. It was fairly level grass, but it was no firm level floor and he felt that he would topple if he moved. He took a step, the right toe immediately hit a clump of grass and he pitched forward—his first fall. He took the shock on his hands. That part was all right, but now he had to get up again. He lay for a while thinking about it. A man came running up and said sympathetically; "Hang on to me, old boy. Soon have you up."

"Go away," he snapped. "I'll do this."

He took his weight on his hands and lowered the rear weight on to his left knee, then pushed hard. In a moment he had fallen back on his hands again. He tried again, pushing up on the left toe, straightening his left knee, and pushing his hands back towards the toe, and came uneasily but without too much difficulty to his feet again. Then he took another step and fell again.

That morning he fell at least twenty times but managed to stumble up and down the grass again and again, arms flailing to keep his balance like a novice on ice-skates, but persisting until his legs were aching and trembling with exhaustion again. Worse, the right stump was sore in spots—obviously chafing. The difficulty of walking on anything but the smoothest floor was worrying him. That was the worst part of all. There would be more rough paths than smooth paths in life, and the airy confidence he had had was rattled. . . . .

★   ★   ★

On a spring Saturday at Hartley Wintney, Adrian Stoop and Tinny Dean, a Harlequins and England scrum-half, were going to play golf at a local nine-hole course and suggested that Douglas and Thelma[4] go and see them hit off. Perhaps Douglas could walk a couple of holes with them. After they drove off Douglas said he would potter about the fairway until they returned, so Stoop handed him a seven iron and a ball and sug-

¹Thelma Edwards, later Thelma Bader.

gested he potter about with them. When Stoop and Dean had gone on he dropped the ball on the grass and took a swing at it, but the club missed the ball by inches and he overbalanced and fell flat on his back. He got up and tried again and the same thing happened. The same thing happened the third time and the fourth time. He tried changing his stance and his swing, and the same thing happened. Luckily the turf was soft and painless. He got a stubborn feeling that he *must* hit the ball and keep his balance before he gave it up.

Again and again he fell until about the twelfth attempt the club hit the ball with a sweet click and, lying on his back a moment later, he could see it in parabolic flight. Something about that click was very satisfying. He tried again, missed and fell over. He kept falling over and missing every time until, on about the twenty-fifth shot, he hit it for the second time (or rather, topped it) and fell over again. In the thirties he hit it twice more, one of them another exciting click, but still fell as before. After he had fallen about forty times Thelma said persuasively: "Now come on, I think you've had enough."

Next day he tried the seven iron again on the Stoops' lawn, this time with Stoop coaching. Several times he hit the ball but still he kept falling over. It was remarkable how precarious the balance was as soon as the swing of shoulders and arms took his weight a fraction over the straddle of his feet. There was no instinct or agility to correct. He had fallen about twenty times again when he tried a shorter and slower swing, hit the ball and just kept his balance. As he looked up with a triumphant grin Thelma said: "Good, now you'll be satisfied."

"Not on your life," he said, got the ball back and kept on trying. Shortly he hit it without falling again, and did it several times more after that.

The following week-end he tried again at the Stoops', until nine times out of ten he was hitting the ball and not falling. It had started off as a determination to do it once and now it was something more, part obsession to be able to do it every time and part pleasure from the feel and the sound of the click when he hit it cleanly and saw it arc away. Stoop said: "You're getting the bug, Douglas. Be careful, there's no cure for it."

Next week-end he improved still more, his brain absorbing the instinctive reflexes needed to keep his balance and thus freeing him to concentrate on hitting the ball. A couple of week-ends later Tinny Dean took him over to the golf course and handed him a three-wood on the first tee. Acutely aware of the concentrated eyes of the usual first-tee onlookers, he desperately wanted to hit the ball, stay on his feet and not let them know he had no legs. "Don't worry," Dean assured him. "Everyone misses on the first tee."

With taut concentration he braced his feet wide apart, took a slow swing and connected. Stumbling, he still kept his feet and saw the ball flight about a hundred yards, fading with a little slice.

"That was a hell of a good shot," said Dean.

"It was a hell of a fluke," muttered Bader, vastly satisfied. . . .

With the outbreak of war, Bader returned not only to the R.A.F. but to flying duties. He took over a squadron, then a wing. His leadership held an inspirational quality, galvanizing men who were browned-off, inadequate, or unlucky, previous commanders into a superbly militant body.

He crossed swords with higher authority to obtain adequate equipment for the men under his command; challenged orthodox tactics and imposed his own creed of gaining superior height and attacking, in mass, from the unexpected quarter. His personal score rose until he was recognized as one of the crack pilots in the whole of Fighter Command, only just behind "Sailor" Malan and the rest.

But he was shot down over St. Omer, and, legless though he was, escaped down a rope of sheets to be succoured by the French. He was recaptured and underwent a severe interrogation.

Sitting on chairs at the other end he noticed the doctor and some soldiers and nurses from the St. Omer hospital. He grinned at them and said a cheerful "Hallo", but they only eyed him sourly. A young Luftwaffe officer motioned him to a lonely chair in front of the table, saying: "Will you please sit down?"

"No, I won't," he answered, conscious that if the officer had told him to stand up he would promptly have sat down.

The judges leaned towards each other and muttered among themselves. A bald, hatchet-faced general in the middle spoke to the Luftwaffe officer who acted as interpreter, and the officer turned to Bader: "Will you swear to tell the truth?"

"No," he answered. "Certainly not."

The officer looked as though he had not heard properly. "I beg your pardon," he said.

"I said certainly not. Go on. Tell the Court."

The officer turned nervously and spoke to the judges, and the bald general's eyebrows shot up.

The officer turned back. "The Herr General wishes to know why you will not tell the truth."

Bader said: "Well, if you're going to ask me questions about the French I will obviously lie."

. . . Hands in pockets, Bader was idly leaning in a doorway three days later when a Luftwaffe captain called Muller passed. Bader kept his hands in his pockets and his pipe in his mouth. Muller stopped, turned and said: "Ving Commander Bader, you should salute me."

"Why?"

"All prisoners of war should salute German officers."

Bader said shortly: "The Geneva Convention says I have to salute enemy officers of equal or senior rank. You're only a captain."

"I am the Kommandant's representative and you should salute me."

"I don't salute the Kommandant either," Bader remarked disagreeably. "He's only a major."

"Those are the Kommandant's orders!" (angrily).

"I don't give a damn if they are. They're wrong and I'm damned if I'm going to salute you. . . ."

Ultimately, Bader was shifted to Colditz, the P.o.W. camp reserved for incorrigibles. Even here, he strove not only to escape but to make as much trouble for his captors as any five whole men.

. . . As Bader's legs had been giving trouble the S B O ' suggested that he be repatriated, too, a suggestion which Douglas emphatically refused, declaring that his legs had not been lost in battle and therefore he was no different as a result of captivity. The S.B.O., however, put his name on the list when the repatriation commission arrived, and then when the Germans called prisoners from Appell to appear before the commission they left out the names of Bader and two very sick men. It was typical of the spirit of Colditz that all the sick and maimed who were called—including some, like Lord Arundell, who were unlikely to recover—refused to see the commission until the three dropped names were restored. . . .

⁵Senior British Officer.

The Colditz Story

by P. R. REID

Peter Reid—once Captain Peter Reid—was himself one of the classical escapists; but he was also one of the organizers of the escapes of others. He was sent to the "bad boys' camp", Colditz—a castle built originally by that fantastic character Augustus the Strong of Saxony (who had, says legend, one illegitimate child for every day of the year); and there he took his place on the Escape Committee, where he controlled the activities of such men as Airey Neave and Douglas Bader, as well as those of assorted Poles, Dutch, and Dominion prisoners.

After the war he recorded the authentic history of Colditz: its bitter disappointments, its bursts of triumph. It is a happy thing to record that Reid himself escaped, in spectacular fashion, with three other prisoners; reached Switzerland; and became a diplomatic servant in that little island of neutrality.

LIEUTENANT MAIRESSE LEBRUN was a French cavalry officer, tall, handsome, and debonair, and a worthy compatriot of that famed cuirassier of Napoleon whose legendary escapades were so ably recounted by Conan Doyle in his book, *The Adventures of Brigadier Gérard.*

Lebrun had slipped the German leash from Colditz once already by what seems, in the telling, a simple ruse. In fact, it required quite expert handling. A very small Belgian officer was his confederate. On one of the "Park" outings the Belgian officer concealed himself under the voluminous folds of a tall comrade's cloak at the outgoing "numbering off" parade and was not counted. During the recreation period in the Park, Lebrun, with the aid of suitable diversions, climbed up among the rafters of an open-sided pavilion situated in the middle of the recreation pen. He was not missed because the Belgian provided the missing number, and the dogs did not get wind of him. Later he descended and, smartly dressed in a grey flannel suit sent by a friend from France, he walked to a local railway station and proffered a hundred-mark note at the booking-office in exchange for a ticket. Unfortunately, the note was an old one, no longer in circulation. The stationmaster became suspicious and finally locked Lebrun up in a cloakroom and telephoned the camp. The Camp Commandant replied that nothing was amiss and that his prisoner complement was complete. While he was 'phoning, Lebrun wrenched open a window and leaped out on top of an old woman, who naturally became upset and gave tongue. A chase ensued. He was finally cornered by the station personnel and recaptured. In due course he was returned to the Castle and handed over to the protesting Commandant.

This adventure lost Mairesse his fine suit and found him doing a month's solitary confinement at the same time as Peter Allan.[1]

One fine afternoon we heard many shots fired in the playground and rushed to the windows, but could see nothing because of the foliage. Terrific excitement followed in the German quarters and we saw posses of Goons with dogs descending at the double from the Castle and disappearing among the trees. Shouts and orders and the barking of dogs continued for some time and eventually faded away in the distance.

We heard by message from Peter Allan what had happened. The "solitaries"—at the time a mere half a dozen—were having their daily exercise in the park, during which period they could mix freely. Being only a few, they were sparsely guarded, though confined to one end of the compound, where the prisoners played football among the trees. Lebrun was in the habit of doing exercises with two other Frenchmen, which included much leap-frogging. Now Lebrun was athletic. It was high summer and he was dressed in what remained to him of his former

[1] Lieut. A. M. Allan.

finery—shorts, a yellow cardigan, an open-necked shirt, and gym shoes—not good escaping clothes, but that was also what he reckoned the Germans would think. While a couple of the latter were lolling rather sleepily outside the wire and looking at anything but the prisoners, Lebrun innocently leap-frogged with the other Frenchmen.

It all happened in a flash. His French colleague stood near the wire and, forming with his two hands a stirrup into which Lebrun placed his foot, he catapulted him upwards. Acrobats can heave each other tremendous distances by this method. Precision of timing of muscular effort is its secret. Lebrun and his friend managed it, and the former sailed in a headlong dive over the nine-foot wire.

This was only half the battle. Lebrun ran twenty yards along the fence to the main wall of the park. He had to reclimb the wire, using it as a ladder, in order to hoist himself on to the top of the wall which was, at this point, about thirteen feet high. Rather than present a slowly moving target during this climb, Lebrun deliberately attracted the fire of the two nearest sentries by running backwards and forwards beside the wall. Their carbines once fired (and having missed), the reloading gave him the extra seconds he needed. He was on top of the wall by the time they fired again and dropped to the ground on the other side in a hail of bullets as the more distant sentries joined in the fusillade.

He disappeared and was never recaught. He certainly deserves the greatest credit for this escape, which was in the true French cavalry tradition and demanded the very quintessence of courage, remembering the effort was made in cold blood and with every opportunity for reflection on the consequences of a false step. A British officer, in a similar attempt a few years later, was shot dead. The escape savours of a generation of Frenchmen of whom the majority disappeared on the battlefields of the First World War and who, alas, never had the chance to sire and educate a generation like themselves to follow in their footsteps.

The loss, which was so deeply felt in the 'thirties and which found physical expression during the critical days of 1940, is happily in these days of the 'fifties fading like a bad dream. The young blood of France is quickening again and there is a new courage in the air.

I met Lebrun again long afterwards, when the war was over, and here is the end of his story.

Lebrun escaped on 1 July, 1941. Although he had the sleuth-hounds and a posse of Goons on his tail within ten minutes, he managed to hide in a field of wheat. (You must walk in backwards, rearranging the stalks as you go.) There he hid the whole afternoon with a search 'plane circling continuously above him. At 10 p.m. he set off. He had twenty German marks which were smuggled into his prison cell from the camp. He walked about fifty miles and then stole a bicycle and cycled between sixty and a hundred miles a day. He posed as an Italian officer and begged or bought food at lonely farmhouses, making sure, by a stealthy watch beforehand, that there were only women in the house. His bicycle "sprang a leak", so he abandoned it and stole a second. On the journey to the Swiss frontier he was stopped twice by guards and ran for it each time. On the second occasion, about twenty-five miles from the frontier, he tripped the guard up with the aid of his bicycle and knocked him out with his bicycle pump. He took to the woods and crossed the frontier safely on 8 July.

Within a week he was in France. In December, 1942, he crossed the Pyrenees and was taken prisoner by the Spaniards, who locked him up in a castle. He jumped from a window into the moat and broke his spine on some rocks at the bottom, was removed, laid down on a mattress, and left to die. A local French Consul, however, who had previously been endeavouring to extricate the incarcerated Lebrun, heard of the accident and insisted on an immediate operation. Lebrun's life was saved. He eventually reached Algeria to carry on the war. To-day, though permanently crippled by his fall, he is a pillar of his own country.

If any German had examined Lebrun's cell at Colditz when he left for his daily exercise on 1 July, he might have nipped Lebrun's escape in the bud. Lebrun had packed up his belongings and addressed them to himself in France. Months later they arrived—forwarded by Oberstleutnant Prawitt, the Colditz Camp Commandant!

★   ★   ★

The most daredevil Polish officer at Colditz among a bunch of daredevils was "Niki", 2nd-Lieutenant (Ensign) N. Surmanowicz. He was a small weedy-looking young man with an untidy face made up of unequal-sided triangles. The fire that burnt in his soul showed only in his eyes, which glowed with fanatical ardour. He was a great friend of mine and we went on many marauding expeditions together through the forbidden parts of the camp. He taught me all I ever knew about lock-picking, at which he was an expert. It was Niki who had been one of the first visitors up in the loft on our arrival at Colditz. The manufacture of magnetic compasses was also a pastime of his. This he carried out with the aid of a home-made solenoid, employing the electric current of the main camp supply, which happened to be "direct" current. The number of compasses fabricated by him alone, together with their pivots, compass cards, and glass-covered boxes, went into the fifties.

His schemes for escaping were, to my mind, mostly too wild to bear serious examination. He, on the other hand, thought my ideas prosaic and I know he inwardly deprecated my painstaking way of setting about escape problems.

Like Lebrun, he relied on "dash", to which he added a depth of cunning hardly to be equalled. In common with all the Poles, he despised the Germans, but, unfortunately also like many Poles, he underestimated his enemy; a form of conceit which, however, is not a monopoly of the Poles.

Niki spent as much time in solitary confinement as he spent with "the common herd". On one occasion in the summer of

54

1941 he occupied a cell which had a small window, high up in the wall, opening on to our courtyard. Another Polish officer, Lieutenant Mietek Schmiel, a friend of Niki, occupied the cell next door. I received a message from him one day, saying that he and Schmiel were going to escape that night and would I join them! I declined the invitation for two reasons; firstly, I thought Niki was crazy, and, secondly, I had given up the idea of escaping myself so long as I remained Escape Officer. With the British contingent on the increase rapidly, this latter course was the only one open to me if I wished to retain the confidence of our group as an impartial arbiter and helper.

I passed on Niki's invitation to a few of the most hare-brained among our company, but Niki's invitation was politely refused by all!

Nobody believed he was serious. Nobody believed he could ghost his way out of his heavily barred and padlocked cell, then open his friend's cell and then unlock the main door of the solitary cell corridor which opened on to the courtyard. Having accomplished this feat, he was inside the prison camp, the same as everyone else! Niki loved a challenge and he would chuckle with laughter for the rest of his life if he could show the Jerries once and for all that it took more than they could contrive to keep a Pole down.

He left the invitation open, giving a rendezvous in the court-yard outside the solitary confinement cells at 11 p.m. that night.

I was at my window watching as 11 p.m. struck, and on the minute I saw the door of the cells open slowly. All was dark and I could only faintly distinguish the two figures as they crept out. Then something dropped from a window high up in the Polish quarters. It was a rope made of sheets with a load strapped at the bottom—their escape kit, clothes and rucksacks. Next I saw the figures climb the rope one after the other to a ledge forty feet above the ground. What they were about to do was impossible, but they had achieved the impossible once already. I could no longer believe my eyes. The ledge they were on jutted four inches out from the sheer face of the wall of the building. They both held the rope, which was still suspended from the window above them. My heart pounded against my ribs as I saw them high above me with their backs against the wall moving along the ledge inch by inch a distance of ten yards before reaching the safety of a gutter on the eaves of the German guardhouse.

Once there, they were comparatively safe and out of sight if the courtyard lights were turned on. I then saw them climb up the roof to a skylight through which they disappeared, pulling the long rope of sheets, which was let loose by Polish confederates, after them.

Their next move, I knew, was to descend from a small window at the outer end of the attic of the German guardhouse. The drop was about one hundred and twenty feet, continuing down the face of the cliff upon which the Castle was built.

I retired to my bunk, weak at the knees and shaking, as if I had done the climb myself.

The next morning the two of them were back in their cells! I find it hard to tell the end of the story. Niki wore plimsolls for the climb, but his colleague, with Niki's agreement, preferred to wear boots of the mountaineering type. As they both descended the long drop from the guardhouse, the mountaineering boots made too much noise against the wall and awoke the German duty officer sleeping in the guardhouse. He opened his window, to see the rope dangling beside him and a body a few yards below him. He drew his revolver and, true to type, shouted *Hande hoch!* several times and called out the guard.

I spent a month in Niki's cell later on without being able to discover how he had opened the door!

After this episode the Germans placed a sentry in the courtyard. He remained all night with the lights full on, which was to prove a nuisance for later escape attempts.

* * *

The French contingent had also been quiet for some time.

They seemed to be resting on the laurels of Lebrun's escape for too long.

It was with pleasure therefore, although with considerable misgivings for its ultimate success, that I received the news of the commencement of a French tunnel. Its entrance was at the top of the clock-tower, a hundred feet from ground-level; that, at any rate, I thought, was a good beginning.

So many tunnels, and exits generally, begin at ground-level, that at Colditz, at least, it was almost a waste of time to start work in the conventional manner. If someone thought of a tunnel, we examined the attics; if someone thought of escaping by glider (do not laugh! for one was made in Colditz and is to this day, as far as I know, concealed there), we started, if possible, underground! The short Laufen tunnel and the Colditz canteen tunnel began at ground-level, although the entrances to both were under German lock and key. Clandestine entrances rose to the second-floor level in the theatre escape; hovered on the first floor with the snow tunnel; then rose to the third floor in the Dutch vertical-shaft tunnel, and now the French capped all by starting their tunnel at the top of the clock-tower!

The most serious danger, of course, for all tunnel attempts nowadays in Colditz was that of sound detectors placed around the Castle. The lightning descents of Priem[2] on our snow tunnel and on the Dutch tunnel were too speedy compared with what we could expect of normal Jerry vigilance. At the same time, as far as tunnel entrances were concerned, German scrutiny of floors and walls decreased in inverse ratio as one increased one's height from the ground!

The French tunnel was a gigantic undertaking. I shall leave it for the present at its entrance.

Further French originality displayed itself shortly after their tunnel had begun. One spring afternoon a mixed batch of French, Dutch, and British were marching through the third gateway leading down to the exercise ground, or park as it was

[2]Hauptmann (Captain) Priem, second-in-command at Colditz.

called. The majority had just "wheeled right", down the ramp roadway, when a gorgeous-looking German lady passed by. She haughtily disdained to look at the prisoners, and walked primly past, going up the ramp towards the German courtyard of the Castle. There were low whistles of admiration from the more bawdy-minded prisoners—for she was a veritable Rhine maiden with golden-blonde hair. She wore a broad-brimmed hat, smart blouse and skirt, and high-heeled shoes; she was large as well as handsome—a fitting consort for a German demigod!

As she swept past us, her fashionable-looking wrist-watch fell from her arm at the feet of Squadron-Leader Paddon, who was marching in front of me. Paddon was familiarly known as "Never-a-dull-moment" Paddon, because he was always getting into trouble! The Rhine maiden had not noticed her loss, but Paddon, being a gentleman, picked up the watch and shouted:

"Hey, Miss! You've dropped your watch."

The Rhine maiden, like a barque under full sail, had already tacked to port, and was out of sight. Paddon thereupon made frantic signs to the nearest guard, explaining:

"*Das Fräulein hat ihre Uhr verloren. Ja!—Uhr—verloren,*"[3] and he held up the dainty article.

"*Ach so! Danke,*" replied the guard, grasping what had happened. He seized the watch from Paddon's hand and shouted to a sentry in the courtyard to stop the lady.

The lady was, by now, primly stepping towards the other (main) gateway which led out of the camp. The sentry stopped her, and immediately became affable, looking, no doubt, deeply into her eyes from which, unfortunately, no tender light responded! "Hm!" the sentry reflected, as she did not reply to his cajoling. "She is dumb or very haughty or just plain rude."

He looked at her again and noticed something—maybe the blonde hair had gone awry. The second scrutiny, at a yard's distance, was enough for him. By the time our guard arrived pant-

[3] "The young lady has lost her watch—yes—watch—lost."

ing with the watch, the Rhine maiden stood divested of her Tarnhelmet, a sorrowful sight, minus her wig and spring bonnet, revealing the head of Lieutenant Bouley (Chasseur Alpin), who unhappily did not speak or understand a word of German.

This escape had been the result of many months of patient effort and was prepared with the assistance of the officer's wife in France. The French were allowed to receive parcels direct from their next-of-kin, which made this possible. He had a complete lady's outfit including silk stockings. The golden hair was a triumph of the wigmaker's art, of real hair, collected, bleached, curled, and sewn together. The wig was put together in Colditz. The large straw bonnet was the product of French patterns and Colditz straw weaving.

The transformation had been practised for weeks and was a conjuring trick which, I regret, I never saw enacted. The "conjurer" had three accomplices and the usual "stooges" to distract momentarily the attention of the guards as he turned the corner out of the gateway leading to the park. At this point, the "conjurer" could count on a few seconds of "blind-spot", which might be drawn out to, say, ten or twelve seconds by a good "stooge" attending to the guard immediately behind him. The guards were ranged along the ranks on both sides at intervals of ten yards.

Part of the transformation was done on the march, prior to arrival at the corner—for instance, strapping on the watch, pulling up the silk stockings, the rouging of lips and the powdering of the face. Once in the gateway, the high-heeled shoes were put on. The blouse and bosoms were in place, under a loose cloak around his shoulders. The skirt was tucked up around his waist. His accomplices held the wig, the hat, and the lady's bag.

There is a moral to this story which is worth recording. I had not been informed of the forthcoming attempt and certainly I sympathized with the French in their desire for complete surprise. It was much better, for instance, that the parade going to the park should be unconscious of what was taking place. The participants behaved naturally in consequence, whereas the least whispering or craning of necks or rising on tiptoe—any conscious movement—might have upset the effort. Yet the fact of having informed me would not have made much difference to all this. Neither would I have been able to warn all the British on the parade; it would have been dangerous. Nevertheless, the moral emerges: the fateful coincidence that I happened to be behind Paddon on the walk; that, if I had been warned, I might have nipped the watch incident in the bud, and the escape would probably have succeeded.

The Naked Island

by RUSSELL BRADDON

Of all the reminiscences of the Second World War, Russell Braddon's
The Naked Island *is that most incandescent with hatred. His experiences
as a Japanese prisoner-of-war have burned themselves into his memory and
those of his readers.*

*Braddon, a raw Australian recruit, was captured early and released late.
His story, essentially personal, is devoted far more to others; and presents
the profound comradeship that defied all that the Japanese—experts in torture—could do to break the spirit of the men who made the Burma Road.*

A NEW field of work was opened up for us by the Jap decision
to move everything in the Austin works from wherever
it was in the building to some other place in the building. The
Jap engineers who supervised this task were quite the most evil-
tempered gentlemen we ever encountered.

During one of our midday breaks, an N.C.O. approached
us to air his knowledge of English and gloat. "War," he
announced, "finish-u soon".

"Go on, eh, Nippon?" Harry encouraged him. "How's
that?"

"Birrama, you know?" asked the Nip—we said yes, we knew
Burma, a word the Japs could never master.

"Indiah, you know?" asked the Nip—we said yes, we knew
India.

"Australiah, you know?" asked the Nip—we said yes, we
knew Australia (and an Argyll added testily, "Och, mon, cut
oot the geography and tell us your news").

"New Zealand, you know?" asked the Nip—wearily we said yes.

"All," said the Nip, with an embracing gesture towards his own bosom, "all Nippon". We laughed heartily and the round yellow face with the shaved eyebrows and the brown eyes glittering went as close to a flush of rage as the Japanese can manage. Exercising all of his limited self-control the Nip produced the daily newspaper printed in K.L.[1]—printed in English because no one could read Japanese—and pointed to the headlines. We Australians took one look and became convulsed at once with laughter.

"Nippon's Warrior Gods of the Air Destroy Outer Suburbs of Broome", the paper announced grandiosely. We laughed and laughed and—determined to back us up, though not really understanding—the Pommies[2] laughed, too. In between outbursts, we explained to the Pommies that Broome—whose outer suburbs the Nips claimed to have destroyed—contained one makeshift air-strip and about four tin sheds. The laughter became louder as this information spread and the Nip flushed deeper. Finally, his hand, as always when in doubt, flew to the bayonet that hung from his second belt.

"Nippon Number One", he screamed. A solid chorus of British voices assured him that Nippon, on the contrary, was Number Ten.

"Tojo Number One", he bellowed, his eyes bloodshot—and slashed the Argyll nearest him, who, looking as indifferent as if he had been stung by a mosquito, replied: "Churchill Number One—Tojo Number Two Hundred". The hysterical Nip looked to the rest of us for confirmation of this astounding statement. We did not fail him.

"Churchill Number One—Tojo Number Two Hundred," we declared with authority. It was on! Our party was at once fallen in in two ranks and the entire guard, armed with lumps

[1]Kuala Lumpur.
[2]Englishmen.

of timber, then marched up and down slugging anyone whose face did not appeal to them—which, I must admit, seemed to be most of us. There is something in the British physiognomy which, it would appear, is most disagreeable to all Japanese.

After twenty minutes, the mass bashing still continued and the Nips—far from getting over it by their outburst—seemed only to be whipping themselves up into a state of murder. Half a dozen of them ran, flailing indiscriminately, their faces contorted, up and down our lines. It was ceasing to be amusing. This was another of those occasions when the lighthearted bashing had passed into the realms of possible massacre. Our survival now depended upon our taking everything standing upright and in silence (to fall to the ground or to complain was a stimulant which, under these conditions, always sent the Japs completely out of control).

Typically, the Nips picked on the biggest man on the parade —an Australian. Standing before him, the smallest guard hit him with everything he had. Lumps of wood, his bayonet, his rifle, his fist. The Australian took it all expressionlessly. Both ranks of men stiffened with revulsion and a muttering broke out. Another few seconds, and, consequences regardless, discretion would be abandoned and the Nips disposed of once and for all. It was an Argyll who saved us.

Leaping out of the front rank, the little Scot, no taller than the Nip, young and furious, sprang on the guard and rocked him to the foundations of his web-toed canvas boots with a clicking left to the chin.

The silence that ensued was startling. The Nip stood dazed with blood trickling from the right-hand corner of the mouth. All the other guards stood with their hands on their bayonets. Two ranks of prisoners waited tense. The Scot faced the Nip.

"Leave the Aussie alone, you animal," the Argyll said quietly, his left foot still forward and his fists, though only half-clenched, at the ready. On his bare forearm two tattooed hands clasped each other firmly. It was the only friendly thing about that forearm just then. "Leave him alone," he repeated. The Nip moved, raising a hand slowly to his mouth to wipe it. Then, as he lowered the hand and noticed the blood on his fingers, the stillness broke. He screamed with rage and flung himself at the Argyll. Simultaneously the other guards hurled themselves forward and, before we could move, the youngster was lying broken on the ground. The episode was over. We Australians carried him back to the gaol. We did what we could. There was nothing he could not have had so long as we ourselves had it. He died a few days later.

★   ★   ★

The oldest member of our party died of what looked suspiciously like cholera. Another fell ill and followed him shortly afterwards. We were now six and I found that my limbs no longer functioned very well. There was an angry swelling in my feet which made them look like purple balloons—the toes mere cocktail-sausages attached to them like teats on an udder.

As I looked at them one of the others, pointing at my bloated extremities, asked: "What's the trouble?"

"Oedema," I told him.

"Christ!" he said, much impressed; then, cautiously, "What's that?"

"Swelling," I told him.

"Silly bastard," he laughed, "why didn't you say so first time?"

But oedema or swelling or whatever the cause, my legs now ceased walking either easily or quickly and whenever any weight was put on my back they folded up. Since Nippon's only object in bringing us all to Thailand had been to put weights on our backs and then get us to carry them elsewhere this condition of mine did not bode well for the future.

And, in truth, things would have gone very badly indeed for me had it not been for the generous help of the men with me. At all times they covered up for me so that the guards did not

64

realize how slowly I worked. And when they had finished their own quota of work then they would do mine too.

In this respect one Snowy Bernard did most. He was unfortunate enough to have paired up with me when we first started work. Now that my arms seemed to have no strength with an axe he would chop down his own timber, then mine. When my legs crumpled under the weight of carrying the timber—particularly the long bamboos—back to the camp, he would deliver his own, then come back and deliver mine. And never was there any suggestion of condescension but only that inexhaustible readiness on the part of the ordinary man to lend a hand whenever it was needed.

And all the time that Snowy and the three other men carried me so steadfastly, I became more and more of a burden. The swelling spread up to my legs so that ankles and knees vanished into two water-filled columns of suet. Then my trunk began to swell with that same ominous suggestion of liquid beneath the skin tissues and even my eyes became merely two slits in a puffy sphere. I was constantly surprised by the slowness of my movements. I was not aware of being slow, but my companions and I had only to start walking and in thirty seconds I was thirty yards behind them. Then Snowy would stop and come back and shove me firmly along until we caught up—whereupon, left to my own devices, I would at once flounder to the rear again.

The guards began to take an unconcealed interest in my condition and daily showed their surprise that I was still alive. "Ashita mati mati," they would say, pointing towards the crop of arms and legs that protruded from the washed-out graves beyond our tent, and drawing a mocking cross on the ground. If I had required any stimulant to prevent me from succumbing to the beri-beri that so bloated me those daily jibes by the guards would have done the job perfectly. Nevertheless the morning at last arrived when I found that not only could I not walk as fast as the others, I could not walk at all . . .

By this time the fluids of the wet beri-beri which swamped me were flopping round in my chest, having crept up from my legs, and a most unwelcome sound it was. The Nips now abandoned their drawings of graves and crosses on the ground and instead mimed a man drowning. I had become indifferent towards many modes of death, but drowning could never be one of them. The only preventative I could think of was to consume sufficient Vitamin B tablets (they would have, of course, to be stolen from the Japs) to overcome the deficiency which caused the beri-beri.

A large force of Japanese reinforcements came sloshing up the jungle trail, shoving mountain artillery along with them. Their hoarse, rhythmic shouts of "Esau, Esau" as they pushed mountain guns along mud tracks sounded harsh and bad-tempered. They were not misleading.

Though we had just finished a particularly heavy shift we were routed out to light fires, boil water, cook food. An officer thrust his waterproof cape at me and indicated that I was to dry it. I was shivering with a malarial rigor.

Standing in front of the fire with the cape I found it impossible not to sway on my unstable legs. Soon the inevitable occurred—the cape caught alight. Before I extinguished the flame one corner of the gentlemen's garment had vanished into a tiny heap of ash and a black cloud of pungent smoke.

The gentleman himself was not slow to notice any of these things. With a hoarse "Currah", he leapt up. He kicked, leaving a perfect impression of his toe-cap in my sodden flesh for hours afterwards; he swiped with his bayonet, cutting open the back of my head: and he then, for good measure, shoved me firmly into the fire. Bloated as I was, I was slow to move. I was surprised to notice that, though the skin bubbled and the flesh smelt singed, I felt nothing. The beri-beri had at least done that for me, I reflected gratefully. On the other hand, however little it hurt, one couldn't afford to remain sprawled in a fire for long. Snowy solved the problem by ignoring the officer's bellows and dragging me out. It was all over in seconds, but it did nothing to heighten in my mind my impressions of *Bushido or Japanese Chivalry*.[3]

Muttering to himself, as Snowy brushed me free of embers, the officer took his charred cape and placed it resentfully over his other possessions. Following his actions with a wary eye, I noticed that from the top of his haversack there protruded a large bottle of Vitamin B tablets.

When I left the guardhouse, so did the bottle. That night I sat up and ate solidly the small brown tablets of bran so rich in Vitamin B. They did not make easy eating, but I was a man who for a hundred days had been mocked by the Japanese as a perambulating corpse, so I continued munching. By morning the bottle was empty. I did not require my small ration of rice.

About two days later I reaped the profits of my theft. We had just gone to our bed-spaces and I was laboriously scrubbing clean (with a few drops of water in my mug and my tooth brush) the burns I had received on my hands, arms and legs as a result of being booted so unceremoniously into a fire. It suddenly became necessary to urinate. I crawled the thirty yards to our make-shift urinal and obliged, and started to crawl back to the tent. I had only gone half-way, however, when it became necessary to reverse. Eventually I stayed there, and every ten minutes or so for two days fluid poured out of me. My chest no longer looked puffy: my stomach lost its thick, pregnant look: my knees reappeared: then my ankles: then my toes. The beri-beri bloated pudding was gone. In its place stood a skeleton which had never in all its life been so pleased with its physical condition than at this moment, when, according to the Japanese quartermaster's scales, it weighed eighty-one pounds. . . .

[3] Title of a book lent to Braddon by a Japanese.
[4]Russell Bradden is five feet, ten inches.

Enemy Coast Ahead

by GUY GIBSON, V.C.

*The late Guy Gibson, V.C., was one of the outstanding leaders of the
Second World War, and stands, also, as a mirror of the spirit of the Royal
Air Force: a man at once incredibly gay and incredibly gallant, superbly
dashing and superbly efficient. Within his short life he was both bomber and
fighter; was in large measure responsible for the successful development of
our night-fighting technique; and set the seal on his career by leading the
assault on the Moehne and Eder dams.*

*Enemy Coast Ahead reflects the very spirit of the age and the arm in
which it was—very hastily—written; but the very quality of the reckless
prose has its true value.*

. . . "BERLIN to-night, chaps," says the Squadron-Commander. "Maximum effort; get cracking."

On the airfield a few minutes later there is a roar of engines as
Lancaster after Lancaster takes off to be given its air test. These
air tests take about half an hour each, and are very thoroughly
done. Everything is tested—wireless, guns, navigational instruments, bomb doors. Sometimes even a few bombs are dropped
for practice to make sure that the bomb-aimer will be on his
target to-night.

Then comes lunch. A short, absent-minded meal taken in the
minimum of time. Not much is said, most minds are pre-
occupied, often the Squadron-Commander does not have time
for lunch at all. The 'phone bell is ringing incessantly.

After this comes briefing. Here all the information is trans-
mitted to the crews who are going to take part in to-night's big
effort. The room is packed, many of the boys, in their roll-

necked pullovers, are standing crowding up against the back of the room. In the corner there may be one or two war correspondents and perhaps a visiting army officer.

The Squadron-Commander comes in, followed by the navigation officer, and the crews get up and stop talking. The babble of conversation dies away and he begins his briefing. "O.K., chaps; sit down. Berlin to-night, aiming point X. This is the centre of a cluster of factories making Daimler-Benz engines. You can see it quite clearly here on the map." He points to a position somewhere in Berlin. "To-night a total of 700 bombers are going. They are all four-engined types, so if you see anything twin-engined you can shoot at it. The bomb-load will be one 4,000-pounder and sixteen cans of incendiaries, so the total load will be about 2,000 tons. It ought to be a pretty good prang. The met. man[1] says the weather will be clear all the way, which is pretty phenomenal. Let's hope he's right. The Pathfinders are going to attack from zero hour minus one to zero hour plus 35; it is going to be a quick, concentrated attack. Your bombing height will be 21,000 feet. Don't get out of this height band or you will run into other aircraft. As it is, we are very lucky not to be the bottom squadron; they will probably see a few bombs whistling past them on the way down. The route is the usual one marked on the board here. The Pathfinder procedure will be detailed by the navigation officer." He cocks his head over to the corner of the room and calls, "Nav."

The navigation officer, a big round man with the D.F.C. and bar, gets up and begins talking. "Zero hour is 18.45 hours. At zero hour minus three and a third minutes the Pathfinders will sky-mark the lane to the target with red flares which will change to green after 120 seconds. At this time, too, they will mark a point on the ground exactly fifteen miles short of the aiming point. With the ground speed of 240 miles an hour this should give three and three-quarter minutes to go to the target. The timing has got to be done in seconds. If anybody is late, he will

[1] Meteorological expert.

probably get a packet, so pilots must keep their air-speeds dead right. The target-indicating marker will go down at exactly zero minus one, and should be right on the factory roof. The sky above will also be marked by green flares in case the T.I.s[2] are obscured by fog or smoke. I will see all navigators after the briefing to give them the tracks and distances."

He turns round to the Squadron-Commander, who gets up again and gives his final orders. "Now don't forget, chaps," he begins; "once you have reached the preliminary target indicator you turn on to a course of 135 degrees magnetic and hold it for four minutes. You are to take no evasive action, but to keep straight on past the target. Once you have dropped your bombs you may weave about slightly and gain speed by going down in a gentle dive. The Pathfinders will drop a cluster of green and red flares thirty miles beyond Berlin, and you are to concentrate on these, and return home in a gaggle. Now don't forget, no straggling. We've had pretty low losses so far and we don't want any to-night; and don't forget to twist your tails a bit so that you can see those fighters, which come up from below. I think that's about all. Don't forget your landing discipline when you come to base. I will see you down in the crew room before take-off. O.K."

The boys go out noisily. Some are on their first trip and look a bit worried. The veterans look as if they are just going to a tea-party, but inside they feel differently. After the briefing a war correspondent comes up and asks the Squadron-Commander a few questions.

"Why all this concentration?" he asks. "What is the exact idea?" The Squadron-Commander is a busy man, but he gives him the whole answer. How there are so many guns in Germany, all depending on short-wave electricity for their prediction, so that if one aircraft were to go over every five minutes, each gun would have that aircraft all to itself. Similarly with the night-fighters. But if all the aircraft go over more or less simultaneously then the guns cannot pick out and fire at any one aircraft nor can the night-fighters be vectored on to any one aircraft. With the result that losses are kept down. Moreover, the bombing takes a more concentrated form when all aircraft bomb together.

"How about collisions?" the war correspondent asks.

"There won't be any," said the Squadron-Leader, "provided they keep straight, and if the Pathfinders are on time. Sometimes this doesn't happen. One night at Stuttgart the Pathfinders were fifteen minutes late and there were some 400 bombers circling the target waiting for them; eighteen didn't come back. Some of those were collisions, I think."

The time after the briefing is not very pleasant. No one knows what to do. Some sit in the Mess, listening to the radio, and wishing they were far away from all this. A few play billiards. But most of them just sit in chairs picking up papers and throwing them down, staring into space and waiting for the clock on the wall to show the time when they must go down to get on their flying-clothes.

The time passes slowly, minutes seem like hours, but it is a busy time for the Squadron-Commander and his Flight-Commanders. First Group telephones to confirm that there is the full number of aircraft on from the squadron. Then the maintenance officer to say that C Charlie has blown an engine, shall he put on the reserve? Yes, put on reserve.

A call from the armament officer—a cookie[3] has dropped off Z Zebra.

"Is everyone all right?"

"Yes, everyone's all right."

"Well, put it on again, then."

The oxygen has leaked from G George—get on to the maintenance flight to have new oxygen bottles put in. And so it goes on, the 'phone ringing the whole time. He does not have time to think, and presently everyone is in the crew rooms dressing

[3] A bomb in R.A.F. slang.

for the big raid, putting on their multiple underwear and electrically-heated suits before going out to the aircraft.

All the boys are chattering happily, but this is only to cover up their true feelings. But they all know that they will be quite all right once they get into their aircraft.

"Prang it good, boys," says an Australian who isn't coming to-night; one of his crew is sick.

Then comes the take-off. A thrilling sight to the layman. Exactly at the right time they taxi out, led by the Squadron-Commander in his own aircraft with a gaudy design painted on the nose. They come out one after another, like a long string of ducks, and line up on the runway waiting to take off. There is a cheery wave of goodbyes from the well-wishers on the first flare. Then the pilot slams his window shut and pushes open the throttles. The ground underneath the well-wishers shivers and shakes, sending a funny feeling up their spine, and the Lancasters lumber off one after another down the mile-long flare-path. And off they go into the dusk.

Over to a farm labourer sitting on his tractor in a field. . . . He has just done his ploughing and is about to go home. He is looking forward to his evening meal. Looking up, he can see hundreds of specks in the sky, black specks, all getting smaller and smaller as they climb higher and higher into the night air. He turns to his tractor and says, "They be going out again to-night. I 'ope they give 'em bastards hell. May they all come back again, God bless 'em. Good boys they be." Then he begins to trudge home.

Over to a girl typist about to get out of a bus in the nearby city. She hears the roar of the aircraft and says to her companion, "Oh, there they go again. I do hope they will come back early; otherwise they will wake me up. . . ."

Over to one of our aircraft flying high. . . . They have just reached their operational height. The engines are throttled back to cruising revolutions. "Hullo, navigator. Skipper calling. What time must I set course for rendezvous point?"

The navigator gets a quick fix. "We are about sixty miles away. If you circle here for five minutes, then set course at 240 miles an hour, you will be there dead on time."

"O.K.," says the skipper. "You all right, rear-gunner?"

"Yes," comes the voice from the back.

In five minutes' time he sets course and the blunt nose of the Lancaster points towards the east. At that moment nearly all the bombers have done the same thing and, with navigation lights on at their various heights, they all converge on to the rendez-vous spot at exactly zero minus two hours. They reach it more or less together, then all navigation lights go out simultaneously and they straighten up on their course for Berlin. The captain yells to his crew to check that all lights are out on board. The bomb-aimer fuses the bombs, the gunners cock their guns and they are on their way.

To describe this big bomber force flying out in this formation is not easy. But imagine a glass brick two miles across, twenty miles long and 8,000 feet thick, filled with hundreds of Lancasters, and move it slowly towards the Dutch coast, and there you have a concentrated wave on its way. The Dutch coast looms up incredibly soon, rather too soon. . . .

It is now five o'clock. At this hour in Germany operational messages have come in from Gruppen and Staffeln of night-fighters scattered throughout German territory. Messerschmitt, Focke-Wulf and other types of fighters are fully loaded with fuel and ammunition, ready for take-off from the operational bases. Aircraft and personnel are ready, mechanics, engineers, armourers are on duty on many airfields ready to supply suddenly arriving aircraft with fresh fuel and more ammunition. Everything has been done to ensure the quickest possible employment of the night-fighter arm.

At this hour it is quiet at the German searchlight and flak batteries. Ammunition stocks have been made up again since the last raid. The enormous power-plants of the searchlights need only be switched on by the young Luftwaffe helpers to convert the electric current, enough to supply a medium-sized town, into shimmering light and send it up into the night sky. The sentries on the large 8.8-cm. guns pace up and down and watch the approaching night. It will soon be pitch dark, as the sky is covered with heavy rain-clouds, and the crescent moon will not rise until later. Even then its light will scarcely pierce the dark clouds. The British prefer nights such as this.

1740 hours. A message comes into the centre near Berlin from the Channel coast. An alarm bell rings. Strong British bomber units are crossing the Dutch coast. A telephone call warns the air-defence forces of the Continent. The night-fighter units in Holland have already taken off and are on the look-out for the enemy on his eastern course, attach themselves to his units, and while the first night engagements between the German night-fighters and the British bombers are setting the stage for the great night battle, the ground crews of countless other Geschwader in the region of Central Germany are putting the final touches to the aircraft as they stand ready to take off.

Behind the great glass map stand female signals auxiliaries wearing head-phones and laryngophones, with a thick stick of charcoal in their right hands with which they draw in the position of the enemy units. From the control room only their shadows moving behind the glass plate can be seen. Ceaselessly the strokes and arrows on the great map give place to new markings.

Every officer and man takes up his position. Each knows exactly what he has to do, and all work together without friction.

The glass map shows that the enemy is advancing along several different directions, but it is clear that the main force is continuing eastwards. The enemy bombers have crossed the frontier of Western Germany. Suddenly they swing round towards the south-east. A few weaker formations are flying southwards up the Rhine. Cascades are dropped over two West German towns; it may be that the main attack is to be directed against these towns, but it may also be that this is a feint movement designed to lure the German night-fighters into the wrong areas. The enemy hopes that a wrong German order will gain him valuable minutes to get his main attacking force into the prescribed target area, where he would then find weaker German night fighter forces.

The control officer, who is fully acquainted with the many different problems and questions, the possibilities of attack and defence, makes his decision after conscientiously checking the situation and a brief talk with the O.C. The British force is still on its way towards Central Germany. The main force of the bombers has made another turn and is again flying east. The last message reads: "Front of enemy formation in Dora-Heinrich area, course east."

1830 hours. At this moment fighter unit X, whose aircraft are ready at the end of the runway with their engines roaring, receives the order "Unit X—village take off by visual beacon Y."

A few minutes later the aircraft are racing over the ground, climbing rapidly, flying towards the flashing light of visual beacon Y. In Berlin the Underground is still running, and traffic goes on as usual. Then the population gets its first warning; the Deutschlandsender goes off the air. The bright lights at the marshalling yard are switched off. The great city sinks into darkness.

The enemy has meanwhile flown past to the north of the first large central German town. In a bare hour he may be over Berlin. At a height of 6,500 m.[4] the four-engine bombers are roaring on their way eastwards.

1845 hours. A message in the head-phones: the enemy has already lost seven aircraft before reaching Osnabrück.

Other night-fighter units are ready to take off to protect the capital. The meteorologist is describing the weather situation. Cloudless sky over South Germany, where night-fighters can land after the battle.

Meanwhile the night-fighter units, which have assembled in

21,000 ft.

75

certain areas, are guided closer to the enemy. The German fighters have already made contact everywhere with the enemy bomber formations. Now the sirens are sounded in Berlin.

Important decisions are taken relating to the activity of the searchlight batteries, taking into consideration the weather situation. Orders are issued to the batteries of the Berlin flak division.

1916 hours. The enemy is 100 kilometres from Berlin. A large number of night-fighters are accompanying the British bombers.

The O.C. sits next to the 1A (Intelligence) officer. In order to clear up a question quickly he asks to speak to the O.C. in another Luftgau; command priority call to X town. In a matter of seconds a female signals auxiliary has made the desired telephone connection.

On the great glass map the arrows draw closer and closer to Berlin. The positions of the night-fighter units are exactly shown.

1941 hours. Is the enemy going straight for Berlin? At 1943 hours fire is opened by a heavy flak battery in the west. It is still impossible to say whether the mass of the enemy bombers will not again make a sharp turn short of Berlin and perhaps attack Leipzig.

Above the inner part of the town the enemy drops streams and cascades of flares. Strong forces are reported over various suburbs. A hail of H.E. shells from the heavy flak rushes up to the heights of the approaching bombers.

In spite of the difficulties of the weather the night-fighters hunt out the enemy. In the brilliant beams of the searchlights the British aircraft are clearly recognizable. The enemy drops his bombs on the city's industrial areas and then tries to get away as quickly as possible. At top speed other German night-fighters chase after him to shoot up as many of his forces as possible.

Over to the leading Pathfinder aircraft.

"How far are we from the target, Nav.?"

"About twenty-five miles."

"O.K. Stand by to drop preliminary target marker."

"Standing by."

A voice from the mid-upper turret, "Flak coming up port behind, skipper."

"O.K."

The guns are just beginning to open up down below. Ahead lies Berlin, still and silent. Berlin seems to be lying down there like a gigantic mouse, frightened to move, petrified. Suddenly it is galvanized into life; hundreds of gun-flashes come up from its roofs, its parks and its railway flak.

"Don't weave, for Christ's sake, skipper; only another minute." This from the navigator.

Again the captain's voice: "O.K."

He is not saying much. Both hands are on the wheel, his eyes are darting everywhere, looking for trouble and hoping not to find it. His aircraft seems huge, it appears to be the only one in the sky, every gun down below seems to be aiming at him, the gun-flashes are vicious, short and cruel.

Down below, to the Germans, he is the first of many hundreds of small spots on cathode-ray tubes. The civilians have long since gone to their shelters, but those of the A.R.P., police and fire-watching services are beginning to hear the loud, angry roar of the invading force.

"Coming up now, skipper. Steady—coming up—coming up —now! O.K. T.I. gone."

A few seconds later it bursts and cascades on to the ground; a mass of green bells, shining brightly, for all the world like a lit-up merry-go-round, an unmistakable spot of light. . . .

Over to one of the main-force aircraft.

"There she is, skip; straight ahead." This from the bomb-aimer.

"Fine; the Pathfinders are dead on time."

The navigator looks at his watch and makes a note to that effect. The bomb-aimer starts his stop-watch. Three minutes and twenty seconds to go. On all sides other bomb-aimers are doing the same, beginning their straight fifteen-mile run through a curtain of steel. Flak is coming up all round, leaving black balloons which float by at an alarming speed. Searchlights are weaving, trying to pick up a straggler. The bomb-aimer begins to count.

"Three mintues to go, skipper."

Like a fleet of battleships the force sails in. Above are hundreds of fighter flares, lighting up the long lane of bombers like daylight. Now and then Junkers 88s and Me.110s come darting in and out like black moths trying to deliver their attack. The sky is full of tracer bullets, some going up, some going down. Others hose-pipe out horizontally as one of our rear-gunners gets in a good squirt.

Two mintues to go.

More flares have gone down. It seems even lighter than day. Searchlights, usually so bright themselves, can hardly pierce the dazzling glow of flares up above. Now the tracers are coming up in all colours as combats take place left, right and centre. On all sides bombers are blowing up, as they get direct hits—great, slow flashes in the sky, leaving a vast trail of black smoke as they disintegrate earthwards. Someone bales out.

One minute to go—bomb-doors open.

The bomb-aimer is still counting.

"Fifty seconds."

"Forty seconds."

There is flak all round now. The leading wave of bombers has not been broken up, a few have been shot down, but the rest have held their course. But the short time they held that course seemed like a lifetime.

There comes the bomb-aimer's voice again. "Red T.I.s straight ahead."

"Good show; there's the sky marker, too."

"Thirty seconds."

Still dead level. Someone in front has already started a fire.

Great sticks of incendiaries are beginning to criss-cross across the target-indicating marker. These sticks are a mile long, but from this height they look about the length of a match-stick.

"Twenty seconds."

"Steady—hold it"—and then the bomb-aimer shouts: "Bombs gone." There is a note of relief in his voice.

The Lancaster leaps forward, relieved of its burden, diving, slithering. But it keeps straight on over the burning city. Throttles are slammed wide open, the engines are in fine pitch; they make a noise as of an aircraft in pain.

A volcano is raging down below, great sticks of incendiaries are slapping across the point where the target-markers had first gone in. Now black smoke is beginning to rise, but as these target-markers burst and drop slowly into the flaming mass, the later bomb-aimers have a good chance of aiming at the middle. Cookies are exploding one after another with their slow, red flashes, photo-flashes are bursting at all heights as each aircraft takes its photographs. This is a galaxy of light, a living nightmare.

As the last wave of bombers roar over, the fires started by the first are beginning to take hold. Against their vivid light can be seen the bottom squadrons, flying steadily on, over the battered city.

The flak is beginning to die, the searchlights have gone out. Once again the ground defences have been beaten.

A few leaflets drift down through the bluish glare, only to be burnt in the flames of the burning houses.

Soon the area is one mass of flames and the last bomber has dropped its bombs. At last the rendezvous is reached and the surviving bombers turn for home.

That is how it is done, by young men with guts, by science and by skill. The Germans do everything in their power to stop it, but in vain. There are too many variations; feint attacks can be made, or the bombers can attack in waves. They can come in at hourly intervals; they might come over one a night when the German fighters cannot get up. And on every raid new devices are carried, made by scientists, to help defeat the German defences.

This was the beginning, the end of three years' hard experiment. The real answer had been found, and the bomber could at last hit hard. It could choose tactical or strategical targets. Both were allergic to bombs.

The Dam Busters

by PAUL BRICKHILL

The shattering of the Moehne and Eder dams was one of the great achieve-
ments of the R.A.F. It took its high rank alike in terms of science and
heroism.

Paul Brickhill, who reconstructed the whole operation in The Dam
Busters, *was himself in the Air Force and was a prisoner-of-war. His*
writing, with its seemingly reckless but actually controlled speed, is the
correct vehicle to record the triumphs of his own arm.

GIBSON[1] slid over the Wash at a hundred feet. The cockpit
was hot and he was flying in his shirtsleeves with Mae West
over the top; after a while he yelled, "Hurry, Hutch, turn the
heat off."

"Thank God for that," the wireless operator said, screwing
the valve shut. The heat in a Lancaster runs down the fuselage
but comes out round the wireless operator's seat, so he is always
too hot, while the rear gunner is always too cold.

The sun astern on the quarter threw long shadows on fields
peaceful and fresh with spring crops; dead ahead the moon was
swimming out of the ground haze like a bull's-eye. Gibson flew
automatically, eyes flicking from the horizon to the A.S.I.,[2] to
the repeater compass in its rubber suspension.

The haze of Norfolk passed a few miles to port. In the nose
Spafford said, "There's the sea", and a minute later they were
low over Southwold, the shingle was beneath them, and then
they were over the water, flat and grey in the evening light.

[1] Wing-Commander Guy Gibson, V.C.

[2] Air-speed indicator.

England faded behind. "G George" dropped down to 50 feet, and on each side Martin and Hopgood came down, too, putting off the evil moment when German radar could pick them up. You couldn't put it off indefinitely; about twenty miles from the Dutch coast the blips[3] would be flicking on the radar screens and the orders would be going out to the flak batteries and fighter fields.

Martin ranged up alongside and there was a light winking as he flashed his Aldis lamp at them.

"What's he saying, Hutch?" Gibson asked.

"We're going to get screechers[4] to-morrow night." Hutchison picked up his own Aldis and winked back, "You're damn right. Biggest binge of all time." Hutchinson didn't drink.

Taerum spoke: "Our ground speed is exactly 203½ miles an hour. We will be there in exactly one hour, ten minutes and thirty seconds. We ought to cross the coast dead on track. Incidentally, you're one degree off course." The last part was the standing joke. The pilot who can fly without sometimes yawing a degree or so off course has yet to be born.

In the ops. room of 5 Group H.Q. at Grantham, Cochrane[5] was walking Barnes Wallis[6] up and down, trying to comfort him. Wallis was like an expectant father, fidgety and jittery, and Cochrane was talking of anything but the bomb, trying to get Wallis's mind off it, but Wallis could think of nothing else.

"Just think what a wonderful job you made of the Wellington," Cochrane said encouragingly. "It's a magnificent machine; been our mainstay for over three years."

"Oh dear, no," lamented the disconcerting scientist. "Do you know, every time I pass one I wonder how I could ever have designed anything so crude."

[3] Slang term for apparition on a radar screen.

[4] R.A.F. slang for drunk.

[5] Air Chief Marshal the Hon. Sir Ralph Cochrane.

[6] Wallis Barnes, C.B.E., chief designer of Vickers-Armstrong.

A black Bentley rushed up the gravelled drive outside, pulled up by the door and the sentries snapped rigidly to attention as Harris[7] himself jumped briskly out. He came into the ops. room. "How's it going, Cocky?"

"All right so far, sir," Cochrane said. "Nothing to report yet." They walked up and down the long room between the wall where the aircraft blackboards were and the long desk that ran down the other side, where men were sitting. Satterly was there, "The Gremlin", the intelligence man and Dunn, chief signals officer, sitting by a telephone plugged into the radio in the signals cabin outside. He would get all the Morse from the aircraft there; it was too far for low-flying planes to get through by ordinary speech.

Harris and Cochrane talked quietly, and Wallis was walking miserably with them but not talking, breaking away every now and then to look at the big operations map on the end wall. The track lines had been pencilled in and he was counting off the miles they should be travelling. It was 10.35 when Cochrane looked at his watch and said, "They ought to be coming up to the Dutch coast now."

The sun had gone and the moon was inching higher into the dusk, lighting a road across the water; outside the dancing road the water was hardly visible, a dark mass with a couple of little flecks.

Taerum said: "Five minutes to the Dutch coast," and the crew snapped out of the wordless lull of the past half-hour. "Good," Gibson said. Martin and Hopgood eased their aircraft forward till the black snouts nosed alongside Gibson and veered out to make a wider target, their engines snarling thinly in gusts above the monotonous roar in "G George". Flying so low, just off the water, they seemed to be sliding very fast along the moonpath towards the waiting flak.

[7]Marshal of the Royal Air Force Sir Arthur ("Bomber") Harris, C.-in-C. Bomber Command.

Spafford said: "There's the coast". It was a black line lying dim and low on the water, and then from a couple of miles out on the port side a chain of glowing little balls was climbing into the sky. "Flak ship," said Martin laconically. The shells were way off and he ignored them. The sparkling moonpath ended abruptly, they tore across the white line of surf and were over enemy territory. "New course 105 magnetic", Taerum called, and the three aircraft swung gently to the left as they started the game of threading their way through the flak.

The northern wave made landfall about the same time, sighting Vlieland and turning south-east to cut across the narrow part and down over the Zuyder Zee. Munro led them across the dark spit; it was so narrow they would see the water again in about thirty seconds and have another seventy miles of comparatively safe water, but without warning there were flashes below and up came the fiery little balls. Munro felt the shock as they hit the aircraft, and then they were past and over the water again. Munro called on the intercom. to see if the crew were all right, but the earphones were dead.

Pidgeon, the wireless op., was standing by his shoulder shouting into his ear, "No radio. No intercom. Flak's smashed it. I think everyone's O.K." Munro flew on several miles, trying to fool himself they could still carry on, but it was no good and he knew it. Without radio he cound not direct the attack on the Sorpe[5]; could not even direct his own crew or get bombing instructions. Swearing, he turned for home.

Inside the Zuyder the water was dark and quite flat, treacherously deceptive for judging height. Geoff Rice slipped down a little to level at 60 feet by his belly lights, but the lights were not working properly and lured him lower as he tried to get a fix. A hammer seemed to hit the aircraft like a bolt and there was a tearing roar above the engines. Rice dragged her off the water, but the belly was torn out of her and the bomb had gone with it. The gutted fuselage had scooped up a couple of tons of water;

[5]The dam he was due to bomb.

it was pouring out of her and the rear gunner was nearly drowning in his turret. Marvellously, she still flew but was dropping back, and when they found the bomb was gone Rice turned her heavily back towards England.

The remaining two, Barlow and Byers, skirted their pin-point on the cape at Stavoren and ten minutes later crossed to the enemy land again at Harderwijk. No one knows exactly how soon it was that the flak came curling up at them again, but there is a report that as Barlow's aircraft hit the ground the bomb went off with a blinding flash, lighting the countryside like a rising sun for ten seconds before it died and left nothing. It was either then or soon after that Byers and his crew died, too. Nothing more was heard from him. Only McCarthy was left of the Sorpe team, flying sixty miles behind, and perhaps that is what saved him.

Over Holland, Gibson, Martin and Hopgood were down as low as 40 feet, playing hide-and-seek with the ground, the bomb-aimers calling terse warnings as houses and trees loomed up, and the aircraft skimmed over them. They were cruising fast and under the cowlings the exhaust manifolds were glowing. Once the three pulled up fast as the pylons of a power line rushed at them, and they just cleared the wires.

Four miles to port they saw the flare-path of Gilze-Rijen, German night-fighter field, and a few miles farther on they passed just to the left of the night-fighter aerodrome at Eindhoven. They could expect night-fighters now; the ops. rooms for miles around must be buzzing. Martin and Hopgood closed in on each side of Gibson for mutual protection. They should be able to see any fighter coming in because he would be higher, while they, low against the dark ground, would be hard to see, and that was their strength. Also their weakness where the flak was concerned. Their aircraft were higher, outlined. Just past Eindhoven, Gibson led them in a gentle turn to the north-east on the new course that would take them round the bristling guns of the Ruhr.

A few miles back the other two vics' of three were on course, too. Dinghy Young pin-pointed over the canal at Rosendaal and turned delicately to take them between the fighter fields, but Bill Astell did not seem sure this was the exact turning point. He bore off a little to the south for a minute and then turned back, but had fallen half a mile behind and was a fraction off track. They did not see him again, and it must have been quite soon after that the flak or fighter, whatever it was, got him.

Fourteen left.

The leading three slid across the border into Germany and saw no light or movement anywhere, only darkness filled with the beat of engines. Taerum thought they were south of track, so they edged to the north, a little nervily because this was the treacherous leg; they were coming up to the Rhine to sneak between the fore-warned guns of Huls and the Ruhr. Just short of the river some twelve light-flak guns opened up without warning; the aircraft gunners squirted back at the roots of the tracer and then they were out of range. No one badly hit. The Rhine was rushing at them and up from a barge spat a thin line of tracer, but they were past before the bullets found them.

Two minutes later more guns opened up, and this time three searchlights lit on Gibson. Foxlee and Deering were shooting at the searchlights. One of them popped out but the two others held, and the air was full of tracer. The rear gunners came into action, the searchlights switched to Martin, blinding him, and Gibson could read the big P on the side of the Lancaster. Every gun was firing, the aircraft shuddering with the recoil, and then they were through with throttles wide.

Ahead and just to the left another searchlight sprang to life and caught Gibson. Foxlee was firing instantly, holding his triggers in a long burst, his tracer whipping into the light. It flicked out, and as they went over in the dying glow they saw the gunners scattering. Tammy Simpson opened up from the

'Aircraft flying in arrowhead formation.

rear turret till they were out of range. You can't take prisoners in an aircraft.

They were past and shook themselves back into formation. Hutchinson tapped out a flak warning, giving the exact position, and way back in Grantham Dunn picked it up and the powerful group radio re-broadcast it at full strength to all other aircraft.

Gibson swung them north around Hamm; those marshalling yards will for years be notorious. Taerum said: "New course, skipper, 165 magnetic," and they then were hugging the ground on the last leg, slicing between Soest and Werl. Now the moon was high enough to light the ground and ahead loomed the dark hills that cradled the water. They climbed to the ridge that rimmed the horizon, crossed into the valley, and down below lay the flat sheet of Moehne Lake.

It was like looking down on the model[10]; the same saucer of water, the same dim fields and across the neck of the lake the squat rampart hugging the water, crowned by the towers. In the half-light it looked like a battleship, but more impregnable. Reinforced concrete a hundred feet thick.

"God," Bob Hay said, "can *we* break that?"

The dam came suddenly to life, prickling with sharp flashes, and the lines of angry red meteors were streaming into the sky and moving about blindly as the gunners hosed the area.

"Bit aggressive, aren't they?" said Trevor-Roper. The pilots swung the aircraft away and headed in wide circles round the lake, keeping out of range and waiting for the others. There seemed to be about ten guns, some in the fields on each side of the lake near the dam, and some—a lot—in the towers on the dam.

Gibson started calling the other aircraft, and one by one they reported, except Astell. He called Astell again at the end, but Astell had been dead for an hour. After a while Gibson gave up and said soberly over the intercom., "Well, boys, I suppose we'd better start the ball rolling." It was the end of the waiting

[10] A scale model of the target had been built and studied.

and the start of action, when thought is submerged. He flicked his transmitter switch:

"Hello, all Cooler aircraft, I am going in to attack. Stand by to come in in your order when I tell you. Hello, 'M Mother', stand by to take over if anything happens."

"O.K., Leader. Good luck." Hopgood's voice was a careful monotone.

Gibson turned wide, hugging the hills at the eastern end of the lake. Pulford had eased the throttles on and she was roaring harshly, picking up speed and quivering, the nose slowly coming round till three miles ahead they saw the towers and the rampart of the dam, and in between, the flat dark water. Spafford said, "Good show. This is wizard. I can see everything." They came out of the hills and slammed across the water, touching 240 now, and Gibson rattled off the last orders:

"Check height, Terry! Speed control, Pulford! Gunners ready! Coming up, Spam!" Taerum flicked the belly lights on and, peering down from the blister, started droning: "Down . . . down . . . down . . . up a bit . . . steady, steady-y." The lights were touching each other, "G George" was exactly at 60 feet and the flak gunners had seen the lights. The streams of glowing shells were swivelling and lowering, and then the shells were whipping towards them, seeming to move slowly at first like all flak, and then rushing madly at their eyes as the aircraft plunged into them.

Gibson held her steady, pointing between the towers. Taerum was watching out of the blister, Pulford had a hand on the throttles and his eyes on the A.S.I., Spafford held the plywood sight to his eye and the towers were closing in on the nails. Gibson shouted to Pulford, "Stand by to pull me out of the seat if I get hit!" There was a sudden snarling clatter up in the nose; Deering had opened up, his tracer spitting at the towers.

The dam was a rushing giant, darkness split with flashes, the cockpit stank of cordite and thought was nothing but a cold alarm shouting, "In another minute we shall be dead", and then

Spafford screamed, "Bomb gone!" loud and sharp, and they rocketed over the dam between the towers. A red Very light soared up as Hutchinson pulled the trigger to let the others know, and then the deeper snarling chatter as Trevor-Roper opened up on the towers from the rear.

It was over and memory was confusion as they cork-screwed down the valley, hugging the dark earth, sightless to the flak. They were out of range and Gibson lifted her out of the hills, turning steeply, and looked back. A voice in his earphones said, "Good show, Leader, nice work."

The black water between the towers suddenly rose and split and a huge white core erupted through the middle and climbed towards the sky. The lake was writhing, and as the white column reached its peak and hung a thousand feet high, like a ghost against the moon, the heavy explosion reached the air-craft. They looked in awe as they flew back to one side and saw sheets of water spilling over the dam and thought for a wild moment it had burst. The fury of the water passed and the dam was still there, the white column slowly dying.

Round the lake they flew while Hutchinson tapped out in code to base. In a few minutes Gibson thought the lake was calm enough for the next bomb and called:

"Hello, 'M Mother'. You may attack now. Good luck."

"O.K., Leader. Attacking." Hopgood was still carefully laconic. He was lost in the darkness over the hills at the end of the lake while the others waited. They saw his bellylights flick on and the two little yellow pools sliding over the water closing and joining as he found his height. He was straight and level on his run; the flak saw him and the venomous fireflies were darting at him. He plunged on; the gap was closing fast when the shells found him and someone said, "Hell, he's been hit!"

A red glow was blossoming round the inner port wing tank, and then a long, long ribbon of flame trailed behind "M Mother". The bomb-aimer must have been hit, because the bomb overshot the parapet on to the power house below.

"M Mother" was past the dam, nose up, straining for height so the crew could bale out, when the tanks blew up with an orange flare, a wing ripped away and the bomber spun to the ground in burning, bouncing pieces. The bomb went off near the power house like a brilliant sun. It was all over in seconds.

A voice said over the R.T., "Poor old Hoppy."

Gibson called up: "Hello, 'P Popsie.' Are you ready?"

"O.K., Leader. Going in."

"I'll fly across the dam as you make your run and try and draw the flak off you."

"O.K. Thanks, Leader."

Martin was turning in from the hills and Gibson headed across the lake, parallel to the dams and just out of effective range of guns. As Martin's spotlights merged and sped across the water Gibson back-tracked and Deering and Trevor-Roper opened up; six lines of tracer converged on the towers, drawing their attention, so that for some seconds most of the guns did not notice Martin rocketing over the water. He held his height and Whittaker had the speed right. They were tracking straight for the middle of the dam between the moon-bathed towers when the gunners spotted them and threw a curtain of fire between the towers, spreading like a fan so they would have to fly through it. Martin drove straight ahead. Two guns swung at them, and as the shells whipped across the water sharp-eyed little Foxlee was yelling as he squirted back, his tracer lacing and tangling with the flak.

A sharp "Bomb gone!" from Bob Hay, and in the same instant a shudder as two shells smacked into the starboard wing, one of them exploding in the inner petrol tank. A split second of flashes as they shot through the barrage. Tammy Simpson opened up from the rear turret, Chambers shot the Verey light and they were down the valley. Whittaker was looking fearfully at the hole in the starboard wing, but no fire was coming. He suddenly realized why and nudged Martin, yelling in his ear, "Thank Christ, the bloody starboard tank was empty!"

Martin shouted, "Bomb gone, Leader."

"O.K., 'P Popsie'. Let me know when you're out of the flak. Hello, 'A Apple'. Are you ready?"

"O.K., Leader."

"Right. Go ahead. Let me know when you're in position and I'll draw the flak for you."

Martin called again, "'P Popsie' clear now, Leader."

"O.K. Are you hit?"

"Yeah. Starboard wing, but we're all right. We can make it."

The lake suddenly boiled again by the dam and spewed out the great white column that climbed again to a thousand feet. More water was cascading over the dam, but it cleared soon and the dam was still there.

Dinghy Young was on the air again. "'A Apple' making bombing run."

Gibson headed back over the lake where his gunners could play with fire, and this time Martin did the same. As Young came plunging across the lake Gibson and Martin came in on each side, higher up, and the flak did not know where to shoot. Young swept past the dam and reported he was all right. The great explosion was up against the dam wall again, beautifully accurate, but the dam was still there, and again Gibson waited till the plume of spray had cleared and the water was calm.

He called Maltby and ordered him in, and as Maltby came across the water Gibson and Martin came in with him, firing with every gun that could bear and flicking their navigation lights on this time to help the flak gunners shoot at the wrong target. The red cartridge soared up from Maltby's aircraft to signal "Attack successful."

In a few moments the mountain of water erupted skyward again under the dam wall. It was uncanny how accurate the bomb was. The spray from the explosions was misting up the whole valley now and it was hard to see what was happening by the dam. Gibson called Shannon to make his attack, and the words were barely out of his mouth when a sharp voice filled his earphones:

"Hell, it's gone! It's gone! Look at it for Christ's sake!" Wheeling round the valley side Martin had seen the concrete face abruptly split and crumble under the weight of water. Gibson swung in close and was staggered. A ragged hole 100 yards across and 100 feet deep split the dam and the lake was pouring out of it, 134 million tons of water crashing into the valley in a jet 200 feet long, smooth on top, foaming at the sides where it tore at the rough edges of the breach and boiling over the scarred earth where the power house had been.

Gibson told Shannon to "skip it".

The others flew over and were awed into silence. In the moonglow they watched a wall of water rolling down the valley, 25 feet high, moving 20 feet a second. A gunner still on his feet in one of the towers opened up at them until lines of tracer converged on the root of the flak and it stopped abruptly. The awed silence was broken by a babble of intercom. chatter as they went mad with excitement; the only man not looking being Hutchinson, sitting at his keyboard tapping out "Nigger".

Soon the hissing steam and spray blurred the valley. Gibson called Martin and Maltby to set course for home, and told Young, Shannon, Maudslay and Knight to follow him east to the Eder. Young was to control if Gibson was shot down.

At Grantham a long silence had followed the flak warning at Huls, and then Dunn's 'phone rang sharply, and in the dead silence they all heard the Morse crackling in the receiver. It was quite slow and Cochrane, bending near, could read it. "Goner," he said, "from G George". Goner was the code word that meant Gibson had exploded his bomb in the right place.

"I'd hoped one bomb might do it," Wallis said gloomily.

"It's probably weakened it," Cochrane soothed him. Harris looked non-committal. There was no more from "G George", and they went on talking. A long silence. Nothing came through, then Hopgood crashed. The 'phone rang. "Goner" from "P Popsie". Another dragging silence. "Goner" from "A Apple". Wallis swears even to-day that there was half an hour between each signal, but the log shows only about five minutes. "Goner" from "J Johnny". That was Maltby, and the aura of gloom settled deeper over Wallis.

A minute later the 'phone rang again and the Morse crackled so fast the others could not read it. Dunn printed it letter by letter on a signals pad and let out a cry, "Nigger. It's Nigger. It's gone."

Wallis threw his arms over his head and went dancing round the room. The austere face of Cochrane cracked into a grin, he grabbed one of Wallis's hands and started congratulating him. Harris, with the first grin on his face that Wallis had ever seen, grabbed the other hand and said:

"Wallis, I didn't believe a word you said about this damn bomb, but you could sell me a pink elephant now."

He said, a little later when some of the excitement had died down: "I must tell Portal immediately." Sir Charles Portal, Chief of the R.A.F., was in Washington that night on a mission, actually at that moment dining with Roosevelt. Harris picked up the nearest 'phone and said, "Get me the White House."

The little W.A.A.F. on the switchboard knew nothing of the highly secret raid. Even at Grantham, Cochrane's security had been perfect. She did not realize the importance of it all, or the identity of the great man who was speaking, and was caught off guard. "Yes, sir," she said automatically and, so they say, dialled the only White House she knew, a jolly little roadhouse a few miles out of Grantham.

Harris must have thought she was a very smart operator when the White House answered so quickly, and there are reported to have been moments of incredible and indescribable comedy as Harris asked for Portal, and the drowsy landlord, testy at being hauled out of bed after midnight, told him in well-chosen words he didn't have anyone called Portal staying at the place;

in fact, he didn't have anyone staying at all, because he didn't have room, and if he did have room he would not have anyone staying there who had people who called him up at that time of night. Not for long anyway.

Harris went red, and there were some explosive exchanges before one of them slammed the receiver down. Someone slipped down and had a word with the little W.A.A.F., and she tried in terror for the next hour to raise Washington, but without success.

Three kilometres down the valley from the Moehne lay the sleeping village of Himmelpforten, which means Gates of Heaven. The explosions had awakened the village priest, Father Berkenkopf, and he guessed instantly what was happening; he had been afraid of it for three years. He ran to his small stone church, Porta Cœli (which also means Gates of Heaven—in Italian), and began tugging grimly on the bell-rope, the signal he had arranged with his villagers. It is not certain how many were warned in time. In the darkness the clanging of the bell rolled ominously round the valley and then it was muffled in the thunder moving nearer. Berkenkopf must have heard it and known what it meant, but it seems that he was still pulling at the bell when the flood crushed the church and the village of the Gates of Heaven and rolled them down the valley.

It went for many miles and took more villages, a tumbling maelstrom of water and splintered houses, beds and frying-pans, the choice from Porta Cœli and the bell, the bodies of cattle and horses, pigs and dogs, and the bodies of Father Berkenkopf and other human beings.

War, as someone said, is a great leveller, but he did not mean it quite as literally or as bitterly as this.

* * *

The Eder was hard to find because fog was filling the valley. Gibson circled it for some time before he was certain he was there. One by one the others found it and soon they were all in a left-hand circuit round the lake. There was no flak; probably the Germans thought the Eder did not need it. It lay deep in a fold of the hills; the ridges around were a thousand feet high and it was no place to dive a heavy aircraft at night.

Gibson said, "O.K., Dave. Start your attack."

Shannon flew a wide circuit over the ridges and then put his nose right down, but the dive was not steep enough and he overshot. Sergeant Henderson slammed on full throttle, and Shannon hauled back on the stick and they just cleared the mountain on the far side.

"Sorry, Leader," Shannon said a little breathlessly. "Made a mess of that. I'll try again."

Five times more he dived into the dark valley but he failed every time to get into position and nearly stood the Lancaster on her tail to get out of the hills again. He called up finally, "I think I'd better circle and try to get to know this place."

"O.K., Dave. You hang around a bit and let someone else have a crack. Hullo, 'Z Zebra'. You have a go now."

Maudslay acknowledged, and a minute later was diving down the contour of the hills, only to overshoot and go rocketing up again like Shannon. He tried again but the same thing happened. Maudslay said he was going to try once more. He came slowly over the ridges, turned in the last moment and the nose dropped sharply into the gloom as he forced her down into the valley. They saw him level out very fast, and then the spotlights flickered on to the water and closed quickly and he was tracking for the dam. His red Verey light curled up as Fuller called "Bombs gone!" but they must have been going too fast. The bomb hit the parapet of the dam and blew up on impact with a tremendous flash; in the glare they saw 'Z Zebra' for a moment just above the explosion. Then only blackness.

Gibson said painfully, knowing it was useless:

"Henry, Henry—hullo, 'Z Zebra', are you all right?" There was no answer. He called again and, incredibly, out of the darkness a very faint voice said, "I think so . . . stand by." They all heard it, Gibson and Shannon and Knight, and wondered that it was possible. After a while Gibson called again but there was no answer. Maudslay never came back.

Gibson called, "O.K., David, will you attack now."

Shannon tried and missed again; came round once more, plunged into the darkness and this time made it, curling out of the dive at the foot of the lake and tracking for the dam. He found his height quickly, the bomb dropped clear and Shannon roughly pulled his plane up over the shoulder of the mountain. Under the parapet the bomb spewed up the familiar plume of white water and as it drifted down Gibson, diving over the lake, saw that the dam was still there. There was only Knight left. He had the last bomb. Gibson ordered him in.

Knight tried once and couldn't make it. He tried again. Failed. "Come in down moon and dive for the point, Les," Shannon said. He gave more advice over the R.T., and Knight listened quietly. He was a young Australian who did not drink, his idea of a riotous evening being to write letters home and go to the pictures. He dived to try again, made a perfect run and they saw the splash as his bomb dropped in the right spot. Seconds later the water erupted, and as Gibson slanted down to have a look he saw the wall of the dam burst open and the torrent come crashing out.

Knight, more excited than he had ever been, was yelling over the R.T., and when he stopped he left his transmitter on for a few seconds by mistake; the crew's remarks on the intercom. were broadcast, and they were very spectacular remarks indeed.

This was even more fantastic than the Moehne. The breach in the dam was as big and there were over 200 million tons of water pouring through. The Eder Valley was steeper and they watched speechlessly as the flood foamed and tossed down the valley, lengthening like a snake. It must have been rolling at 30 feet a second. They saw a car in front racing to get clear; only the lights they saw, like two frightened eyes spearing in the dark, and the car was not fast enough. The foam crawled up on it, the headlights turned opalescent green as the water rolled over, and suddenly they flicked out.

Hutchinson was tapping "Dinghy" in Morse; that was the code to say that the Eder was destroyed. When he had finished Gibson called, "O.K., all Cooler aircraft. You've had your look. Let's go home," and the sound of their engines died over the hills as they flew west to fight their way back.

McCarthy had fought a lone way through to the Sorpe, tucked down in rolling hills south of the Moehne. The valleys were full of mist, so it was a long time before he pin-pointed himself over the lake, dimly seeing through the haze a shape he recognized from the model.

He tried a dummy run and found, as the others found before at the Eder, that there was a hill at each end so that he would have to dive steeply, find his aiming-point quickly and pull up in a hurry. He tried twice more but was not satisfied and came in a third time, plunging through the mist trying to see through the suffused moonlight. He nearly hit the water and levelled out very low. Johnson picked up the aiming point and seconds later yelled "Bomb gone!", and they were climbing up over the far hills when the bomb exploded by the dam wall. McCarthy dived back over the dam and they saw that the crest had crumbled for 50 yards. As they turned on course for England, Eaton tapped out the code word that told of their successful drop.

Wallis's joy was complete. Cochrane radioed "G George", asking if he had any aircraft left to divert to the Sorpe, and Hutchinson answered "None". Satterly, who had been plotting the path of the reserve force by dead reckoning, radioed orders to them.

Burpee, in "S Sugar", was directed to the Sorpe, but he did not answer. They called again and again, but there was only silence. He was dead.

Brown, in "F Freddy", was sent to the Sorpe and reached it after McCarthy had left; the mist was swirling thicker and, though he dived low over the dam, Oancia, the bomb-aimer, could not pick it up in time.

Brown dived back on a second run but Oancia still found the mist foiled him. They tried eight times, and then Brown pulled up and they had a conference over the intercom. On the next run Oancia dropped a cluster of incendiaries in the woods to the side of the dam. They burned dazzlingly and the trees caught, too, so that on the tenth run Oancia picked up the glare a long way back, knew exactly where the target was and dropped his load accurately.

They pulled round in a climbing turn and a jet of water and rubble climbed out of the mist and hung against the moon; down in the mist itself they saw a shock wave of air like a giant smoke ring circling the base of the spout.

Anderson, in "Y Yorker", was also sent to the Sorpe, but he was still later than Brown, and now the valley was completely under mist so that the lake and the dam were hidden and he had to turn back with his bomb.

Ottley, in "C Charlie", was ordered to the Lister Dam, one of the secondary targets. He acknowledged "Message received", but that was the last anyone ever heard from him.

The last man was Townsend, in "O Orange", and his target was the Ennerpe. He searched a long time before he found it in the mist, and made three runs before he was satisfied and dropped the bomb. It was accurate.

Ten out of the nineteen were coming home, hugging the ground, 8 tons lighter now in bomb and petrol load and travelling at maximum cruising, about 245, not worrying about petrol; only about getting home. The coast was an hour away and the sun less than that. They knew the fighters were overhead waiting for a lightening sky in the east.

Harris had driven Cochrane and Wallis to Scampton to meet

the survivors, and in the ops. room at Scampton he picked up the 'phone to try and get Portal again. This time he prepared the ground for smart service by telling the girl that the speaker was Air-Chief-Marshal Sir Arthur Harris, Commander-in-Chief of Bomber Command.

"Yes, of course," said the indulgent girl, who knew the absurd things that plastered New Zealand flight lieutenants were liable to say, "you've been on it again, sir. Now you go and get your batman to put you to bed. He'll give you your course to steer."

There was an explosion in the ops. room and an unusually intelligent intelligence officer hared down the stairs and told the girl the frightful thing she had done. Someone soothed the irate man in the ops. room while the girl beseeched the G.P.O. to get Washington faster than ever before. This time the lines were clear and before long a mollified Harris had the pleasure of telling Portal, "Operation Downwood successful . . . yes, successful!" . . .

. . . Then the decorations came through—thirty-three of them. Gibson was awarded the Victoria Cross. Martin, McCarthy, Maltby, Shannon and Knight got D.S.O.s. Bob Hay, Hutchinson, Leggo and Danny Walker got bars to their D.F.C.s. There were ten D.F.C.s, among them Trevor-Roper, Buckley, Deering, Spafford and Taerum. Brown and Townsend for the Conspicuous Gallantry Medal, and there were twelve D.F.M.s, among them being Tammy Simpson, Sumpter, Oancia and Pulford. . . .

One of Our Submarines

by EDWARD YOUNG, Commander, D.S.O., D.S.C.,
R.N.V.(S.)R.

*The war under the sea is a horrible and terrifying conflict, and it requires a
curiously modern form of courage; valour without glory combined with an
ever-increasing degree of technical proficiency.*

*Edward Young is a fitting historian of this war-long campaign; he is naval
officer enough to have acquired the studied understatement of his Service; but
he was R.N.V.R.—an "amateur"—and has thus escaped the restriction
of "regular" idiom.*

*This account of the sinking of a submarine (by accident) demonstrates the
perils—and how they are conquered—of those who go under the sea in ships.*

*U*mpire's dockyard trials had been successfully completed,
including the usual static basin dive to prove that the hull
was watertight. The last welding leads had been removed, the
bunks, cupboards and other wooden fittings were a bright
mahogany gleam, new curtains hung in the messes, and the
whole boat was resplendent with fresh-smelling paintwork,
white inside and battleship grey outside.

Mervyn Wingfield was plainly delighted with his new command, though he tried to conceal his pleasure behind a demean-
our of severity and icy reserve. The First Lieutenant, Peter
Pannister, I had not met before; he was tall, energetic and
humorous, easy to get on with. Tony Godden, the navigator,
had been in the same training class with me at Fort Blockhouse;
I was delighted now to find we were in the same boat, for he
was a most amusing and endearing shipmate, and we had many
good evenings ashore together during our stay in Chatham.

Upmire moved out at last into the River Medway on a day towards the end of July, spick and span, a brand-new white ensign flying, bound north-about for the Clyde, where we were to carry out sea trials and training with the Third Flotilla based at Dunoon, before setting forth on a "working-up" operational patrol in the North Sea. After that, the Mediterranean.

We stopped overnight at Sheerness to wait for a convoy of merchant-ships leaving the Thames the next day. In the morning we got under way early and found the convoy congregating off Southend under an escort of motor launches and Admiralty trawlers. We took up our station astern, and by the time we turned the corner at Shoeburyness the convoy had more or less sorted itself out.

All day we moved up the East Coast, passing Burnham, Clacton, Walton-on-the-Naze, Harwich, Felixstowe, Orfordness, and when we were somewhere off Aldeburgh a German bomber came in low from seaward and began attacking the leading ships of the convoy. I was officer-of-the-watch at the time, and in accordance with our convoy instructions gave the order to dive.

Now, we had never dived before at sea and under way. Normally a brand-new submarine carries out numerous dives in slow motion, with the crew already at diving stations, before it is committed to a full-speed dive. We had to make our first dive on the klaxon, and it is to the great credit of all concerned—the Chatham men who built her; Wingfield, who as Captain had thought ahead and trained his officers and men to his satisfaction; Bannister, who as Number One had organized the crew in their duties and had also worked out the first trim; and the crew, who went calmly to diving stations and performed their jobs correctly—it is to the credit of all these that *Umpire's* first dive was a complete success. Within two minutes Bannister had caught a trim[1] and the captain was able to concentrate on the periscope. We did not want to stay down longer than we need, because

[1]"To catch a trim" means to "achieve proper balance".

the convoy was drawing ahead of us. Five minutes later the Heinkel seemed to have vanished, so we surfaced and pressed on to regain our station in the convoy, which had sustained no damage from the attack.

We felt very pleased with ourselves, and boyishly proud of our boat that had behaved so well. Then, about nightfall, one of the diesels developed trouble and had to be stopped. At first this did not affect our speed, our propulsion being diesel-electric, and we continued to maintain our station. But as the evening wore on, the engine-room staff were unsuccessful in their attempts to get the defective engine going. The other one produced insufficient power by itself to balance the batteries' output when driving two propellers, and we were obliged at last to reduce our speed. The Captain flashed a signal to the Commodore of the convoy, reporting the situation. An M.L.[2] was detailed to drop back and act as our escort, and we were to catch up as soon as possible.

We knew from the latest W/T[3] situation report that, some twenty miles to the north of us, a southbound convoy was approaching down the same buoyed channel. The two convoys were due to meet somewhere about midnight.

The international rule at sea is that in a channel-way ships must keep to the starboard side. Ships meeting in a channel should therefore pass *port to port*. It was revealed afterwards that when the two convoys met, some miles ahead of us, they passed on the *wrong* side, starboard to starboard. So when Tony Godden, the officer-of-the-watch, presently sent down a message that the southbound convoy was approaching, Wingfield was surprised to find on reaching the bridge that the oncoming convoy was not on our port bow, as he expected, but right ahead, with part of it actually extending across our starboard bow. It was a calm night, very dark, but with reasonably good visibility; lights could have been seen at a fair distance. But the German E-boats

[2]Motor launch.
[3]Wireless telephone.

were raiding the East Coast convoys nearly every night, and no one was showing any lights. Our escorting M.L. had lost touch with us some time earlier. We were quite alone and almost invisible to other ships even at close range.

The normal action would have been to alter course to starboard, but this would have taken us across the bows of the approaching merchant-ships and we might not have had room to get clear. Wingfield altered a few degrees to port, and the first six ships of the convoy passed safely down our starboard side about two hundred yards away. Although we did not know it, our own convoy, now several miles ahead, had taken the same action.

Suddenly a dark shape appeared ahead of us, detached from the nearest column of the convoy. Examining it through his binoculars, Wingfield saw that it was a trawler, presumably part of the convoy's escort, and that we were directly in its path. In the next second he realized that it was alarmingly near to us and apparently unaware of our presence. He had to decide quickly what to do. The trawler was fine on his starboard bow and seemed certain to pass dangerously close. By the rule of the road it was the trawler's right of way and our duty to keep clear. According to the rules Wingfield should have altered course to starboard, but only two hundred yards to starboard was the endless line of southbound merchant-ships forming an impenetrable barrier. With every ship fully darkened, this was a predicament not visualized by the authors of the Regulations for Preventing Collision at Sea. Wingfield ordered "Hard-a-port". But, even as we began to turn, the trawler seemed to see us, low and dark in the water, and turned instinctively to starboard. This made collision inevitable. Wingfield yelled his last order down the voice-pipe, "Full astern together!"—but before the order could be carried out, the bows of the trawler struck *Umpire* with a sickening metallic crash, some twenty or thirty feet abaft the starboard bow. The submarine lurched to port, and for a few seconds the two vessels stayed locked together, held by the impetus of the trawler's headway. During these seconds Wingfield clutched the trawler's side as it swung in towards him and shouted furiously, "You bloody bastard, you've sunk a British submarine!" Then the trawler fell away, and Wingfield found his boat sinking under him by the head. In less than thirty seconds she plunged under, leaving Wingfield, Godden and the two look-outs in the water. In the darkness there was shouting and confusion, but the four kept together at first. But presently one and then the other of the look-outs dropped out of the small circle. Tony Godden, who was wearing long, fur-lined seaboots, gasped out that he could not kick them free and that he was sinking. For a while Wingfield helped to support him, but Tony finally let go and sank out of sight. It seemed a long time before the trawler's boat appeared, and Wingfield was unconscious when he was hauled on board. When he came to and realized that he, the Captain, was apparently the sole survivor, his feelings can be imagined.

When the Captain left the wardroom to go up on the bridge in response to Tony's message about the approaching convoy, Peter Bannister and I were sitting at the wardroom table, decoding a routine wireless signal that had been passed to us by the telegraphist on watch.

The wardroom was divided from the control-room only by a thin steel partition, and by curtains from the passage-way; at sea these curtains were drawn back, and Peter and I could hear the helmsman repeat the orders which came to him down the voice-pipe from the bridge.

When we heard him repeat the Captain's emergency order, "Hard-a-port", we pushed back our chairs and stood up, our eyes meeting in question and alarm. We stumbled out into the passage-way, and Peter at once gave the order to "Shut Water-tight doors!" Almost immediately we heard another urgent yell down the voice-pipe, but before this last order from the bridge could be repeated by the helmsman there was a violent crash for'ard in the torpedo-stowage compartment, followed by the blue-white flare and muffled thump of an electrical explosion. The boat rocked to port, stayed there a few seconds, and then slid drunkenly forward and over to starboard as she began her plunge to the bottom. If the water were deep here, its weight would crush us like an egg-shell. Most of the lights had gone out. Then men were running past us from the next compartment, Peter was yelling, "Shut that door!", and I had my hand on it, letting the men run through, disobeying Peter because I hadn't the courage to deny any of them a chance so long as the water was not yet actually at their heels. Somehow the farther door to the damaged compartment had shut, whether blown to by the explosion or deliberately shut from the inside by a last nameless act of self-sacrifice as the sea came flooding in, we shall never know. "Shut that bloody door!" repeated Peter in a fury, but by now all the men from the intervening compartment were through. With some difficulty, because of the angle of the boat, I pulled the door up towards me and clamped it shut.

I turned, and struggled up the tilting deck into the control-room. The boat was listing to starboard and sloping forward at an angle of about ten degrees. Water was pouring in from what seemed to be a hundred places. Peter was struggling with the outboard battery-ventilation-valve overhead, desperately seeking an explanation for this inrush of water, and acutely aware of the fatal danger of chlorine gas if the sea-water should find its way into the battery cells under the deck. I reached up to help him, glad in my numbed state of something positive to do. But the valve was already shut, as we knew it should have been, and we must look elsewhere for the breach in our defences. To my paralysed brain it seemed that the shock of the collision had cracked the hull and started rivets along the whole length of the ship. Surprisingly enough, no water was coming down the conning-tower; presumably the upper hatch had fallen shut when the boat took on a list immediately before she went under.

Peter was now calling for more light, and one or two of the men searched about for the emergency hand-lamps. I remembered that I had a torch in my drawer in the wardroom, so I retraced my steps, moving with difficulty down the wet and sloping deck. In the passage-way the water was already knee-deep. I sloshed through it and pulled myself up into the wardroom. Streams of ice-green water were cascading from somewhere overhead, drenching the beautiful new curtains and bunks in a universal deluge. If I had brought a conscious intelligence to bear on the source of this waterfall I should have hit on something that ought to have been obvious to all of us. But not until the whole thing was over did I realize that all this water must have been coming from the *ventilation shaft,* now open to sea pressure through the damaged torpedo-stowage compartment. By reaching up my hand over the Captain's bunk I could have shut the valve on the bulkhead quite easily, and the flow of water would have stopped. But my brain, as though stunned by the catastrophe, had become incapable of constructive thought.

I found the torch and splashed my way back to the control-room. As I did so, it occurred to me to wonder what depth we were at. I shone the torch on the depth-gauges and found, to my surprise, that they were both reading only a little over 60 feet. This meant we were in very shallow water, with the bow presumably resting on the bottom at something like 80 feet. I asked Peter whether it was possible to *blow* her up.[4] It seemed unlikely, since we had been at full buoyancy at the time of the collision, and a vast quantity of water must have entered for'ard to have overcome that buoyancy so suddenly. It was obvious that a large gash had been torn at the top of the pressure hull in the torpedo-stowage compartment, and that the compartment had filled up in a matter of seconds. We should never get her up with all that weight of water in her. However, Peter thought it

[4] To "blow up" does not mean to dynamite; but to "blow the tanks" clear of water—an operation which forces a submarine to the surface.

would do no harm to try, so one by one he opened up the valves of the high-pressure air-panel until all five ballast tanks and the two main internal tanks were blowing. But it was no use: the depth-gauges did not even flicker.

The sea continued to pour in on us, with a terrible and relentless noise, and the water in the compartment grew deeper every minute. As the level crept up the starboard side, live electrical contacts began spitting venomously, with little lightning flashes. Vaguely I wondered if we were all going to be electrocuted.

In the half-darkness the men had become anonymous groping figures, desperately coming and going. There was no panic, but most of us, I think, were suffering from a sort of mental concussion. I discovered one man trying to force open the watertight door that I had shut earlier. "My pal's in there," he was moaning, "my pal's in there." "It's no good," I told him; "she's filled right up for'ard and there's no one left alive on the other side of that door." He turned away, sobbing a little.

For some reason we decided it would be useful if we could find more torches. I knew there must be one or two others somewhere in the wardroom, so I made yet another expedition down the slope, wading through the pool that was now waist-deep and already covering the lowest tiers of drawers under our bunks. I spent some time in the wardroom, shivering with fear and cold, ransacking every drawer and cupboard, pushing aside the forsaken paraphernalia of personal belongings—underclothes, razors, pipes, photographs of wives and girl-friends. But I could find only one torch that was still dry and working. Holding it clear of the water, I returned to the control-room.

It was deserted.

The door into the engine-room was shut. Had I spent longer in the wardroom than I thought? Perhaps they had all escaped from the engine-room escape hatch, without realizing that I had been left behind. Even if they had not yet left the submarine, they might have already started flooding the compartment in preparation for an escape, and if the flooding had gone beyond a certain point it would be impossible to get that door open again. I listened, but could hear nothing beyond the monotonous, pitiless sound of pouring water. In this terrible moment I must have come very near to panic.

I could at least try hammering on the engine-room door. Looking round for a heavy instrument, I found a valve spanner and began moving aft towards the door. As I did so I heard a voice quite close to me say, "Christ, who's that?" I looked up and found I was standing under the conning-tower. In it, to my infinite relief, I saw Peter with an able-seaman and one of the E.R.A.s.[5] "Where the hell have you come from?" said Peter. "Where the hell's everybody gone?" I retorted. "Any room for me up there?" "We ought to be able to squeeze you in. The others are going to escape from the engine-room."

I climbed up through the lower hatch, grateful as never before for the company of my fellow-creatures. Four of us in the tiny space made a tight squeeze. Peter at the top of the ladder with his head jammed up against the upper hatch, the A.B. half-way up the ladder with his bottom wedged against the side of the tower, leaving just room for me and the E.R.A. standing at the foot of the tower, with our feet on the edge of the lower hatch-opening. The E.R.A. was in a bad way, vomiting continuously and hardly able to stand.

In the centre of the upper hatch was a small port, or round window, made of glass thick enough to withstand tremendous pressure. Number One said that he could see a glimmer of light through it, and supposed it to be caused by a searchlight from some vessel waiting overhead. This encouraged him to think we ought to be able to swim to the surface and be picked up without much difficulty. We knew the control-room depth-gauges were reading just over sixty feet; the upper hatch was something like fifteen feet higher than the normal surface water-line (the point of reference for the depth-gauges) and was

[5] Engine Room Artificers.

therefore probably only about forty-five feet from the surface, say the height of eight men standing on top of each other. It ought to be easy.

"Shut the lower lid," said Peter, "and let's just think this out." I bent down, shut the hatch and pulled the clip over. We then discussed exactly what we were going to do. We agreed that to wear Davis escape gear would be an unnecessary complication in the confined space. One of the dangers was that on our way up we might crack our skulls on the cross-bar between the periscope standards; but we decided there was little chance of this owing to the starboard list. We hoped (vainly as it turned out) that we might be assisted in our rise to the surface by the bubble of air which would be released from the conning-tower as the hatch opened. The drill was simple. Peter would open the hatch, and as the water came in each man would fill his lungs with air and climb out as fast as he could. Except for the poor E.R.A., who was sick beyond comfort or encouragement, we were by now quite calm, even cheerful.

How long we considered the situation I cannot remember; but at last Peter said: "Well, the next thing is to see if we can open this hatch against the sea pressure." Bracing himself against the side of the tower, he pushed upwards with all his strength. The hatch remained firmly shut. Somehow we must raise the pressure inside the tower.

It occurred to me that while we had been talking the pressure had still been building up in the control-room below us, owing to the continuing inrush of water. I eased off the clip of the hatch under my feet, and sure enough there came the sharp hiss of air forcing its way into the tower. I allowed the air to come in until, after a minute or two, I became aware of a peculiar, faint smell. "Hullo," I said, "I think I can smell chlorine gas." "All right," said Peter; "shut the lid again and I'll have another shot at opening this one." This time he managed without much effort to lift the hatch slightly off its seat, allowing a trickle of water to come through.

"O.K.," said Peter. "Well, boys, take your time. There's no hurry. You say when you feel you're ready."

I said I was for having a go at once, before we weakened ourselves any further by breathing foul air, and the others agreed. We stripped down to vest, pants and socks.

"Ready?" asked Peter.

"Ready," we all replied, though I think the E.R.A. had reached the point in his sickness where he wanted to die more than anything else.

"Right. Stand by," said Peter cheerfully. "Here we go for fourteen days' survivors' leave. We're off!"—and he pushed up the lid with all his strength.

I took as deep a breath as I could, and then the sea crashed in on us. There was a roaring in my ears, a blackness everywhere, and there was nothing for it but to fight for life with all one's primitive instincts of survival. Hauling myself up by the rungs of the ladder, I found my head obstructed by the A.B.'s bottom. With the strength of a desperate man I pushed up at him, his heel struck me in the face, I pushed again, and then we were through the hatch and clear of the submarine. I swam upwards with quick, jerky breast-strokes. It seemed a terrible distance. Time stretched out of its normal span until I thought my lungs must surely crack before I reached the surface. And then suddenly I was there, coughing, spluttering, gasping in great draughts of the sweet night air and drinking in the blessed sight of the stars shining in the immensity of space.

The sea was fairly calm, with no more than a gentle popple. Seeing two heads in the water not far away, I called out and found they were Peter and the A.B., both in good heart. Of the E.R.A. there was no sign. We could make out the dark shapes of several ships around us, so we began shouting to attract attention. Some of them were throwing searchlights on the water, and one of these seemed to me nearer than the rest. "Come on," I said, "let's swim to that nearest one," and began swimming towards it with my rather feeble side-stroke. I pressed on for a few minutes, imagining the other two were following me, but after a while I turned and could see no sign of them, although I heard them shouting at intervals not far off. The vessel I was making for was farther away than I had thought. I am not a strong swimmer, so I turned over on to my back and relaxed into an easy backward leg-stroke, calling "Help!" at the top of my voice from time to time. Sometimes a wave lopped over my head and I swallowed a little more water. I seemed to be swimming for a long time. Whenever I looked round, the ship seemed to be as far away as ever. Surely, after all this, I was not going to drown in sight of safety? I began to feel rather exhausted. Suddenly I heard voices shouting, the churning of propellers going astern, and I turned to find a searchlight blazing in my eyes and below it the shape of an M.L. quite close, with a scrambling-net down over the side and men running along the deck. A heaving-line shot out, I grabbed it and was hauled in. A sailor clambered down the net and helped me on to the deck, where I fell into the arms of two R.N.V.R. officers. Exhausted and groaning for breath, with my lungs half full of sea-water, I must have appeared in a worse state than I was, but while they wrapped me in blankets and hustled me below I managed to tell them that there were some more of us out there in the water and many others still down in the submarine trying to escape from the engine-room.

In a cabin below they rubbed me down, gave me dry clothes, and put me into a bunk, where I lay shivering from delayed shock. About half an hour later they came and told me our men were starting to come up from the bottom. I couldn't bear to stay in my bunk while this was happening, so I wrapped myself in a blanket and tottered along to find out what the situation was. They were coming up at fairly frequent intervals, strange Martian creatures with their D.S.E.A.[6] goggles and oxygen buoys, and rendered almost unrecognizable by black oil which had floated up from the bilges when they flooded the engine-room

[6]Davis Submerged Escape Apparatus.

for the escape. But they were in extraordinarily good spirits, half-intoxicated with their unexpected return to life. Every one of them was full of praise for the way in which the Chief E.R.A. and the Torpedo Gunner's Mate had organized the escaping party and carried out the escape drill. When finally these two reached the surface, the Chief E.R.A. last of all, they reported there was no one left in the engine-room. There had been enough D.S.E.A. sets for all but two of the party. Two men had volunteered to go up without them, each holding on to the legs of one of the others; one of these was never seen again. A final roll-call showed that the only other casualty of the engine-room party of twenty was a civilian technician from Chatham Dockyard, who had joined *Umpire* as passenger for the trip north; the Chief E.R.A. and the T.G.M. had fitted him with a D.S.E.A. set and patiently explained its simple operation to him several times, but the man was so unnerved by the catastrophe that, although he succeeded in getting out through the hatch, he failed to reach the surface. But altogether the engine-room escape was a remarkable justification of the submarine escape drill.

It was only afterwards I discovered that, halfway through the escape, the Chief E.R.A. thought it would be advisable to make sure none of the escapers was getting caught up in any obstruction outside the hatch. He therefore clipped on the oxygen mouthpiece of his D.S.E.A. set, made his way up through the hatch, walked about on the outside casing of the submarine in the vicinity of the hatch, and then, although he could easily and without shame have made his ascent to safety, he climbed down through the hatch into the engine-room once more and carried on with the business of supervising the escape of the remaining men. Not until every other man had left the compartment did he make his own getaway.

For his part in the escape Chief E. R. A. Killen was later awarded the British Empire Medal.

It was not until the M.L. landed us at Yarmouth that I heard

Peter Bannister was missing. I had been told that another vessel had rescued some survivors from the water, and I had assumed that these were Peter and the A.B. who had been with us. In fact only the A.B. had been picked up. When I saw him later at Yarmouth, he said that he and Peter had swum together for some time and that when they were rescued he had thought Peter was immediately behind. A long search failed to find him. I was staggered by this news, for Peter was a strong swimmer and had seemed in excellent fettle when we spoke together on the surface. To have got so far and be lost at the last moment was an appalling tragedy.

It was daylight when we reached Yarmouth and were met by Lieut.-Commander J. F. B. Brown, who had flown up from submarine headquarters in London to get the facts at first hand. During the day, in the intervals of answering questions, we enjoyed the generous hospitality of the Naval Base.

That evening I strolled along after dinner in a small grassy courtyard. A gentle drizzle of rain was falling, and it was what one would call a miserable evening, but to me the sound of the soft rain falling like a benediction on the living grass seemed inexpressibly sad and sweet, and life itself so desirable, that I could not imagine myself ever again being dissatisfied with it. For the first time I knew the delirious joy of not being dead.

At the same time I felt that in the emergency I had failed to act in the manner expected of a submarine officer. Running over again and again the sequence of events following the moment of collision, I was tortured by two nagging thoughts. First, why had I not had the sense to realize that all the water coming into the control room had been pouring in through the ship's ventilation system? Second—and this has haunted me ever since —I knew that I should have been in the engine-room with the men.

There was also the problem of the future. At first I was sure I never wanted to see the inside of a submarine again. But the conviction grew in me that to ask to leave the submarine service would be such an admission of defeat that I should never recover my self-respect. For the purely egoistic reason of patching up my pride, I therefore decided to remain in submarines—if I was allowed to. On the principle of immediately remounting the horse that has thrown you, I resolved to ask to be sent on an operational patrol as soon as possible.

With thoughts like these crowding my brain, I was still awake when Wingfield walked into my cabin about midnight. He had just landed, having stayed on the scene of the collision until nightfall. He was looking ten years older, grey and haggard from worry and lack of sleep. He told me how Tony Godden had been drowned, and asked about Peter Bannister. I told him the story up to the point where we had separated after reaching the surface. He said the final casualty total was two officers and twenty men, almost half the ship's complement.

The next day, after further interrogation, they sent us off on fourteen days' leave. In the middle of it we were recalled to attend the official Board of Inquiry at Chatham, a dreary and gruelling experience.[7] At the end of my leave I reported to H.M.S. *Dolphin* at Gosport, and in answer to my request for an early return to sea I was appointed to relieve Freddie Sherwood[8] as Torpedo Officer of the submarine *Sealion*, then based on Fort Blockhouse and operating off the French coast under the command of the famous bearded Ben Bryant.

Extract from the Engine-Room Register
of the submarine Sealion.

Twelve little S-boats "go to it" like Bevin,
Starfish goes a bit too far—then there were eleven.

[7] The Admiralty apparently did not attach too much blame to Wingfield, for he was given another command soon afterwards and remained in command of operational submarines until the end of 1944, winning a D.S.O. and two D.S.C.s.

[8] Lieut. F. C. Sherwood, the first Royal Canadian Naval Volunteer Reserve officer to join submarines in this war.

Eleven watchful S-boats doing fine and then
Seahorse fails to answer—so there are ten.

Ten stocky S-boats in a ragged line,
Starlet drops and stops out—leaving us nine.

Nine plucky S-boats all pursuing Fate,
Shark is overtaken—now we are eight.

Eight sturdy S-boats—men from Hants and Devon,
Salmon now is overdue—and so the number's seven.

Seven gallant S-boats trying all their tricks,
Spearfish tries a newer one—down we come to six.

Six tireless S-boats fighting to survive,
No reply from *Swordfish*—so we tally five.

Five scrubby S-boats patrolling close inshore,
Snapper takes a short cut—now we are four.

Four fearless S-boats too far out to sea,
Sunfish bombed and scrap-heaped—we are only three.

Three threadbare S-boats patrolling o'er the blue,
. . . .

Two ice-bound S-boats . . . .
. . . .

One lonely S-boat . . . .
. . . .

His completion of the list, leaving the blanks to be filled in
later (I am glad to say it was not necessary: *Sealion, Seawolf* and
Sturgeon survived to the end of the war), is an example of the
buoyant sense of humour, fatalistic but far from defeatist, which
inspired most of the *Sealion's* crew.

Return Ticket

by ANTHONY DEANE-DRUMMOND

Anthony Deane-Drummond was a born parachutist and a born escaper. He was one of the first to land from the air in Italy on a raid in 1941 and—only after his mission was completed—he was taken prisoner. Twice he escaped: once from prison, once from hospital; on both attempts he reached the Swiss frontier and, on the second, he crossed it.

He joined the First Airborne Division and was dropped at Arnhem. It was during this third spell of imprisonment that Deane-Drummond underwent the ordeal recorded here, in the course of his third—and finally successful—escape.

THE game was up and I was a prisoner again. Once more I went through the indignity of being searched by the enemy, but on this occasion I at least had no weapons to surrender. I had to let go my sten gun and pistol while swimming across the Rhine.

No longer was I a free man and the anti-climax suddenly made me remember my hunger, and how every bone and muscle in my body ached for rest. Wearily, so wearily, I was marched down the road to the Company H.Q., watched by sleepy-eyed Germans from slit trenches dug into the verge.

We stopped at a farmhouse and I was shown into a room, after pushing aside a blackout blanket which had been nailed over the doorway. Inside, a hot aroma of unwashed bodies, the acrid stench of stale German tobacco smoke and seasoned sausage combined to stifle my nostrils. A hurricane lamp turned low gave the only light, and in the gloom my smarting eyes could now see gently-heaving bodies wrapped up in greatcoats lying all over the floor, with mounds of equipment taking up every vacant space. The only sounds were wheezes and snores except for the faint noise of a conversation in German coming from a next-door room.

One of my escort of three pushed by and, after mumbling what I took to be swear words, woke up one of the prostrate Germans. He turned out to be an N.C.O. and was soon kicking the other bodies to life, who grunted in a dialect I did not understand, and then stood up and stretched. A piece of paper passed hands and I was off again out of the house with three new guards to Battalion H.Q. which was about a mile away.

This time everything was much more orderly, and after a German sentry had examined the piece of paper carried by my escort, we went down some steps into a cellar whose roof had been chocked up with large baulks of timber. A clean-shaven, middle-aged German subaltern sat at a table with a lamp on one corner. He motioned me to sit down and said in broken English:

"I must to you questions ask. You will answer."

"Oh."

"Your name, please?"

I told him.

"What day you jumped?"

"I can't say."

"How many more are you?"

"I can't say."

His eyes seemed to bulge a bit behind his glasses, and an angry flush spread up his neck.

"O.K. You no speak. We will see."

He ended with some instructions in German and I was shown outside into the back of an open *Volkswagen* car, in which I was driven along the road towards Arnhem.

We crossed the Rhine using the main bridge for which so many lives had been sacrificed. I could see many marks of the bloody fighting which had taken place as we threaded our way in and out of shell holes and burnt-out German tanks. Smoke was still coming from the ruins of the buildings on the north side of the river.

We sped on through deserted streets to the outskirts of the town and stopped outside a newly-built church which had sentries posted all round it. I was told to get out and wait inside. There I found the church full of newly-captured prisoners of war standing in little groups everywhere. In one corner I could see a few officers, none of whom I knew, and I learned from them that the division was now fighting inside a small perimeter round Oosterbeek, a suburb about three miles from the centre of Arnhem.

In another corner I saw Lance-Corporal Turner and three others who had shared the lavatory[1] with me. They, too, had been captured that morning in various places not far from where I had been taken. All touch had been lost while swimming across, and Turner had been caught while trying to find a hiding-place in a farmhouse. Daylight had come before he had reached a point anywhere near the railway bridge.

We all looked pretty scruffy in that church. I had a five-days' growth of beard, not having had a chance to shave, and many were like me. All had the slightly haggard and drawn look of soldiers who have been without sleep, and seen their best friends die, not knowing when their own turn might come. Some were rummaging in their pockets or haversacks for any crumbs left over from the once-despised 48-hour concentrated ration that we all carried. Many were lying down full-length on pews fast asleep, snoring away with mouths slightly open and heads twisted at any angle.

As the morning drew on, the air in the church became warmer, and more and more of us lay down where we were on the hard tiles and went fast asleep. I followed suit after checking that all doors were guarded and there was no way of getting out.

The Germans still gave us nothing to eat and by midday we

[1]During the house-to-house fighting at Arnhem.

were all getting very hungry and thirsty. Some men I spoke to asked me if I could get the Germans to do something about it.

After some argument I managed to get hold of an officer who could speak some English and in a mixture of two languages I told him that we expected to be given food within an hour, or else I would see that his name was remembered after the war when the time came to deal with the war criminals who disobeyed the Geneva Convention.

He became quite angry and spluttered:

"You can all think yourselves lucky to be alive and you will get food when it pleases us. Anyhow, what do you know about Geneva Conventions?"

"You would be surprised," I replied, "but food we must have, and it is your responsibility to provide."

"Let me tell you, Herr Major, I have just received orders to march you all to a prison near here run by the S.S. I am sure they will feed you."

With a glint in his eye, he turned on his heel, and five minutes later we were on the march with guards on all sides. For two miles we went through the suburbs and saw very few civilians, one or two of whom were brave enough to wave and smile as we went by.

Eventually we arrived at a house on the outskirts of Arnhem in another suburb called Velp. This was used as a prisoner-of-war cage and was guarded by an under-strength company of fifty-five men. It was a typical large suburban house, about twenty yards back from the main road and with exactly similar ones on either side. Two monkey-puzzle trees stood on the front lawn.

Inside the house were about five hundred all ranks of the Division, whose spirits were high except for the ignominy of being prisoners. Here I met Freddie Gough, Tony Hibbert, and many others. I learned all their news and told them mine. The Germans fed us on tins of lard and coarse brown bread, but we were not fussy and I wolfed my share down. I had not had a really square meal since leaving England, my last being breakfast on the 17th, and to-day was the 22nd. What months it all seemed and yet it was only five days.

I heard that the bridge had been captured by the Germans soon after dawn on the 21st, when nearly all the original defenders were killed or wounded, and all ammunition had been expended. Colonel Johnny Frost had himself been wounded, and for the last twenty-four hours Freddy Gough had been in command. For three days and nights this gallant force had held out against overwhelming odds, including tanks, which came up and gradually knocked down or set on fire every house that was being used for the defence. Some of these tanks had been stalked on foot and blown up with grenades. Fighting patrols had gone out every night to drive the Germans out of houses which overlooked the bridge. Deeds of heroism were done which are matchless in the history of the British Army, but received little publicity at the time because nobody returned to tell the tale. The Division had been ordered to hold the bridge for forty-eight hours until the arrival of the Second Army. It had been held for seventy-two hours by six hundred men, but unfortunately to no avail.

We now realized what a failure the whole operation had been but we still hoped that the Division could hold on where it was and provide Second Army with a bridgehead from which the advance could continue. Many were our speculations on what was happening to the rest of our units still fighting, but our hearts were heavy and we could not help thinking about ourselves and our present plight.

I remember the latrines inside the house were hopelessly inadequate for the numbers of men, and some deep trenches had been dug at the bottom of the garden at the back of the house. In this garden were growing carrots and onions, and we quickly dug these up and distributed them on the basis of half a carrot or onion per head. It took some of the hunger away.

All this time I was looking for ways out of the house or garden. I was determined to escape and not be a prisoner longer than I could help. Now would be the time and it would be infinitely easier than later on.

Some of the officers were already saying that they would leave trying to escape till they arrived at the German prison camp. It would all be "laid on" there. It is so easy to put off action till to-morrow and all this sort of talk was so reminiscent of my experiences in Italy. I told everybody I saw that their one and only chance of getting away would be before they left Holland. The farther they went back along the evacuation channels, the more difficult would escape become. I think they believed me, but most of them could not see any possible way out with any hope of success. When I started looking over the whole house and the garden there were many smiles cast in my direction. It was not possible to get away, they said, they had already been over the place with a fine-tooth comb. The trouble was that most of them were numbed by the anti-climax of being prisoners, and they did not realize that small though the chances of getting away were at the moment, they would be better now than at any future date.

I reasoned that the cage would only be temporary and would last as long as the Division did. From all accounts this would not be long, so one solution would be to hide up in the house itself till the Germans left and then to get out. Again it was just possible that the Second Army would continue their advance through the Division's bridgehead, and then the area would be liberated.

I could not see any way to escape that gave a better than fifty-fifty chance of success, so I looked everywhere for a hiding place that would hold me for two or three days. The only possible place seemed to be a wall-cupboard in one of the ground floor rooms, which had a flush-fitting concealed door. The whole door was covered with the same sort of wallpaper as that of the rest of the room, and was difficult to see except on close examination. The cupboard was about four feet across, twelve inches deep, and about seven feet high. Its interior was divided horizontally by adjustable shelves, but by removing the shelves I was able to stand inside in tolerable comfort. Fastening the door was a problem. The cupboard was fitted with the normal type of mortice lock let into the thickness of the door, with a keyhole on the outside complete with key. By unscrewing the lock, and turning it back to front, the keyhole came on the inside of the door and I was able to lock myself in. A piece of wallpaper, torn from another part of the room and pasted over the outside keyhole, helped to conceal the cupboard's presence.

The next job was to lay in a stock of water and food. All I had was my waterbottle, and I found an old two-pound jam jar that I also filled up. A one-pound tin of lard and half a small loaf of bread completed all the provisioning I could do. Some of the officers very kindly offered to give me their waterbottles, but I refused. They would need them for their own escape, which, I reminded them, they must try to make or be a prisoner for the rest of the war.

Little did I think that I would be confined to my cramped little cupboard for thirteen days and nights before getting out. I thought that the limit of my endurance would be reached after three or four days, because I did not start off in the best condition for an endurance test. The Germans came round on the evening of the 22nd to take all names, and in order to avoid a record being taken I started standing in my cupboard. Pole squatting is, I believe, a time-honoured sport in the U.S.A. I cannot recommend cupboard-standing to anybody who wants to try out something new. I stood first on one leg, then on the other; I leaned on one shoulder and then on the other. There was no room to sit down because the cupboard was too shallow. I managed to sleep all right, although occasionally my knees would give way and would drop forward against the door, making a hammer-like noise. Every bone in my body ached, and I felt quite light-headed from lack of food, water and rest.

The day after I locked myself in the cupboard the Germans turned the room into an interrogation centre. Every officer and man going through that cage was first interrogated in the room where my cupboard was. It was certainly an interesting experience, which I believe had never before been rivalled, though I scarcely appreciated its uniqueness at the time. We in the army had always been instructed that if ever we were made prisoner, the only information that we should give would be our army number, rank and name. The Germans knew this, of course, but tried every guile to get more information. The usual trick was to pretend that they were filling out a card for the Red Cross, and ask a series of innocuous questions until the prisoner was at ease, when a question of military importance would suddenly pop up. It was a surprising thing to me that very few officers or men gave only their number, rank and name. Almost everybody gave a little additional harmless information, such as the address of their parents or wives, or whether they were regular soldiers or had been in the T.A. before the war.

Only two gave away military information. One was a captain in the Glider Pilots, and another was the batman to a company commander of the leading battalion of relieving Second Army. This battalion had assaulted across the Rhine opposite the division's perimeter in order to allow the successful withdrawal of the division. These two men, who shall be nameless, gave all the information they knew or were capable of giving. Luckily neither was in possession of any real military secrets and no great harm was done, except to my pride. The officer talked so much, and seemed so promising a source of information, that he was given lunch just in front of my cupboard door. What agonies of mind and tummy! To hear all this coming out, and to smell what seemed to be a delicious meal only a few yards from my hiding place. I nearly burst out of the cupboard on several occasions to stop the wretch giving information. I think I would have done so if he had started to say anything serious. Luckily he did not know much and I kept my peace and exercised self-control over my mental anguish.

The questioning went on for several days, four or five I think, and by night the room was used as sleeping quarters for the German guard. I had no chances to get out at all, but as I had lasted so far, I resolved to try to remain a little longer. My luck must come to my rescue. It had always done so up till now.

Little by little I eked out my rations of water and bread. Four mouthfuls of water every four or five hours and just a bite or two of bread. The water was the chief shortage, and after nine or ten days I could not eat any more bread because my mouth was so dry. For the benefit of the curious, I was able to direct my urine through a paper funnel into one corner of the cupboard where there was a gap in the floorboards to allow some pipes to pass down to the cellar. It interested me to see that I continued to pass water in spite of drinking practically nothing. I did not feel the need to do anything more solid during the whole time, perhaps because there was nothing in my tummy. My system started to function again quite normally as soon as I started to eat when I got out. My only legacy was a series of bad boils, followed by styes which persisted for about a year afterwards.

It was now 5 October, 1944, and the thirteenth day of my voluntary confinement. My water was nearly at an end, and the cramp in my muscles hurt acutely most of the time. Patience and caution were now finished and I told myself that I would have to make an attempt to escape that evening or fail in the effort.

The room outside my cupboard was still full of Germans but provided no new prisoners came in that evening there would be a good chance of the whole guard leaving the room empty for half an hour or so at sunset. On the previous evening they had all cleared out of the room and hung over the garden wall adjoining the main road outside my window, to watch the passers-by in the twilight. I suppose it is a world-wide habit to come out of the houses on a warm evening for a breather before going back inside for the night. The only thing that might spoil it would be new prisoners; but there had not been any last night, so with any luck I would get away to-night.

I slowly shifted my weight from one leg to the other, and leaned alternately on my right shoulder and then my left. By now, shifting my position had become almost automatic, and no longer required any thought or even consciousness. My mouth was dry as a bone, but I had already had both my dawn and midday mouthfuls. My evening one was not due for another two hours yet. To-night I would take three mouthfuls of water. What bliss this promised to be!

It was due to get dark about 7.30 p.m. or 8 p.m., and I hoped the room would clear by about 7 p.m. I would then have to hide up in the bushes near the house for an hour, till it was really dark, before it would be possible to move round to the back of the house and get away.

The minutes slowly crept by while I waited anxiously, my ears taut for the sound of the Germans leaving the room. Occasionally one of them would go in or out, but I could hear snores from two or three having an after-lunch nap. At about 6 o'clock I pulled on my boots and smock and gathered all my equipment. Dressing in that cupboard was a work of art, and to avoid making a noise it was three-quarters of an hour before I was ready. While I was dressing I heard two Germans stumble out of the room, but I was fairly certain that there were one or two more. Sure enough, by their grunts and the bumping of boots on the floor, I heard two more get up and go out talking about a *fräulein.*

"The time had come. Cautiously I unlocked my door. There might still be the odd squarehead making up arrears of sleep. I opened the door an inch and had a quick look round. Damnation take it, there, not six feet away, was a solitary German soldier sleeping with his hands crossed over his tummy and his mouth wide open. As I had to walk across the floor and open the big french windows, which were both noisy operations, I decided to give him another half-hour.

A few troops came clattering into the building with a couple of girls, all talking at the tops of their voices. I heard them go upstairs and enter the room directly over my head, and they soon had quite a merry party going with songs and a gramophone, and an occasional girlish giggle or scream. I was in luck. They were probably not expecting any prisoners to-night, and if the noise increased as the wine flowed I should have no worries about covering up squeaks as I opened a window.

The noise upstairs woke my sleeping soldier after about twenty minutes, and he got up and walked out. This was my chance and, taking a couple of mouthfuls of water, I gently pushed the door open again. This time the room was empty. I could see the guards lining the garden fence on the main road and not ten yards away. My plan was to get the window open and then wait for a lorry or tank to go by before slipping out and into the shrubs growing almost under the sill. The Germans would be most unlikely to look back towards the house when anything interesting was passing.

I was in luck and no sooner had I opened the windows when a large truck went clattering by. This was my cue, and I was quickly out and had dropped into the shrubbery. My luck held good on the thirteenth day in that Dutch cupboard.

I quickly crawled into the bushes where it was thickest at the corner of the house, and concealed myself as best I could with dead leaves. From where I was I could see eight or ten of the guard idly leaning against the garden fence a few yards away and could hear them chatting unconcernedly about the war in general and their sweethearts at home. From the window above came occasional strains of gramophone records and the semi-delighted, semi-frightened squeals from the not-too-particular girls.

The Siege

by ARTHUR CAMPBELL, M.C.

Kohima was besieged for 16 days in April, 1944. During that time, between 12,000 and 15,000 crack Japanese troops—the 31st Division—ringed the little town which was defended by 500 Territorials of the Royal West Kents, 4th Battalion, led by a professional soldier of Irish blood, Lieut.-Colonel John Laverty. In Kohima there were also some 2,000 non-combatant Indian troops.

The siege of Kohima, as a fight against overwhelming odds, ranks with the 300 Spartans of Leonidas at Thermopylae, with Revenge's defiance of 53 men-of-war, with Horatius at the bridge. The perimeter contracted, but it never vanished.

Earl Mountbatten's verdict on this action is quoted in the author's preface: "The Battle of Kohima will probably go down as one of the greatest battles in history. It was in effect the Battle of Burma."

But for the valour of that British half-thousand, Japan would have reached—perhaps crossed—perhaps conquered—the sub-continent of India.

LANCE-CORPORAL JOHN HARMAN was bored. He had been bored ever since the coming of war compelled him to join the Army, dragging him away from the complete life he found on the island of Lundy where he loved so well the rugged coastline and the friendship of animals and birds in the rocks and on the crags. His father, city engineer and stamp collector, bought the place some years before, when his son was still a boy and, since an early age, the boy's interests had lain there as much as in the normal fellowship of the world outside. The sea sounds thrilled him; he found exhilaration in the weird wailing of the wind round the great house; he would watch for days on end the busy life of ships and boats in the wide estuary. School meant little to him, though the masters were kind and he was good at games, because the work bored him so that he spent each term looking forward with passionate longing to the holidays and to the wild loneliness of Lundy.

Like most young men with wealthy parents he travelled abroad during holidays, though these journeys held little appeal for him unless they took him to Spain. In this country of wide space and warm people he was at ease, and it was only a few miles from Madrid that he met the remarkable old sage who held more influence over him than any other being. This dried-up old man had introduced him to spiritualism while he was little more than a boy, arousing in him a warm interest. The sage was able to tell him what was happening at his home on Lundy at any given time and always, on the boy's return from Spain, the sage would be proved right. The old man foretold that John Harman would live to be seventy years old. There were times when the young man took the prophecy in complete confidence; there were times when the lance-corporal entertained doubts.

He was a well-built youth, five feet ten inches tall, with huge shoulders and a great barrel of a chest. His square head, set on a thick neck, was crowned by a mop of unruly black hair which had no parting and fell in a fringe over his low forehead. He could have looked moronic but for his eyes, two startling features which would cling to the memory when the rest of his face was forgotten. They were the eyes of an introvert; they seemed always to be looking inwards, examining, criticizing, yet in them lay kindness and a deep understanding.

Army life was the antithesis of everything he was used to. Men were everywhere, crammed up against him on the square, in the dining-halls, in canteens, sleeping, even, within a yard of him, one each side. Though naturally untidy, he cleaned and polished and stamped his feet endlessly, at the beck and call of loud-mouthed N.C.O.s and indifferent officers. Somehow he had to get along with these men, being kind and helpful to them, as they helped him; he had to do this because they were training together for war. To a degree he succeeded, for he made a few friends and many acquaintances. But he was essentially an individualist; what he had to do he liked to do alone. If there was blame attached he would accept it; if kudos, he would revel in the limelight, though he never boasted of his achievements.

He trained initially as a trooper in the Household Cavalry so that he was able to enjoy the companionship of the magnificent troop horses placed in his charge. Soon these were removed and their places taken by impersonal monsters, tanks and armoured cars. John Harman transferred to the infantry. There followed more training, then a succession of reinforcement camps all over the world, in which he waited endlessly with nothing to do until some unit in the desert, in the jungles or in the mountains claimed him.

In the course of time he was drafted to the Royal West Kents, joining them in the Arakan. He knew nothing of the regiment, but was at once forced to absorb their customs and traditions. These were things he understood, milestones in the history of a proud regiment and a great nation, and he took to them readily. But the jungle was dull, with never enough action to fill his days and nights; all the time looking for the enemy, for the Japs, always looking, patrolling, reporting, with only now and then a short action, a little excitement which soon died away when the enemy disappeared, only to have to be found again. Even the few actions left him with little stimulation.

As a private his job was to obey orders, stupid as some of them were; he seldom had to think. When it was a matter of pushing a bayonet into a man's guts before he pushed one into yours, there was not much time to think; you just pushed and pushed until the man on the end of the bayonet went limp and then you pulled it out and looked for another one. He thought, sometimes, of taking a stripe himself because of the idiocy of some of the orders he was given. As a private, if he objected or suggested a better way, as he often did, officers and N.C.O.s would be angry and tell him to do what he was told. Perhaps the best way out was to start giving orders himself, but, though his education fitted him for leadership, he did not really want to lead and he was by no means sure that men would follow him. No, he was an individualist, one who found it easier to go out and kill the Japs on his own, an exercise which gave him no qualms for they looked little better than the wild beasts they were.

So he stayed as a private with few friends, until he met Donald Easten, a friendly and charming officer in his own company who at last persuaded him to take his stripe. This was only a week or two before and the young man was not yet used to the feel of the thing on the arm of his bush shirt. But even with his stripe the lance-corporal was bored, never more so than now, shuffling, as he was, along a dusty road through the darkness with eight men behind him; the eight men who made up his section. He was responsible for these men; he had to think for them; he had to see that they were provided with clothing, food and ammunition and anything else they might need to fight with. It was not an arduous job because there was always someone else above who seemed only too keen to interfere; he was happy to let them do it. Now and then on the march he looked back to ensure that the men were closed up behind him, but they knew how to march as well as he did and he had little doubt that they would be.

*   *   *

There were only five Japanese, but they had one machine-gun and two light automatics and it would need a properly-planned attack to drive them out. They were well placed, and properly protected, but they had not yet finished with Sergeant Tacon.

He had foreseen such an incident as this and the evening before had crawled down to see Lance-Corporal Harman in charge of the section immediately on his right. He and Harman discussed what might happen in the night and they agreed that, should

Tacon's men be driven back, Harman with his section would counter-attack into the flank of the attacking enemy. Then Tacon saw Harman's platoon commander who agreed to the arrangement.

When Harman saw the Japs entrenched on the ridge, he decided to counter-attack. He said to Jim: "I can do this best by myself. If I sneak up behind them they won't see me coming, but if we all go they're bound to spot us."

Jim answered: "Now don't be a clot, John, we can all muck in on this and give the bastards a proper bashing."

Harman ordered, "Now do what you're told—take your Bren over there behind that tree and keep the bastards' heads down."

Jim said, "O.K., Corp.," and moved away. Harman noticed the other men conforming with his order; it was strange how readily they obeyed him.

He climbed out of the trench and walked forward, deliberately, making no use of the cover offered by the few bushes still standing, or by the trees. He walked to and fro, searching for the best position from which to overlook the enemy, until he found a place which gave him a good view of one of them. He stopped there and, raising his rifle, shot him dead. Then, still walking slowly, he moved on. By now they had seen him and were shooting back, but Jim Matthews was not giving them a moment's peace, even though he found it awkward handling the Bren with his left hand.[1] As Harman moved in, his head thrust forward, his hair falling over the low forehead, his solid body a little ungainly on its odd-sized feet, he must have looked to the Japs like some monster, sent by a strange god they had offended, and equipped with a shield, proof against the bullets they fired at him in a constant stream. They could hardly realize that it was a shield of some skill, of immense courage and unshakeable faith.

Still moving forward he raised his rifle a second time and shot

[1]Matthews had been recently wounded in the right arm.

dead another Jap. Then he paused, crouched low behind a bush, to fix his bayonet, before going forward again, now a little faster, though still at little more than walking pace. He held the rifle out in front of his barrel chest, pointing towards the three remaining enemy whose fire was now panicky and ill-aimed. He advanced deliberately, his head lowered so that the thick neck was barely visible, until he topped the small ridge. Then he leapt down into the machine-gun post and disappeared from Jim Matthews' view. The young soldier saw occasional glimpses of the cut and thrust of his rifle, of the quick movements of his tousled head; he heard one scream of agony, then another, then one single shot. A moment later John Harman appeared on the ridge, holding the Jap machine-gun high above his head for all the soldiers to see before flinging it down on the ground.

A cry went up from the nearest soldiers, "Good old John, he's done it again," and the cry spread through the trees to the rest of the company, and then up the ridge to the other companies, until the whole area was ringing with cheering and shouting. The officers, although they realized the danger, let the men shout and yell because they knew it was good for them to let loose their pent-up feelings; they were all living on nervous energy, and many on borrowed courage. It would do no harm to borrow courage from John Harman who had enough for a whole army. The Japs, too, must have heard the cheering and can have drawn little comfort from it.

John Harman clambered off the ridge and started walking across the small valley to rejoin his section. Soon he became aware of men shooting from the other side and saw Jim Matthews standing up, yelling frantically, "For Christ's sake, run, you bloody fool, run, run, RUN," but he continued his steady march forward. His mind was clear, his blood cool, his heart steady. He had done what anyone else might have done in the same circumstances; he was going back now to take his place at the head of his section.

As he reached the middle of the little valley a Jap machine-gun fired from farther along the ridge behind his right shoulder. The burst of fire caught him at the base of his spine, hurling him to the ground. Jim at once dashed out, while the others poured a hail of fire into the Jap position, until now unseen. The red and green tracer bullets of the defenders wove patterns over his head, the clamour of battle echoed all round as Jim Matthews heaved his friend's body on to his back. Spasms of agony wrenched at his wounded right arm as he staggered up the hillside, gasping for breath, pouring out sweat, driven to his knees by the weight of his burden. At last, as the action died away and smoke drifted quietly across the battleground, he lowered John Harman gently into the trench they had shared. Harman's eyes were closed, and Jim, kneeling over him, slapped him gently on the face to bring him round. The eyes opened and John Harman spoke, "I'm dying. I've got to go."

Jim answered, "Don't be a fool, John, you ain't finished yet. Think of all them judies waiting for you outside. I'll get the doc. down in a minute."

"No, Jim, I don't need a doctor. He has enough to do without another on his hands." His eyes closed again, while his head dropped back on to his friend's knee. Jim waited, murmuring urgent, meaningless phrases.

Five minutes later John Harman raised his head once more. He said, "I got the lot—it was worth it." Then he died.

Escape from Germany

by AIDAN CRAWLEY

Aidan Crawley, before the war a journalist, was himself a prisoner-of-war. That, perhaps, is why his book, of all others, has the very feel of barbed wire. He was himself an escaper who reached the very border of Switzerland before recapture. His Escape from Germany is a classic.

The story of W/O Grimson is one with an unhappy ending. Grimson, who made no fewer that six bids to escape, succeeded in organizing the successful escape to Sweden of two comrades; but himself was recaptured and, it is believed, shot.

IT IS ironic that the most accomplished escaper of all never reached England. The story of the late Warrant Officer G. T. W. Grimson, R.A.F., is unique. He not only escaped six times from the various camps in which he was held, but spent several months in Germany during his last period of freedom arranging a route from the camp at Hydekrug to the Baltic ports by which prisoners could reach Sweden. The route was completed, and proved helpers, most of them Poles, were stationed at various addresses to provide shelter and set prisoners on their way. Unfortunately the first man selected to use it was arrested as he left the camp, and in the round-up which followed Grimson himself was caught. He was never seen again and was believed to have been shot by the Gestapo.

Grimson was an unusual man. He was thick-set, of medium height with mouse-coloured hair which looked almost grey when it was cut short. His character was a mixture of aggressiveness and reserve. He had joined the R.A.F. in 1938 as an observer and was shot down in 1940. At first he made an unfavourable impression on his fellow-prisoners, boasting about well-connected relations in England and being apt to show off; but before the war was over he commanded the admiration of all.

His first escape was ostentatious and unsuccessful. While on a working party at Barth he caught a guard unawares, kicked him violently from behind, and made off. He was caught within a few minutes, but received no more severe sentence than usual and spent two weeks in the camp gaol. As the war went on Grimson's character developed. He was in his late twenties when shot down, and spoke only a little German, but he began to learn the language thoroughly and to take the business of escape seriously. In the Centre Compound of Stalag Luft III, to which he and the rest of the prisoners at Barth were moved in 1942, he lived for little else.

His first escape from this camp was an impersonation. Grimson noticed that in build and appearance he was very like a German corporal who was in charge of the issue of stores. After working on him for some time he managed to borrow the corporal's pay-book and gate pass and have copies made. As it was summer, most of the Germans wore white fatigue jackets while on duty and there was little difficulty in making one of these from German towels. A converted Air Force field service cap, German badges of rank, leather belt and pistol holster, completed the uniform.

A day was chosen when the German corporal was on leave. Grimson put on his disguise and walked from the equipment store to the compound gate carrying a fourteen-pounder German jam tin which had been converted into a bucket. This contained a few new scrubbing brushes and floorclothes, under which were concealed his food and a camp-made civilian cap. He wore a camp-made civilian coat under his fatigue jacket.

The sentry opened the gate as he approached, merely glancing at his pass as he went by. Grimson walked across the outer compound, which housed the camp stores, coal dump and sick quarters, and was treated in exactly the same way at the gate leading into the German compound. Although he could have managed a short German conversation he was not called upon to speak at either gate. After passing through the second gate he spent the following five or six hours in the German compound, mostly in an air-raid shelter and in lavatories, and when it was dark left through a wicket gate at the side of the German Officers' Mess. He was recaptured a few days later because of a fault in his identity papers.

His second escape occurred six months later, just after Christmas, 1942. At that time of year, even in prison compounds, social events took place, and the N.C.O.s' camp-leader arranged a concert to which he invited members of the German staff. Grimson and a companion were to escape as two of them while the concert was in progress. The concert was in the evening, and soon after it had begun Grimson and his companion left their barrack in the uniform of two German corporals. When they reached the gate the sentry was some yards away and they had to wait for him. They produced their passes and at the same time rated him for not being there to meet them. With many apologies the sentry unlocked the gate and let them through. As they went they remarked that they did not like the show.

At the second gate the sentry on duty asked for their numbers. This took them by surprise as they had not known that the German Security Officer had just introduced a system whereby each German entering the compound was issued with a number. But they again cursed the sentry so thoroughly for keeping them waiting while he unlocked the gate that he let them pass without further question. They left the German compound by the gate near the officers' mess and, after altering their disguises in the woods, walked to Sagan railway station as foreign workers. They travelled by train to Bayreuth, where they were caught two days later through a check of documents as they left the station.

The following summer Grimson escaped again in an even

more brilliant style. German electricians in uniform occasionally repaired the telephone wires which ran along the top of the perimeter fence, and in doing so climbed up and down both sides. Grimson decided to pretend to be an electrician and to carry out tests on the telephone wires, and in doing so he hoped to cross the fence and walk off. His equipment consisted of a dark blue boiler suit, German Air Force field service cap and leather belt, an imitation electrician's meter, several spurious identity documents, a quantity of concentrated food, and a civilian coat which he wore under the overalls.

An elaborate system of signals between himself and his colleagues was arranged and shortly before three o'clock in the afternoon he put on his disguise and made his way to the compound theatre, where he borrowed the ladder used for the stage. He carried this to the guard-rail opposite the spot where telephone wires from the German compound crossed the perimeter fence, and called out in German to the guard in the tower, explaining that he was going to test the telephone wires. The guard waved to the man in the other tower covering this zone, then indicated that it was safe for Grimson to cross the strip of ground between the guard-rail and the fence.

Grimson stepped over the guard-rail, propped the ladder against the wire, climbed it, and then with his dummy meter made a show of testing telephone wires. After a few moments he informed the guard in the tower that the fault must be farther over, climbed down the ladder and walked to where a plank was lying near the fence a few yards away. He carried this up the ladder and placed it across the top of the double fence. Unfortunately the plank was too short and it fell down on top of the barbed wire entanglements between the fences. Unperturbed, Grimson climbed down the ladder, swearing volubly in German, recovered the plank and put it back where it had been lying, then walked to another part of the compound and found a longer plank with which he returned. He then climbed the ladder once more and placed the plank firmly across the gap between the fences. After clambering on to the plank he again began testing the telephone wires, gradually working his way to the outer fence. At this stage the sentry patrolling outside stopped opposite him and asked what he was doing. Not satisfied with the reply, he demanded to see his identity papers. Grimson produced his false camp-pass and told the guard to mind his own business. After looking at them the guard handed back the papers and continued on his beat.

A few moments later Grimson, who was once more on top of the wire, deliberately dropped his test meter in the barbed-wire entanglement between the fences, but closer to the outer edge. Swearing loudly in German, he climbed down the fence within the German compound and recovered the test meter. After examining it he grumbled to the guard in the sentry tower, who had watched the whole proceedings with a bored air, about the amount he would have stopped from his pay because the meter was damaged. He was about to walk away, but after a moment's hesitation climbed back up the fence, removed the plank which spanned the top and laid it on the ground a few yards within the German compound. This done, he walked off through the German camp. His colleagues persuaded a German N.C.O. to fetch the ladder back to the theatre, alleging that it had been removed by one of his staff. Travelling by train, Grimson reached Stettin, but while looking for a neutral ship was picked up on the fifth night after his escape.

When the N.C.O.s were sent to Hydekrug on the Memel Peninsula, in the summer of 1943, a fresh enthusiasm for escape was born. The camp was so near both the Lithuanian frontier and the Baltic coast that there was the double chance for anyone who got away of crossing to Sweden or being hidden by the civilian population and either going east or joining the Partisans. Attempts multiplied and the organization improved. However, no one reached England during the rest of that year, and in analysing the failures the Committee came to the conclusion that exhaustion was one of the chief causes, because it led to carelessness. They therefore decided to try and arrange a hiding-place in Germany or Poland where escaped prisoners could go and rest before making their final preparations to get out of the country.

About this time a member of the Escape Organization received a letter from a friend of his family, an Englishwoman married to a Swede, who lived in Stockholm. This letter contained a partly disguised message saying that when in Germany, her husband, the captain of a Swedish merchant vessel, frequently visited "The Parson's House" near the camp. The Committee came to the conclusion that "The Parson's House" must either be the name of an inn used by Swedish sailors in a Baltic port, or the residence of a Swedish clergyman doing welfare work among Swedish sailors. In any case, here was an address where help might be forthcoming.

In order to try and find "The Parson's House" Munkert[1] was sent to Memel to investigate. He made several visits and carried out exhaustive inquiries but without success. Shortly afterwards one of the prisoners engaged in trading with Germans told the Escape Committee that one of his "contacts", another conscripted Pole, was connected with the Polish Underground Movement and was willing to shelter escapers in his own home. The Committee investigated this offer, found it genuine, and accordingly, about October, 1943, decided to organize an escape route by sending Grimson to the Pole's home, which he was to use as a base for visiting all the Baltic ports, until he found "The Parson's House". He was to keep in touch with the Escape Committee by means of code messages in letters written in German to Munkert, who would pass them on.

As soon as the escape route was established, another prisoner was to be sent out to go to Sweden and arrange for the co-operation of Swedish seamen visiting German ports on the Baltic.

[1] Eddie Munkert, an interpreter, and—on account of his Roman Catholic faith—an anti-Nazi, whose activities in helping Prisoners-of-War are recounted in other chapters of Aidan Crawley's *Escape from Germany*.

This second man was to keep in touch with both the camp and the first man by code messages in letters written in English or German; the first letters from him would indicate how replies should be addressed. It was hoped that when all arrangements were complete, prisoners would be able to leave the camp and travel along the route from point to point until they were taken on board a neutral ship and hidden.

By mid-January, 1944, all was ready, the only decision which remained being the method by which Grimson should escape from the camp. Arrangements were made with the driver of a horse-wagon, a Pole, that he should be taken out of the camp hidden in the large inverted box which served as the driver's seat. However, on the appointed day and for some weeks afterwards, the Pole failed to appear, and after Grimson had waited fully dressed in civilian clothes for several days this scheme was abandoned. It was then decided that he should repeat a trick which had already been performed successfully, of examining a new drainage system which was being constructed from the north-east wash-house, and leave the compound disguised as a civilian foreman at the point where a trench passed under the fence of the wash-house enclosure. While Grimson was putting on his civilian clothes to do this, the German Security Officer visited the site and gave orders that the trench should be filled in.

Undeterred, Grimson and the Committee completed arrangements for a third scheme within a few hours. Because of the comparatively mild weather, roll-call then took place on the compound football field. Shortly before each parade a party of guards, usually about twelve in number, entered the compound and took up positions in various parts of it, remaining until the parade had been dismissed; they then made their way individually through the compound and Vorlager gates to the guardroom. Afternoon parades took place at three o'clock, and it was arranged that on this day the parade would last for about an hour instead of the usual twenty minutes, owing to artificially created miscounts. This would mean that the guards would leave the compound at dusk and it was planned that Grimson should leave disguised as one of them.

Shortly after midday on 21 January, 1944, Grimson put on his civilian disguise, the lower half of which consisted of long boots and riding breeches, and over it a German Air Force greatcoat, cross-belts, ammunition pouches and dummy bayonet. When dressed, Grimson lay down on a bed in a dimly-lighted part of the room and was covered with a blanket. Meanwhile arrangements were made that the prisoners should be counted in their barrack rooms, ostensibly because of the colder weather, and for a prisoner who resembled Grimson to take his place. The arrangements worked smoothly and Grimson was counted as a man sick in bed. There were several miscounts, and it was not until 4 p.m. that the whistle blew signalling the end of parade.

At its sound Grimson rose, slung a beautifully-made dummy rifle on his shoulder, put a German field service cap on his head, and walked out through the compound and Vorlager gates as the third or fourth "guard" to leave. As there was no commotion when the last guard left it was obvious to those left behind that the sentries on duty at the gate had not counted them as they passed. In the Vorlager, Grimson went to a lavatory close to the guard-room, where he disposed of the dummy rifle. Then he walked across to a locked clothing store of which he had the key, where he found in a packing-case a trilby hat and a brief-case containing all the documents and equipment which had been prepared for him. The packing-case also contained food for consumption on the spot. Grimson took off his German uniform, put it in the packing-case, and the following day this case was taken back to the compound by the Camp Quartermaster and a party of prisoners accompanied by Munkert.

Grimson remained in the store until an hour before the train on which he intended to travel was due to leave Hydekrug. After locking the store he left the key in a prearranged place to be picked up by his colleagues next day. Dressed as a civilian he walked through the German camp to the railway station, a distance of about two miles. He bought a ticket and a few minutes later boarded the train for Insterburg. He travelled by train, in stages, nearly four hundred miles, to the home of a forester who was a friend of the Polish guard at the camp and lived in the woods in German-occupied Poland about ninety miles south-east of Danzig. The guard's home was in a nearby village.

When Grimson arrived at the forester's house on 22 January he was well received and stayed there for several days. During this time he wrote a letter to the Escape Committee which contained a message saying that he had arrived safely at the forester's house and had the nucleus of a good organization already in being. He asked that tobacco and other things which he required for trading should be sent to him. This was done through a guard who went home on short leave soon afterwards. A few days later this man returned to camp and conveyed a verbal message from Grimson saying that he was obliged to leave the forester's house because a woman in the family was talking too much to other Poles in the neighbourhood; also that he intended to try to find "The Parson's House".

As has been explained, the Escape Committee had planned that a second man should escape and join Grimson when the latter indicated that he had made arrangements for him to be received. After a lapse of two weeks, when no further communication was received from Grimson, a letter was sent to him which contained a message stating that the second man would be sent on 18 February to join him unless instructions to the contrary were received. This letter was taken by a guard who went home on three weeks' leave who also carried a parcel of supplies for Grimson. The Escape Committee did not receive any reply to this message before 18 February, and the second man escaped from the camp that morning as planned. Later that same day, the Escape Committee received a brief letter from Grimson which had been sent through Munkert. It contained the message: "Send the second man but no route arranged".

On the following morning Munkert received a further letter

from Grimson which had been posted in Memel. This contained a direct request to Munkert that he should meet him that day at a specified place in the town of Hydekrug at 6.30 p.m. Munkert took the letter to the Escape Committee and, after the matter had been discussed, they told him to meet Grimson. He was given a written report of developments in the camp since Grimson's departure, including the instructions given to the second man who had escaped, and was told to give this to Grimson together with a parcel of supplies and a map of Danzig docks.

Munkert met Grimson in Hydekrug and handed over the report and supplies. Grimson gave him a written report of his activities since he had left the camp, also a personal note for one of the members of the Committee. These were delivered by Munkert the following morning. The gist of Grimson's report was that he had found "The Parson's House" in the seamen's quarter of Danzig and that the parson was a Swede. When Grimson had approached him, he denied all knowledge of any Swedish ship's captain whom Grimson sought, and refused to help. Eventually he was persuaded to allow a search to be made of the register of Swedish seamen who visited the parsonage, but no person bearing the required name had been there during the previous fifteen years. Afterwards Grimson had reconnoitred Danzig harbour and he gave details of the position of guards and Swedish ships. He stated that he had visited all the Baltic ports from Lubeck to Memel, but had not been able to find another "Parson's House" nor to obtain any information about the ship's captain whom he was seeking. He said that Memel was not used by Swedish shipping.

In his personal note to the member of the Escape Committee who had been his closest friend in the camp, Grimson described how he had spent the greater part of his time since leaving the camp in trains and snatching a few hours' sleep in waiting-rooms whenever possible. He mentioned that he was suffering from a form of gastric influenza. He said that he was dissatisfied with

143

the result of his work during the month he had been at liberty and felt that the Committee must be disappointed; he was prepared, however, to continue if the Committee thought he should do so. He had made contact with a number of Polish workers and outlaws in Danzig and the surrounding district who might prove to be useful. Latterly, he had stayed occasionally at the home of the forester's brother, also a forester, in a wood some distance from his original shelter. He had been able to obtain food coupons from an innkeeper and had paid for them with the chocolate and cigarettes which had been sent to him by the Committee. He concluded by saying that he wanted some more supplies, including clothes for the children of the man who was sheltering him, and that he would collect these the following week from Munkert, whom he had arranged to meet at the same time and place. Finally he said that he was travelling to the original forester's house to meet the second man, as it was not safe for him to be in that area.

Meanwhile the second man, Warrant Officer (later Squadron-Leader) C. B. Flockhart, D.C.M., R.A.F., had escaped from the camp and met Grimson on 21 February at the home of the forester's brother. The two discussed all that had happened during the previous month, and Grimson explained that he had not succeeded in arranging a passage to Sweden, but he believed it might be possible to board a Swedish ship in Danzig harbour. They decided to travel to Danzig that day. After a few hours' sleep they left, taking different routes because their documents were identical. They met in the waiting-room of Danzig railway station at ten o'clock that evening as arranged. Grimson was familiar with the dock area and he led Flockhart to within a few hundred yards of a Swedish ship which was being loaded with coal. Flockhart then handed his money, papers, brief-case and raincoat to Grimson and arranged to meet him in the station waiting-room before daylight should he fail to get on board the ship.

While Grimson walked off towards the city, Flockhart

entered the prohibited dock area through an open gate across a railway track and crawled fairly close to the side of the ship. There was quite a lot of activity on the quayside, which was lit by arc lamps, and a German sentry was posted on the end of the ship's gangway. Flockhart lay in the snow for about four hours looking for a way of boarding the ship. Eventually he crawled to a position behind a crane about thirty feet from the ship's side, but the arrival of some German workmen and a railway engine made him decide that he could not board the ship that night. He returned to the railway station and met Grimson, who told him that the nightly examination of identity papers in the waiting-room had taken place some time previously, and they spent the rest of the night there.

Next morning Grimson, who was an experienced oarsman, suggested that it might be possible to board the same ship from a rowing boat that night. He proposed that he should search for a rowing boat while Flockhart travelled to Gdynia to find out whether Swedish shipping used that port. Flockhart went by train and found that it was a German naval base so heavily guarded that it was impossible to enter the harbour area in daylight. He returned to Danzig and met Grimson, who had failed to find a rowing boat. However, he had seen another Swedish ship in a different part of the dock and had discovered that this might be reached through a hole in the dock fence.

After dark that evening Grimson led Flockhart by train and ferry to a point near the hole in the fence and close to an anti-aircraft battery. Within a few seconds Flockhart had handed over his raincoat and papers and lay down by the side of the road, while Grimson walked on. Flockhart crawled about a hundred yards over snow-covered ground to the fence and after some searching found a small gap. He crawled through and across railway tracks towards the ship which Grimson had pointed out. This part of the harbour was well lighted and Flockhart was able to see that there were two ships flying the Swedish flag alongside the quay. He chose the larger, a vessel of about three thousand tons, and reconnoitred from the cover of some railway wagons. There was an armed sentry patrolling near the ship's gangway. Flockhart walked some distance along the quay away from the ship, keeping the railway wagons between himself and the guard, then crossed to the water's edge and approached the ship. He was helped in this by the cover afforded by the leg of a crane. He succeeded in getting within about three yards of the gangway while the sentry was walking towards the opposite end of the ship, but he turned and saw him. Flockhart was walking quite slowly, and when he saw that he had been observed he stopped, had a look round, then sauntered slowly away. At that moment two Swedish seamen arrived to go on board the ship and the guard, being engaged in examining their papers, did not challenge Flockhart, who left the dock area immediately by climbing the fence some distance from the hole through which he had entered.

He returned to the railway station and saw Grimson, but they pretended not to recognize one another and sat in different parts of the waiting-room until morning, leaving about 7 a.m. Flockhart then described his experiences and they discussed various means of boarding the ship under cover of darkness. Both men were suffering from lack of sleep, but Grimson wanted Flockhart to make one more attempt that night. Flockhart said that he would prefer to make the attempt openly in daylight and asked Grimson to try to obtain a suit of workman's blue overalls, a black cap with a shiny peak, and one of the badges worn by Poles in Germany. Grimson said that he thought he could get these without difficulty from a cousin of the forester who was living in Danzig. They parted and about three hours later Grimson returned to the station with a parcel containing the clothes which were required.

Flockhart went into the station wash-room and put on the overalls over his civilian clothes, packed his trilby hat in his brief-case in case he should need it later, and substituted the peak cap. After a suitable interval Grimson knocked on the door of the compartment to indicate that there was no one else in the main room, and Flockhart handed him his raincoat as he passed. As Flockhart stood outside the railway station at a tram stop, Grimson, who had followed him, stood beside him for a moment and whispered "Good luck".

Flockhart travelled by tram and ferry to the dock area and walked to the hole in the fence which he had used the previous night. As he approached he noticed that a path had been trodden in the snow between the hole and the roadway. He assumed that this must be a short cut used by dock workers, so he followed the path and crawled through the hole. Although there were a number of people on the road, no one showed any interest. Feeling elated by the ease with which he had gained access to the dock, he walked across the railway tracks to a small wooden hut near a concrete mixer, which he had observed the previous night. This was about two hundred yards from the larger of the two Swedish ships. He observed the quay through a knothole and, after hiding his brief-case under some wood in the hut, soiled his hands and face, then walked towards the ship. Some Russian prisoners were loading the bunkers with coal under the supervision of a guard, and a similar party was working on the quay near the smaller ship. As it was then midday no other workers were about, and Flockhart stood near the Russians for about half an hour in the hope that one of them might leave the others for a few minutes so that he could ask his help in boarding one of the ships; but none did.

Noticing that the sentry on the larger of the two ships was walking up and down the quay near the gangway, Flockhart decided to try to repeat his trick of the previous night and approach the ship along the water's edge under cover of the crane leg. He returned to the hut by a circuitous route and removed the Polish badge from his overalls. He approached the ship noiselessly, and after ensuring that there was no one else near, stepped from behind the leg of the crane when the sentry was walking in the opposite direction and began to examine one of the ship's moorings. He hoped that when the sentry turned and saw him he would assume that he was one of the ship's crew who had come down the gangway. The sentry turned and saw him but made no sign, so Flockhart walked to the next mooring, which was closer to the gangway, and examined it very carefully. The guard turned again and walked towards the other end of the ship and Flockhart walked slowly up the gangway.

The ship sailed at 10 a.m. on 25 February, after having been searched by Germans, but Flockhart was not discovered. On the afternoon of the following day he went on deck and revealed himself to a member of the crew who took him to the captain. The captain said that his ship was already in Swedish waters and would arrive in Stockholm the following day; he placed a cabin at Flockhart's disposal. On arrival in Stockholm the captain handed him over to Swedish plain-clothes police, and next morning he was taken to the British Legation. Ten days later he travelled by air to the United Kingdom.

On 4 March Grimson again visited Hydekrug and returned every week until 13 April. He told the Escape Committee that he had decided to confine his activities for the rest of March to the Danzig area because of the amount of Swedish shipping there and because he had succeeded in finding lodgings which he considered to be reasonably safe. He was living on food obtained through the black market and was forced to pay very high prices. About mid-March he stated that he had rented two other rooms in different parts of Danzig and that each contained a stock of food; the rents had been paid for some time in advance and they could be used to house escapers until they could be put on board Swedish ships. In another report he said that he had several Poles working for him and had established contact with helpful foreign workers who lived in a camp close to Danzig docks. Subsequently he outlined a scheme whereby any escaper from the camp who reached Danzig could establish contact with him. He intended to be at a specified place in Danzig railway station between noon and 1 p.m. and 7.30 and 8.30 p.m. daily. Should the escaper not find it possible to be there at either of these times, he should make a mark on a particular ferry time-table against a time when he would return. This notice board would be under constant observation by one of his Polish helpers and the escaper would be met at the time he indicated. In the report which he made towards the end of March, he said that he had made some friends among Swedish seamen who lodged in hotels in Danzig, and that he was ready to receive escapers.

At the end of March it was arranged that the first man to use the route should escape from the camp on 6 April. Grimson undertook to meet him at the house near Hydekrug and accompany him to Danzig.

About the same time, two prisoners proposed to the Escape Committee that they should escape together and go into Lithuania. It was their intention to explore the possibility of organizing a route through that country to the Russian lines, or by fishing-boat to Sweden, for use by prisoners who could not speak German. The Committee approved this proposal on the condition that these two men undertook to remain in Lithuania for two weeks before travelling to Danzig to make contact with Grimson in the event of failure to establish a route. The details of Grimson's scheme for establishing contact in Danzig were explained to them after they had complied with the Committee's condition.

On 3 April, 1944, these two men, Warrant Officer R. B. H. Townsend-Coles and Aircraftman, later Sergeant, J. Gewelber, M.M., were escorted from "A" Compound to "E" Compound by Munkert, escaping the following day disguised as a "ferret"[2] and an engineer. When they reached the Lithuanian frontier, about six miles from the camp, near Nowemiasto, they decided it would be impossible to cross it because of the swampy nature of the ground. It was also intensely cold. They therefore decided

[2]Ferret—slang P.o.W. name for German spy within the camps.

149

to go at once to Danzig by train, and arrived without incident on 6 April. They waited in the station at the place which had been specified by Grimson until 7.30 p.m., but he failed to arrive. It was too late then to go to the ferry notice-board in the dock area, and they decided that Gewelber should seek help from Poles. He spoke to three Poles standing at a street corner and explained who he was, and one of them agreed to take them to his home. They stayed there for two days, later moving to a foreign workers' camp.

After the Poles had failed to find them a ship, they went to the ferry notice-board and made the sign specified by Grimson. During the next few days they visited the docks several times, but there was no sign of Grimson and they tried to persuade Swedish sailors to hide them on their ships, but without success.

Meanwhile Grimson visited Hydekrug on 6 April in order to pass on his report, collect supplies and escort the first escaper to use the route to Danzig as planned. He was told that this man had not been able to escape that day because the forged documents which he was to use had not been completed, but that they would be ready within a few days. Grimson arranged to return on 13 April. The Escape Committee also told him through Munkert that Townsend-Coles and Gewelber had escaped on 4 April and had been instructed to make contact with him in Danzig at the end of two weeks should they be unable to make their way through Lithuania. He therefore returned to Danzig.

On 12 April the first man selected to use the escape route was escorted from "A" Compound to "E" Compound by the same method as before. He was a fluent German speaker, having been a prominent member of the Escape Organization as a "trader", and was in possession of the usual forged identity documents and a camp pass. He, too, was to escape disguised as a "ferret".

At noon on 13 April he was advised that there were no Germans in the compound and left the barrack room in which he had dressed. He walked to the gate in the northern fence and showed his camp pass to the guard. He was allowed to pass through, but when he headed towards the sewage farm the guard called out that he must "book out" at the guard-room which was nearby. The "ferret" replied that he did not think this was necessary, but the guard was insistent. The prisoner walked to the guard-room and reported to the sergeant in charge, who inquired whether he was new to the camp. This query was answered in the affirmative, whereupon the sergeant wanted to know to which Company he was attached. Without hesitation the prisoner answered that he belonged to the third Company. At this juncture the sergeant examined the "ferret's" camp pass and said that he thought that the bearer must be a prisoner-of-war. He arrested him and took him into the guard-room. The prisoner attempted to destroy his forged identity documents on the fire, but a member of the German Security Staff arrived before they had been burnt and rescued them. After being searched the prisoner was marched off to the office of the German Security Officer and interrogated briefly. Later he was taken to the camp gaol where he was questioned by members of the Security Staff and a member of the Criminal Police.

That evening Grimson arrived at the rendezvous at Hydekrug and was met by Munkert and Sommers. They handed him a letter from the Escape Committee which explained the circumstances of the prisoner's arrest earlier that day. Because of the similarity between Grimson's documents and those taken by the Germans that morning he was advised to return to Danzig and remain under cover for about two weeks. It was suggested that he should return to Hydekrug on 29 April.

Grimson gave a message to Munkert for delivery to the Escape Committee. The gist of this was that he had learned through one of his helpers just before he left Danzig that Townsend-Coles and Gewelber had arrived there. He proposed to return there immediately to make contact with them. He stated that travelling was becoming increasingly difficult because of much more frequent and closer examination of papers by Civil Police, Criminal Police, Railway Police and Gestapo officials. On one journey alone his papers had been inspected on twenty-seven occasions. He had tried to establish contact with various Allied nationals, including prisoners-of-war and workers in Germany, but seven attempts had been made to betray him. He concluded by saying that he would return on 29 April.

On the morning of 13 April, Townsend-Coles and Gewelber visited the ferry notice-board and found a message from Grimson. This gave a time later that day and the initials "G.G.". They returned at the time indicated but failed to see Grimson. Presently they noticed a man watching them and eventually he addressed them in Polish. After some discussion he stated that he was one of Grimson's assistants and gave them a parcel of food and arranged to meet them the following day; they returned to the workers' camp. They met Grimson's assistant on 14th and 15th, when he informed them that he expected Grimson to return to Danzig that night with another escaper from the camp. They arranged to meet again that evening. They kept their appointment and met the Pole, who was accompanied by Grimson. Grimson took them to an address in Gdynia, where they were lodged with another of his assistants.

On 19 April Grimson escorted them to the docks and led them through the hole in the fence which had been used by Flockhart. He instructed them to board the Swedish ship which was lying there while he distracted the attention of the sentry guarding the gangway, then left them. He walked along the quay and engaged the sentry in conversation. Townsend-Coles boarded the ship quickly, but Gewelber approached more slowly, and when he had reached Grimson's side the sentry noticed Townsend-Coles moving on the ship. He went after him and, on instructions from Grimson, Gewelber boarded the ship and hid. The guard caught Townsend-Coles, but Grimson remained on the scene and accompanied the party when Townsend-Coles was taken to an office for questioning. Later he was taken to a prison at Marienburg. The Germans searched the ship twice before she sailed on 21 April, but Gewelber was not discovered. He remained in hiding until the ship arrived in Sweden four days later, then got ashore without being seen and reported to the British Legation in Stockholm. He was handed over to the Swedish police and repatriated to the United Kingdom, where he arrived on 8 May.

Immediately following the arrest of the prisoner who was trying to leave the camp disguised as a "ferret" on 13 April, the Escape Committee ordered the cessation of all escape activities and all equipment was hidden securely in anticipation of extensive searches. On the following day the man who had been captured was interviewed by the Camp Commandant and asked to make a statement about his intentions after leaving the camp. He refused and requested that his R.A.F. uniform should be brought to him. He was told that this was a matter for the Security Staff. On the following day he bluffed one of the cell guards into fetching his uniform from the compound and discarded his civilian clothing. He was detained in the camp gaol until 11 May, being interrogated daily, then released into the compound.

For a few days following his arrest conditions in the camp were comparatively quiet, but the Escape Committee learned through Munkert and other Germans that an investigation was being made about the forged documents which had been recovered from the guard-room fire. When it was discovered that some of these had been reproduced by photographic means, the camp photographer, Sommers, was suspected and questioned. It is believed that he was able to clear himself. At the same time Munkert was under suspicion because of his known association with the man who had attempted to escape. On about 19 April one of the members of the Escape Committee gave a message to Munkert for delivery to Grimson on the occasion of his next visit to Hydekrug. The message was:

"Get out of the country, position hopeless."

Two days later Sommers arrived in the compound under escort and all the prisoners who lived in one of the barrack blocks were ordered to parade. Sommers scrutinized them but did not pick out anyone. At a propitious moment he pulled up one of his trouser legs which revealed that there were no laces in his boots. This was noticed by members of the Escape Committee, whom he knew, and it was concluded that had instigated the identification parade in order to get into the compound so that they might learn that he was under arrest. Later he and the man being held in the camp gaol were confronted with one another, but each declared that he did not know the other.

About this time the Camp Commandant sent for the Camp Leader and the Senior Medical Officer, an officer of the Royal Army Medical Corps. He informed them that it would be dangerous to continue escape activities at that time, and requested the Camp Leader to hand over to him all existing copies of forged documents. He stated that the surrender of these would enable him to report to higher authority that the whole matter was closed; failure to do so would cause untold complications in the form of searches and arrests. The Camp Leader said he knew nothing about such matters but he would make inquiries in the compound. Upon his return there he consulted with the Escape Committee, and it was decided that after a suitable interval he should return to the Commandant and inform him that there were no other forged documents in existence; this was done. On 23 April a note from Munkert was conveyed to the Escape Committee by another German collaborator. The note stated that Sommers had asked him to inform the Committee that a colleague of his in the Polish Underground Movement had been killed in a shooting affray with the German Police, and that a message connecting him, Sommers, in his real name, with this Movement had been found on the man's body. He had been in the hands of the Gestapo on a previous occasion and did not trust himself not to divulge information under interrogation.

He desired the Committee to supply him with poison or a pistol, so that he could commit suicide. The Committee conferred and decided to meet his request; early next morning it was learned that Sommers had died during the night and later that day this information was confirmed. It was learned also that the guard who had arranged for Grimson and Flockhart to stay with the forester had been arrested at the same time as Sommers. They had occupied the same room in the German camp and were known to be associates. When arrested this man had broken away from his escort in an endeavour to get himself shot, but had been recaptured uninjured. However, he knew very little about the Escape Organization within the camp or about Grimson's movements after he had moved to the Danzig area. He is believed to have been shot some time later.

On this day the Escape Committee learned from other Germans that Munkert was being watched very closely and was virtually under open arrest. However, a few days later a note was received from him through the agency of a German who had not been very co-operative, and whom the Committee did not trust. In the note Munkert stated that he was cleared of suspicion and wanted instructions for the meeting arranged between himself and Grimson which was to take place later that week. The Committee was reluctant to accept Munkert's assertion that he was cleared of suspicion, but decided that it was imperative to try to transmit a final message to Grimson. A letter was accordingly written giving full details of the developments within the camp during the previous two weeks and instructing Grimson to leave at once for Sweden; this was not signed. Grimson's friend on the Committee wrote a personal letter to Grimson and signed it. No Germans were mentioned by name in either of these letters. The letters and one thousand Reichsmarks were enclosed in an envelope and handed to Munkert's messenger at noon on 28 April. This German did not return to his normal place, the carpenter's workshop in the Vollager, that afternoon.

That evening one of the members of the Escape Organization was informed by a "ferret" that Grimson, posing as a civilian working for the German Air Force, had been arrested at Insterburg; also that Munkert had been arrested that afternoon and removed from the camp. None of the Germans or Poles, service or civilian, who had been really useful to the Escape Organization were seen again in the camp after that day, but nothing is known concerning their fate.

On the following morning, 29 April, six prisoners-of-war, including the member of the Escape Committee who had signed the letter to Grimson, were arrested and placed in the camp gaol without being charged with any offence. Next day the Escape Committee learned that Townsend-Coles was being held in the cells, but was not allowed to make contact with any other prisoner in the gaol; also that he was still wearing the civilian clothes in which he had escaped. All efforts to get an R.A.F. uniform to him during the next few days were unsuccessful, but it was learned that he was in possession of his prisoner-of-war identity disc, and the member of the Escape Committee who had been arrested managed to talk to him for a few moments. Apparently Grimson had travelled as a passenger on the same train when Townsend-Coles was being escorted from the prison at Marienburg to the camp, and he had seen him on several occasions, but they had not had an opportunity to speak because of the vigilance of his escort. He last saw Grimson when the train stopped at Insterburg. He had learned from his guards that a country-wide check-up was being made to find Grimson.

On and about 6 May, Townsend-Coles was taken from the camp gaol under escort to an unknown destination, but a little later it was learned from one of the Germans in the camp that he had been seen in Tilsit Civil Prison. Subsequently the British Government made inquiries through the Protecting Power and a reply was received from the Germans that he had been charged with espionage and collaboration with the Polish Underground Movement, and that on 15 July, 1944, he had offered resistance at Tilsit and had been shot dead. The British Government demanded an inquiry, but before this could be carried out by the Protecting Power the area was occupied by Russian forces and no further investigation was possible.

The six men who were arrested on 29 April were removed from the camp under escort to an unknown destination on 10 May. Subsequently it was learned from the Germans that these men were regarded by them as the Escape Committee. Although nothing was known in the camp at the time concerning their fate, they were split into two parties of three and sent to separate camps in other parts of Germany. Apart from periods of detention in cells, no further action was taken against them.

Little more is known about Grimson, although extensive inquiries have been made. Nearly a year later, in another camp, one of the members of the Escape Organization met a German whom he had known at Hydekrug. This man stated that about April, 1944, he had been a member of a party of guards which had escorted Grimson and Munkert from a military detention barracks to an undefined destination. He had not been a member of the firing party, but he believed they had been shot.

The escaper who was arrested as he attempted to walk through the camp gate on 13 April was tried by court martial about January, 1945, at Stalag 357, Fallingbostel. He was charged with using forged documents to the confusion of the German military and civilian authorities. He was found guilty and sentenced to three months' hard labour, but was never called upon to serve the sentence because of the chaotic conditions prevailing in Germany at that time.

Tobruk Commando

by GORDON LANDSBOROUGH

It is the peculiarity of the British that, upon occasion, they exalt their defeats into victories; Dunkirk, Arnhem, Tobruk. The North African town that for years was a thorn in the enemy flank was the scene of one of the earliest and most disastrous combined operations of the war: one to rank with Dieppe.

But the valour exhibited—both by the Royal Navy and by the Commandos engaged—must stand with the charge of the Light Brigade—of which an expert bystander commented: "It is magnificent, but it is not war." The men on the beaches fought to the last round and the last breath. The men on the sea . . .

AT 0505 on Monday, 14 September—D2 for Operation Agreement—one solitary searchlight suddenly abandoned aerial targets and flung itself out from the north shore. It wavered, touched *Sikh,* passed on, came back. Then it held the destroyer.

Sikh was picking up a dead motor-launch and two lighters. The sea had brought them suddenly out of the darkness on to the stern of *Sikh* before anyone spotted them, and for a few frantic moments it seemed as if all the occupants would go under. The boats crashed against the *Sikh,* and some equipment went overboard, including a marine's rifle. Then someone cut a tow rope and the situation eased. Scrambling nets were thrown down and everybody hauled themselves up in the white light of the searchlight. Aboard the *Sikh* there was quiet activity around the guns.

As the marines came on deck an officer saw a man without his rifle. He gave the poor devil a lot of Army language, and then they were all sent below. Last man out of the boat was Able-

Seaman Robinson, acting coxswain in a dumb lighter. It saved
his life, being last.

A salvo came from some coast defence guns. As yet only *Sikh*
was held by the searchlights, and *Zulu* turned and went out to
sea for five minutes and then came in bow-on to the searchlights. Shells screamed through the night towards *Sikh*, beginning to turn away from shore after taking on the stranded
marines. *Sikh* and *Zulu's* gunners went into action and fired
back, trying to hit the searchlights. South of their position it
seemed as if every gun in Tobruk was now hurling tracer across
the harbour towards other unseen targets close to Scioa Bay.
Then M.T.B.s were seen caught in searchlights and assailed by
a fury of machine-gun and cannon fire.

More guns were firing all along the coast opposite *Sikh* and
Zulu. Shells were coming closer. Then they began to hit. Mostly
it was 88-mm. ack-ack stuff, and while it was disconcerting and
did some damage, no one in the *Sikh* felt seriously perturbed.
What was unpleasant was the fire from a coast defence battery
about a mile west of the landing beach. This was bigger stuff,
probably something like 5-inch guns.

Commander White could see the *Sikh* held now by two
searchlights. He was perturbed to see the sister ship's behaviour.
She was circling, losing speed. *Sikh* was already hit, mortally
wounded at the start of the battle.

A big shell landed in the forced lubrication system of the
main engine gearing. The steering had also gone. Another shell
had hit them for'ard and started a fire in the fo'c'sle. It had also
hit some ammunition stowed forward for "A" gun, and the
blast came down into the mess decks and through a passage into
which the returning marines were crowding.

Able-Seaman Robinson saw it all from the rear of the crowd.
He saw the marines—those fine, healthy young commandos of
a few moments before—go wilting in agony before the searing
heat of the blast. Their bodies protected the *Sikh* seamen. The
alleyway and mess decks were a shambles of burned and dying

men. Worse, the fire for'ard had trapped many of the second flight of commandos, and it was impossible to get through to them.

Fire parties were being organized, and the wounded were being dragged out of the flames. But the ack-ack and coast defence batteries ashore were firing as fast as they could load at the crippled, almost motionless *Sikh*. She was a sitting target.

Her director-tower was next hit, and now her guns had to fire independently.

The Chief Engineer came to Captain Micklethwait and made his report. After which he said, in the emphatic way of engineers, "We must stop the engines or they'll seize up without lubrication." Which is an engineer's way of seeing things.

Captain Micklethwait said, tersely, "To hell with your engines. I don't care a damn what happens to them, so long as we get out of range of those guns."

They were trying to steer a straight course, but the ship would only turn slowly in circles. Then at last even that stopped as the engines abruptly halted. *Sikh* lay helpless and took the thrashing of her life.

At 0520 *Zulu* had been signalled that *Sikh* was badly hit. At the same time Captain Micklethwait made a signal for all naval forces to retire. He knew that Operation Agreement had flopped. It was true that Colonel Haselden held a bridgehead, and the land commando had succeeded wonderfully in its task. But judging by the fireworks display at the mouth of Tobruk harbour, nothing else had succeeded. Clearly the M.T.B.s hadn't landed their forces, and now never would in the face of such furious opposition. And judging by the firing around Mersa Matruh the marines had run into trouble, too.

It was a moment to write off losses, and Captain Micklethwait was a man who could do it. He gave the order to retire—but there was no retiring for the old *Sikh*.

Commander White in *Zulu* now received a signal from *Sikh* ordering him to take the helpless destroyer in tow. This was at

0545. Since 0520 *Zulu* had been caught in the searchlights and was being hit by shells, too. Both ships had about this time begun to make a smoke screen, but it was not very effective.

Commander White at once came racing in to take *Sikh* in tow. It was coming light and suddenly they were hailed from the water. They saw a motor-boat and three dumb lighters drifting. Not only Colonel Unwin had had trouble in keeping going, apparently. But *Sikh* was in greater need of attention, and the tossing, awkward-looking craft had to be left behind.

The first attempt to pass a line failed. *Sikh* was still moving, very slowly but sufficient to upset calculations. *Zulu* manoeuvred beautifully, bringing her stern round to meet *Sikh's* bow. But the swell and the *Sikh's* dying motions beat the manoeuvre. *Zulu* just scraped the port bow and took away some stanchions. The line missed.

It was now almost daylight. *Zulu* circled again. More guns were ranging on them, hitting almost every time at targets no more than 2,000 yards out. *Sikh* was still firing all guns that could be brought to bear, smoke rising in a dense column from the bow where the fire raged. Another big-calibre shell hit them aft and started a second fire.

Then a shell exploded on deck near "B" gun. When the smoke cleared, and the effects of the stunning violence had dissipated, they saw that only three men were left alive on the gun. Immediately a gun's crew formed from nowhere and got the gun into action again.

Zulu made another run. She came in, taking a lot of the fire on to herself, swung in from the port quarter, and a heaving line was thrown and made fast. It broke.

Zulu circled for yet another run.

Sikh was swinging. Now only "X" gun in the stern could be brought to bear. With one gun only she was talking back to a triumphant enemy that was hurling everything it had got against the destroyers.

But not just gunners were being heroic at that moment. The

marines were fighting the fires now completely beyond anyone's control, and helping the crew wherever directed. Down in the engine-room *with a temperature of about* 180 *degrees,* the Chief Engineer, Lieutenant-Commander (E) T. Lewis, was making attempts to get at the engines. The Gunner's Mate, H. W. Seymour, D.S.M., was down below, too, trying to fight his way through to rescue the marines trapped forward. Gillick, Rope, McManus—Electrical-Artificer Taylor, Chief Yeoman Thatcher, P.O. Finn, Chief Petty Officer Moseling, D.S.M.— all were distinguishing themselves in those chaotic moments while *Zulu* came in for the third time to pass a tow-line.

Captain Micklethwait had a fine crew and some very brave and gallant officers. In the agony of those long hours of helplessness he knew it. It might have helped if he had known that his men had those same feelings about their captain—that they took their inspiration from him; his bearing, his calmness, the way he gave his orders, kept them together and left them without personal thoughts that could embrace fear.

A shell exploded on the bridge, demolishing it and killing a rating. Captain Micklethwait had just gone for'ard.

Then *Zulu* came in. Commander White's handling of the craft was magnificent. Shells ranged her as she came across for the third time. Beautifully for a moment the ships were almost poised stern to bow. A line was cast—was caught. *Zulu* wasn't firing now, though "X" gun continued on *Sikh.* Commander White had got every man on to the awkward wire hawser— every marine, including their O.C., Major Sankey. Hitting the enemy was of less importance than taking the *Sikh* in tow.

A rope was hauled across. The hawser was attached and began to go over. *Sikh* men grabbed it and made it fast. *Zulu* swung as her engines began to take the strain. *Sikh* started to move through the water. The batteries ashore were going frantic, cheated at the last moment of their target . . .

A shell landed on the quarterdeck of *Zulu.* The hawser snapped. The tow had parted. Two men were killed on *Zulu* by that shell, and *Sikh* was helplessly adrift again. It was a million to one chance, that happening—that a shell should land on a taut wire like that. But it had happened. And Captain Micklethwait knew it was the end. It was now broad daylight.

He refused to let *Zulu* take any more risks. He ordered her to stand away and not make another attempt to tow. Commander White at once signalled, "Shall I come alongside and take off the ship's company?"

At 0636 hours Captain Micklethwait signalled back, "Wait ten minutes." Commander White thought this might be to give *Sikh* a chance to hide herself in a smoke screen, and thus protect *Zulu* during the transference, and he also came round on *Sikh* making smoke.

Around seven o'clock *Zulu* was being repeatedly hit. The big guns could get her range easily, and nothing Commander White could do could silence the shore opposite. The coast seemed alive with heavy guns pounding at the two ships.

At 0708 Commander White received a signal, "Leave me and rejoin *Coventry*."

It was a dreadful decision for Captain Micklethwait to have to make, and yet his old friend, commander of the *Zulu*, knew it was the correct one under the circumstances. Even so, to *Sikh* it seemed as if *Zulu* was going to disobey and come in yet again to try to take her in tow. Certainly for a few minutes longer she laid down smoke to help her stricken sister ship. Captain Micklethwait repeated his order for *Zulu* to retire.

Then slowly, reluctantly, *Zulu* turned her bows seawards. She made a signal to *Sikh*—"Goodbye. God bless you."

Back came the *Sikh's* reply: "Thanks. Cheerio." Captain Micklethwait was an undemonstrative man.

When *Zulu* was six miles to seaward, she ran out of range of the shore guns. The last she saw of *Sikh*, the destroyer was on fire for'ard and aft, with tall columns of smoke lifting to where enemy aircraft were beginning to circle.

But "X" gun was still firing back at the shore batteries.

They Have Their Exits

by AIREY NEAVE

Airey Neave's They Have Their Exits *has an unusual twist to it: first, he saw Goering when the Reichsmarschall swept by him as he stood, a prisoner-of-war newly captured, on a road in France. Five years later he again saw Goering, when the leader of the Luftwaffe was in a prison cell and Neave was one of the legal luminaries concerned in the Nuremberg Trials.*

But Neave was much more than either lawyer or soldier. He was an indefatigable escaper whose incorrigible evasions drove him first to be condemned by his captors to the toughest of all P-o-W camps, Colditz; and then to escape from that "impossible" fortress.

The three sections incorporated below deal with his final, successful escape; the first, in Germany; the second, in France; the third on the Pyrenean borderland between France and Spain.

WE CAME again to the station waiting-room and sat there, tired and cold and anxious. The numerous passengers in the waiting-room, many poor and infirm, assembled for the night trains. Then came the men in uniform, elbowing all the civilians aside. I watched them closely. The bullying S.S. men, the clod-like infantrymen, and the pale and spectacled administrative clerks. All in uniform, they tramped over the gloomy station like locusts, demanding refreshment or newspapers or anything they wanted. Such is total war.

Luteyn bought the tickets to Ulm. We had decided to change there and, if all went well, to take tickets to the Swiss frontier. At the barrier of the platform for the train to the south, military police stood to check the soldiers but there seemed no control of civilians. We waited beside the train before it started, preferring to find standing room than risk conversation in a compartment. As it began to move we climbed the steps of a carriage and stood in the corridor.

The compartment opposite was occupied by a single figure in the uniform of the S.S. I could see the man as we stood outside, a great ape-like person with a heavy jaw. His uniform was new and spotless and he crossed his legs which were in fine black boots as he read a newspaper with screaming red and black headlines. I caught only the word "Rommel". So that he should not watch us, we moved into the shadow at the end of the corridor and looked into the darkness where only a few pin-points of light showed the effective blackout of the city. The train jolted over the points and gathered speed with piercing whistles. Above its rattle I heard the door of the compartment open, and turning my head saw the big S.S. man standing in the doorway. His hands were on each side of the entrance door and he spoke to us in a soft voice.

"Are you Jews?"

"Certainly not. We are Dutch," replied Luteyn.[1]

"Good. Come in and sit here. This compartment was reserved, but my friends are not coming."

We took our seats beside the big man who spoke very slowly to us, using simple phrases. His friendliness alarmed me.

"Where are you travelling?"

"To Ulm."

"Why?"

"We are Dutch electrical workers transferred there from Leipzig."

Luteyn was doing the talking. He had his genuine Dutch passport ready to produce in an emergency. Then the man turned to me and his stupid eyes examined my face, searching for something he did not understand.

"You are Dutch, too?"

"Yes."

[1]His fellow-escaper, Lieut. Toni Luteyn of the Netherlands East India Army.

165

"How are things in Holland?"

"We have not been there for some months. We have been in Leipzig since the summer."

It was Luteyn who spoke. The S.S. man turned to me.

"I am going to Munich," he said unexpectedly. "Then I go to Vienna for a conference."

We nodded politely and the conversation stopped. Men and women passengers were walking up and down the corridor and were soon invited into the reserved compartment. They bowed respectfully to the high S.S. officer, took their seats and gave our shabby clothes a scornful stare.

There was no further conversation about Holland. I was glad of this. My sole visit to that country had been the journey in the barge up the River Waal to Germany as a prisoner in 1940. As soon as the passengers began to snore, Luteyn stayed awake according to our arrangement and I slept for a few hours until his turn came to sleep. I was awakened by a loud tapping on the glass of the door and two military policemen looked in. They checked the passes of the soldiers and even scrutinized the documents of the S.S. officer. They stopped for a moment to stare at our queerly tailored clothes. I wondered for a moment whether they would recognize the colour of R.A.F. trousers, but the S.S. officer intervened importantly.

"These are foreign workers (*fremdarbeiter*). Dutch," he said with conviction.

The military police hesitated, then turned away as if suspicious civilians were nothing to do with their department. Now it was Luteyn's turn to sleep and I listened to the endless rattle of the express as we passed through Plauen and Hof and sped southwards into Bavaria. Lifting the blind, I glimpsed the snow outside or studied the sleeping faces in the dim light of the compartment. Towards four in the morning the train began to slow down and came to a halt amid the sounds of a large station. I woke Luteyn, rose and stretched my limbs, and walked over to the doorway. In the gloom there was shouting and the bustle of passengers. I leant out of the window and saw on a sign before me the word Regensburg.

It was here that we were due to change for the train to Ulm and we stepped on to the platform in the sharp cold.

"Good-bye, Dutchmen," said the S.S. man pompously from inside the compartment.

★   ★   ★

I was near to collapse from the heat and the smell of cooking. My appetite had been impaired by my last meal of curry in Geneva and the excitement which had turned my stomach. I dared not refuse her hospitality and swallowed the eggs and coffee. Spots circled before my eyes thicker than ever, and I searched for a means of escape into the cool sweet air. A knock at the door came as a welcome and hopeful diversion. A young girl entered, her head covered in a blanket.

She removed the blanket, revealing long black hair. Her face was very white as if she had spent her life in the shadows of a cloister. The forehead was high and the black hair parted in the centre. Her nose was sharp, a little ugly, and her mouth too hard for beauty. She sat quietly at the table for a moment and then spoke to Louis. Her voice had the tone of a vesper bell.

"All is ready," she said, gravely. Louis turned to us.

"Mademoiselle Jeanne is your next guide. She will take you to the other side of the town. I myself am responsible only for the first lap. We expect two more 'parcels' to-morrow. But please, gentlemen, finish your breakfast. You have half an hour at least before you must leave."

The struggle against the desire to vomit[2] passed as I watched the girl. Her eyes were cast down as if in prayer. She said nothing until she rose, ready to go. Then I saw her face clearly. Her eyes

[2]After the poor food of P.O.W. camps and the exiguous rations of escape, Neave was fed not wisely but too well on innumerable fried eggs once he reached the Underground of France.

had the fervour of a deep faith, and in her sallow features were the lines of suffering willingly borne. She restored the blanket to her head and turned to the door with solemn grace.

We walked with Mademoiselle Jeanne through allotments and smallholdings into Annemasse. We two, light-hearted and often cynical, were afraid to speak, so deeply had her faith impressed us. In a side-street, she knocked on the door of a decrepit house where another young, sad-faced French woman led us through a dark passage to a kitchen. The smell of frying met us once more and caught me cruelly by the throat. Fried eggs were ready in profusion and the young woman seemed prepared to out-do Louis's wife in the size of her English breakfast. Sick and perspiring, I drank two further cups of coffee and with enormous effort swallowed more fried eggs. An hour passed without conversation. A small child played beside us in the stuffy kitchen. Sitting at the table, Mademoiselle Jeanne seemed as if carved in stone, the figure of a saint in meditation. Once I ventured to ask a question about our escape route and its organizers. She lifted her eyes reproachfully.

"All I ask of you is that you should send a message on the B.B.C. if you get back to England in safety," she said. "Here, everyone listens to the B.B.C."

Her olive cheeks glowed faintly and she spoke with a sudden warmth. Her eyes for a moment held mine. In their strange sacrificial light I read no womanly interest in myself or Woollatt. There was mystic devotion and courage which placed her far above the desires of the world. Virginal and fanatical, Mademoiselle Jeanne fought her lone intense battle against the powers of darkness without fear. Her work for the French Resistance was but a part of an inner struggle of the spirit. Like other heroines of the great Resistance Movement she inspired the respect and reverence of those she helped. With her there could be neither intimacy nor companionship.

★   ★   ★

A little dark man dressed in the costume of a guide and wearing pure white boots now took his place at the table. He began by asking briskly in a mixture of French and Spanish for money, and large quantities of notes in bundles were taken from money belts or unpicked from the lining of coats and placed before him as if he were a croupier at a Casino. René[3] supplied the money for most of his party, but the Roberts[4] paid their own passage. The funds for our journey had been entrusted to René by Solon[5] in Marseilles. I looked at the notes, mysterious in their crisp new bundles under the candlelight, and wondered where they came from. José, the guide, collected the bundles and counted the notes with care. He appeared satisfied with his payment, for he handed them to the woman who vanished into the darkness of the house.

José was a determined character, thin and wiry, and his eyes were always watchful. His face was the colour of a walnut and deeply lined. When he laughed his teeth showed very white in the candlelight. He earned his living by smuggling. The war had brought him great prosperity on account of the valuable cargoes of spies and escapers requiring safe passage over the Pyrenees.

When the money had been taken away, José said he must inspect the belongings of all those who intended to cross the mountains. Woollatt[6] and I stuffed our pockets with dry socks and packets of chocolate and left our suitcases in the house. The others were asked to discard all unnecessary possessions. Poor old Mr. Roberts vainly pleaded to be allowed to take his suitcase of Bibles and devotional books. José was adamant and the holy books were left behind. His other suitcase of clothes Mr. Roberts insisted on taking, much to our consternation, for it was heavy and the weather in the mountains promised to be stormy.

[3]René—a member of the French Resistance.
[4]An elderly Irishman, and his son who later joined the Commandos.
[5]Solon—another member of the French Resistance.
[6]Hugh Woollatt, another escaper.

At midnight we shook hands with the staunch René. José opened the door gently and, one by one, we stepped on to a path which led to the hills. The night was clear and starlit, but deep clouds moved threateningly towards us over the Mediterranean. I could see the mountains dark and formidable as we began to climb the foothills. For me they were the last barrier but one to cross. In that cold air, as I climbed the path, listening to the others struggling among the steep banks of scrub and the sound of boots now on chalk, now on flint, I steeled myself to meet new dangers. At that stage of the war, the Fascist Government of Spain might have found British officers useful pawns in the game with Hitler. Not till I reached the Rock of Gibraltar would I be safe from the enemy.

José's white boots in front of us stood out clearly as we climbed with him to a height of 1,000 feet and then stopped for a short rest. It was three in the morning and we could see the clouds advancing from the sea behind us. I stood and drank from a small flask of brandy and turned to look towards the heights above. Around me, the remainder of the party lay panting and whispering to each other on the peaty turf. The path continued up slopes of heather. Then came slippery shale and stones. We pulled ourselves from tuft to tuft and then clambered among rocks where icy streams flowed. Slipping backwards and sometimes falling in the darkness, we began to feel our energy draining from us.

At four o'clock we rested again beneath a sharp face of rock. My breath came in painful gasps and I felt my heart would burst. Woollatt and I were young and fit after many adventures, yet we were badly exhausted. The two Canadian priests, spare and ascetic, and the Poles, lay panting and helpless; Mr. Roberts, comforted by his son, was groaning. He had begun to fear that he would be left to die among the mountains. He complained miserably in a mixture of Irish and French. José, unmoved by the climb, silenced him with heartless laughter. In half an hour we moved again towards the summit, lifting frail old Mr.

Roberts like a parcel from man to man, hoisting him by his arms and legs. Some of us cursing and panting took turns at carrying his heavy suitcase.

Daybreak found us among black rocks near the summit eating a breakfast of cheese and hard-boiled eggs and drinking brandy. I had time to study our party in the grey light. The priests reticent and pale, the Poles talkative and full of suggestions. Hugh Woollatt stood with his long dark lock of hair hanging below his beret.

Then suddenly a storm descended on the mountain like a great bird with outstretched wings. Soon everything was drenched in fine rain. The wind blew so that we could hardly stand upright. Above and around us were only the rain cloud and the desolate mountains. In this misery and confusion old Mr. Roberts's suitcase was by general consent hurled among the rocks. There was a feeble round of applause but the old man was near to tears.

For many hours the rain lashed us with pitiless force. The mountain paths filled with waterholes as we splashed through the mist, dragging the old man till he could walk no more. The youngest of us, Woollatt, Roberts jun., and I, took it in turns to carry him on our shoulders. Once, when he was on my back, he seemed to be unconscious and swayed from side to side. Only with great difficulty could I maintain my balance among the wet rocks.

There was a moment when we had to consider whether we should leave him in some farmhouse, but he cried so piteously that we had not the heart to leave him.

At noon the rains ceased as suddenly as they had come, leaving only a blank fog as we began to descend the mountain on the Spanish side, along shepherd tracks in the direction of the town of Jonqueras. In an hour the sun shone and we were on level ground. Mr. Roberts was just able to stumble along with us among farms and wide green pastures. We headed away from Jonqueras towards the railway which, crossing the frontier at

Cerbère, led to Figueras. All that day we tramped heavily through wet fields and along tracks, sometimes carrying Mr. Roberts, sometimes helping him to walk. Once we nearly ran into frontier guards. "That way is no bon," said José laconically, leading us out of their sight. I caught a glimpse of light-green uniforms and black cocked hats in a valley.

And so we marched on in a drawn-out column, crossing the River Muga and trudging through fields, heading towards the railway. As the sun set we were among small villages and ploughed fields. Every one of us was exhausted. Several times it seemed impossible to carry the old man any more and he was left to walk far behind in the dusk calling to us. And then, realizing his danger, we would go back and pick him up again.

The end of the journey came quickly. In the darkness we crouched beside a roughly plastered wall in a Spanish village, waiting for the signal to advance, and then, still following the white boots of José, we reached the railway panting and cursing in our exhaustion. We came to a rough wooden platform and a faint light showed from a shed. In its doorway was the stout figure of a man who stood aside as we blundered into the shed and flung ourselves on narrow bunks.

When I had recovered a little I rose to examine with interest the stout man who welcomed us. He was dressed in a smart pale grey suit with a pearl in his tie and wore a hat at a rakish angle. There came from him a strong Parisian scent and I could see his fat white hands, carefully manicured, adorned with rings. He looked at us humorously through his thick black-rimmed glasses and said in broken English: "Welcome to Spain, gentlemen. Rest yourselves. It is now one o'clock and the train for Barcelona arrives at six."

No Passing Glory

by ANDREW BOYLE

Leonard Cheshire, V.C., succeeded Guy Gibson in the command of 617 Squadron—the men who bombed the Moehne Dam. As portrayed by Andrew Boyle, his official biographer, Cheshire underwent a strange metamorphosis: from a supreme "line-shooter" with a wicked, almost irresponsible, sense of humour to an impassioned and dedicated leader. After the war, as Boyle recounts, another metamorphosis supervened; and Cheshire, profoundly religious, now devotes himself to a mission of healing.

Perhaps Cheshire's greatest single contribution to the bombing-war was his unremitting campaign to be allowed to mark from low altitudes and by the naked eye, instead of by instruments from thousands of feet up; this technique brought to the R.A.F.'s raids a precision undreamed of hitherto. Against all established precedent, against all accepted theory and practice, Cheshire, with split-second timing, flew his Mosquito to a raid and dived it through the flak to lay his markers from a few hundred feet only.

IN THE week 617[1] took delivery of its two Mosquitos, the future of Bomber Command and of the American strategic air force based in Britain was thrashed out at the highest level. The most effective contribution which the Allied heavy bombers could make to the invasion preparations had been the subject of prolonged and acute dispute, and the controversy came to a head between 25 March and 17 April. Day after day there were meetings between political as well as military leaders in Whitehall and elsewhere, for the problems went much deeper

[1] The squadron which under Wing-Commander Guy Gibson shattered the Moehne Dam.

than the nicely balanced technical viewpoints of the professional partisans.

Apart from the vexed question of targets, the operational control of the bombers was at stake; and as Supreme Allied Commander, General Eisenhower was in no mood for pedantic time-wasting arguments. He had only two months left to complete the aerial prelude to D-Day. He wanted the strategic bombers to paralyse all railways leading to the Normandy beaches; only thus could he win the vital race for reinforcements and keep a firm foothold on the shores of France. Without such a campaign of interdiction, D-Day might go down in history as the bloodiest and most foolhardy gamble ever taken by a responsible commander.

In Eisenhower's view, the success or failure of the Allied landings hinged on the success or failure of what became known as the Transportation Plan, drawn up by experts on the staff of Trafford Leigh-Mallory, his air commander, and wholeheartedly backed by Tedder, his deputy at S.H.A.E.F.

It was Tedder's resolute support for the plan, and Eisenhower's deep faith in Tedder, which gradually overcame all opposition and led to its adoption; but the Supreme Commander and his brilliant deputy had first to meet a fierce cross-fire of criticism from Churchill, the Ministry of Economic Warfare, Spaatz[2] and Harris.[3] The time was certainly overripe for sending out the bombers. Yet with Allied air supremacy unchallenged from Norway to Sicily, there seemed ample room for more than one opinion about the best strategic use to which the bombers could be put.

Spaatz had cut-and-dried strategic ideas of his own. He was on the eve of an independent campaign with his Flying Fortresses and long-range fighters against Germany's synthetic oil plants. He believed that the enemy's power to resist an invasion would be fatally undermined if the life-blood of his war-

[2]U.S. Air C.-in-C.

[3]"Bomber" Harris, Chief of Bomber Command.

machine were drained away. Harris thought otherwise; oil plants were what he called "panacea targets", and he would have none of them. But, like Spaatz, he was reluctant to be diverted from area attacks on industry. Both could argue with some show of realism that to sidetrack them now from campaigns which promised such rich results was wrong-headed strategy, since the enemy would be allowed a breathing space for industrial recovery and reorganization.

But Harris, as rigid as ever in his advocacy of mass raids on cities, had a second line of argument that could not be disputed so readily. He expressed his genuine doubts whether Bomber Command was fitted to undertake such a campaign of precision bombing as Eisenhower and Tedder envisaged. His force had been employed almost exclusively with the saturation bombing of sprawling built-up areas; what likelihood was there now that it could suddenly be turned against small targets with any hope of quickly knocking them out? As he put it in *Bomber Offensive*:

"All previous experience had gone to show that the R.A.F.'s heavy bombers, with their futile 0.303 defensive armament, could not operate by day in the face of serious opposition, and could not hit small targets by night except when the opposition was negligible and the weather and light exceptionally good. Any sustained campaign against a large number of small tactical targets could not be carried out in any reasonable period of time if the bombers had to wait for such unusual conditions."

The Prime Minister's objection to the Eisenhower-Tedder plan was political and therefore unanswerable. With other members of the War Cabinet, Churchill was concerned with the possible effect of the proposed bombing campaign on Anglo-French relations, especially if the attacks resulted in grievous casualties among French civilians. Finally Roosevelt was asked for his view, and the President's firm reply to Churchill on 11 April settled the question.

"However regrettable the attendant loss of civilian lives is, I am not prepared to impose from this distance any restriction on military action by the responsible commanders that, in their opinion, might militate against the success of 'Overlord' or cause additional loss of life to our Allied forces of invasion."

This, as Churchill says, was decisive.

On 14 April, the control of the strategic air forces was handed over to Tedder, who was admirably suited for the task of co-ordinating them by his diplomatic touch and great experience as an Allied air commander. He needed every ounce of tact and patience, not only to smooth over inter-service and inter-Allied jealousies but to assert his rather nominal authority without winning unnecessary enemies in the process. Lacking a staff and a headquarters of his own, Tedder was in the invidious position of a Minister without portfolio suddenly saddled with some of the responsibilities of a Premier. It is a measure of his statesman-like stature and strategic acumen that he managed to defy the odds and make the Transportation Plan work.

Tedder had acquired a wealth of valuable experience in Sicily and Italy, where, acting on the advice of scientists like Professor Zuckerman,[4] he had perfected a novel method of paralysing enemy rail communications. Instead of following the traditional text-book technique of blowing up bridges and cutting lines, both of which the enemy could speedily repair, he directed his aircraft against the railway workshops and repair sheds. Since most of these were situated close to big marshalling yards, he gradually deprived the Germans not only of communi-cations but of the means of restoring them. Only when this had been done were the tactical bombers turned loose finally against locomotives and rolling stock.

The Transportation Plan before D-Day followed the same pattern, except in one vital particular: it had to be carried out so deceptively that the German High Command would be given no inkling whether the invasion was likely to be launched against the Pas de Calais, Brittany, or Normandy. Fortunately for Tedder, the geography of France and the original builders of

[4] Professor Solly Zuckerman.

the railways in the north aided his strategy of deception: for the lines to Normandy nearly all branched off from the main network linking the Pas de Calais and Brittany to Paris. In other words, the gutting of rail junctions and maintenance centres near the Belgian frontier, in Paris or along the Seine would hamper the movement of German troops and supplies just as effectively as if Normandy itself were turned into a "railway desert"; and German intelligence would be none the wiser about Allied intentions.

The Transportation Plan was given a trial run more than a month before Eisenhower won control of the heavy bombers. On 6 March the R.A.F. attacked the marshalling yards at Trappes, a busy rail centre some miles west of Paris. Seven more of the eighty targets finally allotted to Bomber Command were attacked during March by the standard method used against cities in Germany: Bennett's Pathfinders flew in at great heights to drop markers from "Oboe" Mosquitos, then the main force followed to bomb the markers. To prevent unnecessary loss of life the crews were forbidden to bomb if they were unable to see the markers.

Even so, there were the inevitable early mistakes with the inevitable outcries from politicians here and Resistance leaders in France. The latter did not contest the necessity for destroying rail communications; they were apparently less apprehensive about the political repercussions of severe civilian casualties than Churchill and some of his advisers. But they believed that it could be done at a far cheaper cost in human lives by sabotage than by air bombardment. When General Koenig, the Commander of the French Forces of the Interior, offered to destroy any targets the Allies cared to name, Eisenhower had to refuse.

The Supreme Commander dared not court the risk of failure.

The edginess of Harris and his staff during the trial phase of the railway offensive can be well imagined. They had practically no experience of precision attacks to guide them, except the evidence of 5 Group's raids on Friedrichshafen, Peene-munde[6] and the ski-sites,[7] as well as the rather startling results achieved by Cheshire and 617 Squadron since the beginning of 1944. Even though the Pathfinders inflicted considerable damage and spilled comparatively little French blood during March the prickly vigilance of the politicians ruled out all complacency. Slowly the marking methods were overhauled in the interest of greater accuracy, and in the changes the influence of Cochrane's[8] tactical ideas stood out unmistakably.

A master-bomber and a deputy were introduced to control the attacks and direct the target marking. Then, with irresistible logic, it was decided that 5 Group should be given a virtual monopoly of target marking because of its proven experience. Finally, as the supreme vindication of Cheshire's lonely persistence, his low-level technique was fully tested over France in mid-April.

It had taken him less than a fortnight to prove that the Mosquito was too fast for the defenders at low level. On 5 April, the whole of 5 Group was sent to attack an air-frame repair factory at Toulouse, and Cheshire was ordered to mark the target in his Mosquito. It was the first large-scale precision raid he had ever led, and he prepared for it with even more thoroughness than usual.

One small incident beforehand perfectly illustrates the scrupulous, almost finicky care he gave to technical minutiae. Cheshire was not blessed with a mechanical mind, and as a rule he trusted the judgment of his own experts; but none of the experts could answer a simple conundrum which worried him: could the Mosquito, which had been designed for high altitudes, carry him at low level to Toulouse and back without running out of petrol?

Without more ado, Cheshire telephoned direct to John de

[6]The plant where the secret weapons were developed.

[7]The "doodle-bug" (V.1) launching sites.

[8]Air-Chief-Marshal the Hon. Sir Ralph Cochrane.

Havilland at Hatfield, who realized at once that the problem was no figment of an apprehensive imagination:

"I'll come over to-morrow, and we'll decide what's possible after a test," he said.

The informal arrival of de Havilland on the morning of an important raid created a mild stir among those who had dismissed Cheshire's doubts as fussiness carried to the *n*th degree. There *was* some uncertainty about the Mosquito's petrol range after all. De Havilland wasted little time, and few words.

"It can be done, but only just. My advice is—don't try without long-range tanks."

Cheshire hesitated for a second, then replied:

"Thanks, John. But I think I'll chance it."

Too much depended on the raid to "scrub" it at the last minute, and clear knowledge of the odds gave him a sense almost of relief. By spending less time identifying and marking the target, he could just scrape home. With so little margin for error, he could not afford to slip. Risks for Cheshire had little in common with the conventional phantoms of aircraft trapped by guns or night fighters. The risks he really feared were the stupid, avoidable ones, the loose screw, the wrongly-fused marker, or the badly-tuned engine. That explained his endlessly roving eye and the pains he took to inspire every man with pride in his work and faith in the work of others.

Pat Kelly, the short, dark, charming Irishman who was his navigator, had some trouble keeping a straight course to Toulouse. The Mosquito's speed was deceptive, and they arrived after the main force. The bright moonlight over the target, however, guided them to the aiming point at once. Hurtling through the light flak, Cheshire put his markers on the roof of the central repair hangar on his third low-level run. The backing-up by Munro and McCarthy in Lancasters was excellent, and for a few minutes he watched the bombing with satisfaction. The needle on the petrol gauge told him when to leave.

At St. Cyr less than a week later, Cheshire was baffled by the darkness. The squadron had been ordered to "destroy at all costs" the Field Air Park and Signals equipment depot of the Luftwaffe, the most important single target of its kind in France. But the light was so faulty that he could not see even the ornate, formal gardens of the Versailles Palace, which practically ad-joined his aiming point. Not to be outwitted by the weather, he did something he had longed to do for five years. Turning the Mosquito's nose straight down he dived towards the ground, identified the T-shaped central depot as it loomed up out of the gloom, pulled back the control column 700 feet above it, and released the markers. They landed on the western fringe of the target area.

When the squadron turned for home, says the diary, "all six sheds were burning fast and were beyond any shadow of doubt destroyed".

Less than a fortnight had passed since the two borrowed Mosquitos had appeared at Woodhall Spa; in that brief span Bomber Command policy had been turned upside down as a result of the strategic arguments in London. The entire force was committed now to an indefinite campaign against the type of target in which the squadron specialized; the whole of 5 Group was keyed up for action; and Harris readily agreed to let 617 act as the spearhead in two mass attacks on marshalling yards in the Paris region.

Never a man for niggling half-measures, the Commander-in-Chief[9] moved energetically to implement a policy in which he disbelieved; and on 14 April he ordered the transfer to 5 Group of two Lancaster squadrons and a whole Mosquito squadron from Bennett's Pathfinder Force. Since Cochrane had made a study of precision bombing, Cochrane should be given as free a hand as possible against precision targets. It was as simple as that. But Bennett, conscious of the blow to his prestige, was sickened by what he still regards as his greatest "let-down".

617 Squadron received two more Mosquitos; Shannon,

[9] Sir Arthur ("Bomber") Harris.

Kearns and Falke learnt to fly them; and on 18 April Cheshire led his team to the Juvisy marshalling yards, south of Paris, to mark for two hundred Lancasters of 5 Group. In the morning Shannon and Cheshire spent nearly an hour dive-bombing on the practice range at Wainfleet, calculating the exact moment for dropping markers so that they would stay put and not bounce. They found a way together, and it was one problem less for Cheshire. Hardly any bombs shattered the homes that shut in the labyrinth of railway tracks at Juvisy. "The bombing was exceptionally concentrated and well aimed," said the diary, "especially when it is considered that this was achieved by Main Force crews practised in area and not precision onslaughts. All squadron aircraft returned safely, and so was opened a new phase in the history of Bomber Command."

That hackneyed, overworked phrase expressed the bare truth. Harris at any rate was sufficiently impressed by the results of this raid and the second against La Chapelle two nights later to send for Cochrane and Cheshire. Low-level marking seemed an unscientific, impracticable way of clinching a bombing operation; and false heroics had no appeal for the unsentimental Harris. Yet he had to acknowledge that this intent-looking squadron commander had reduced a crazy technique to a teachable art. Could it be used, he wondered, against targets in Germany? When the question was raised over dinner in the Commander-in-Chief's home, Cheshire's heart thumped madly. There could be no better test on earth for his methods than a heavily defended German target. He said so.

Harris leaned across, fixing him with his stony smile:

"There aren't many German targets that fit into the present campaign. Have you any particular preference yourself?" The answer tripped off Cheshire's tongue:

"Yes, sir. Munich."

Munich! 5 Group had come nearest to pounding this remote Bavarian city and rail junction where the Hitler Movement had been born; but even 5 Group had been defeated by the distance, the weather and the defences. Munich was protected by more guns and searchlight batteries than any other place except Berlin and the Ruhr. Even the stern Harris paused, consenting at last with a shrug which seemed to say:

"Right, but it's your funeral. *You* suggested it."

It was an exclusive 5 Group affair, and there was an indifferent dress rehearsal over Brunswick, where Cheshire discovered that controlling a force of nearly 300 aircraft by radio could be a confusing business. The two squadrons of Lancasters recently transferred from the Pathfinders carried flares to enable 617 to mark accurately; but one of these Lancasters had its radio transmitter turned on, and every order Cheshire tried to give was effectively jammed.

There was no radio jamming at Munich on 24 April. The four Mosquitos set out two hours after the main force. As they weaved through the flak and searchlights on the outskirts of the city they could see the occasional outline of bombers high above, pinned like gulls against the angry sky. Cheshire put the nose of his machine down and dived steeply at nearly 400 miles an hour towards the little white house near the main railway station that was his aiming point. He pulled sharply out at 500 feet, and Kelly shouted excitedly: "That's it, sir, dead on."

As far as they could see, the markers were just right, and the white walls of the house were stained red in the glare. The backing-up by the other Mosquitos was perfect. So was the bombing, at first. Then a clump of markers suddenly appeared on the far side of the river, half a mile away. As he flew over the city at less than 1,000 feet, weaving wildly through the barrage of heavy bullets and pattering shell fragments, Cheshire tried to warn the main force off the wrongly-placed markers. But the ex-Pathfinder controller, too, had seen the error and corrected it with an accurate cascade of green spot-fires.

For days before the raid Cheshire had badgered Cochrane's headquarters for long-range petrol tanks. He had not forgotten the lesson of the Toulouse raid, but apparently everyone else had. His repeated demands were "not taken seriously". Once again, to his lasting regret, he had to leave the target area early. Yet if he had stayed over Munich much longer it is questionable whether he would have lived to tell the tale. As it was, the guns and searchlights pursued him "for fully twelve minutes before he got clear".

Cheshire still believes that the Munich attack was his greatest single triumph of the war, and the undeniable fact that 90 per cent. of the bomb load fell in the right place for once, doing more damage in a night than the whole of Bomber Command and the American Air Force had done in four years, supports his opinion. Characteristically, he takes little credit for helping to revolutionize Bomber Command tactics in the far more critical campaign against the French railways. The only victories Cheshire could recognize were the victories he contrived himself. The Munich raid is usually accepted at his valuation, partly because it was specifically mentioned in the citation which accompanied the award of his Victoria Cross in the late summer of 1944. But Cochrane, in his detached way, does not altogether endorse the popular sentiment:

"Munich was a triumph, but not nearly so important as is often claimed," he said. "Its significance as a matter of air history is simply that, for the first time, Bomber Command managed to hit a difficult German target by the low-level marking technique which Cheshire pioneered. Later, other squadrons, notably 627, achieved far more striking successes with the same method, and Pathfinder techniques steadily improved, too. They got no V.C.s for a good reason: Cheshire was the first man to understand the problem, to grapple with it in his own thorough fashion, and to solve it in action. The entire burden of proof was his, and his greatness as a tactical thinker was established in the process."

Walker, R.N.

by TERENCE ROBERTSON

The late Captain Frederick John Walker, R.N., was one of the outstanding officers in the Battle of the Atlantic. The peril of the U-boat was even more acute in the Second World War than it had been in the First when—until the introduction of Q-ships—it brought Britain to the edge of starvation.

Walker served in "little ships"—destroyers, corvettes, sloops. The section of Terence Robertson's biography presented here deals with some of his operations in Starling *in* 1944.

CAPTAIN WALKER[1] took over a Flag Officer's command on 29 January, 1944, when he led his Group from Liverpool to rendezvous off Northern Ireland with the aircraft-carriers, *Nairana* and *Activity*, for a hunting strike into mid-Atlantic. The Group was back to full strength—*Starling*, *Wild Goose*, *Kite*, *Wren*, *Woodpecker* and *Magpie*. After the appalling storms of December, fresh paintwork gleamed dully in a pale wintry sun. Leaks had been plugged, damage repaired, tailwags stopped, and there was every reason for this striking force to be fit, ready and eager to destroy the enemy if he could be found. The carriers' aircraft would be their eyes.

To his officers, Walker confessed his dislike of having to operate with carriers but found some consolation in the hope that they would act as irresistible bait for the U-boats. He grinned appreciatively on the first night out when a bleak half-obscured moon showed both "flat tops"[2] clearly visible at five

---

[1] The late Captain Frederick Walker, R.N., C.B., D.S.O. and three bars.
[2] R.N. slang for an aircraft carrier.

miles or more. He mentioned this on the bridge, but the carriers were left in ignorance of their nakedness, it being considered bad for their morale to tell them.

On 1 February they were drawing near to the battleground, steaming in hunting formation, the sloops in line abreast, a mile apart, and the carriers zigzagging independently a mile behind them. Shortly after 10 a.m. all seemed peaceful enough; it was a crisp, cold morning with a slight swell and calm sea. In *Starling*, Alan Burn[3] had exercised his gun crews, *Woodpecker* had carried out depth-charge drill, and in *Wild Goose*, on the port extreme of the line, Commander Wemyss[4] was discussing their "dead reckoning" position with his navigator in the chartroom. Suddenly a shout came down the bridge voicepipe.

"Captain, Sir, submarine echo to starboard."

Wemyss rushed to the bridge, and a quick report from the asdic operator made it clear that it was a U-boat trying to penetrate the screen for a close shot at the bait. Wemyss turned to look back at the carriers and, to his horror, saw *Nairana* turn on a zig to port, bringing her in the enemy's direction. At any moment she would be sitting squarely in the U-boat's sights. Wemyss rapped out orders.

"Hard a'starboard . . . Full speed . . . Hoist attacking flag . . . Tell Leader on R/T I am attacking."

The enemy had passed between *Wild Goose* and her neighbour, *Magpie*, by the time Wemyss had turned his ship and was slithering in for the first attack. Wemyss blinked a warning to *Nairana* to get out of the way and without waiting for a perfect run-in dropped a ten-charge pattern more to scare the enemy than to sink him. *Nairana* was still in danger.

As soon as he received Wemyss's report, Walker flashed a signal to *Nairana* ordering her to head out to starboard at full speed. He repeated the order to *Activity* and told off *Kite*, *Wren* and *Woodpecker* to screen them. Then he headed towards the

[3]Lieut. Alan Burn, R.N.V.R.
[4]Commander D. E. G. Wemyss.

battle while *Wild Goose* was drawing off and *Magpie* about to follow with another attack. This yielded no result and *Magpie* was sent off to assist in screening the carrier, leaving *Wild Goose* and *Starling* to continue the hunt.

"Unquestionably, *Nairana* was saved by *Wild Goose's* exemplary speed and decision," Walker said later. "Another minute or two and she would have been a sitter. When *Magpie* had left to join the remainder of our force, *Wild Goose* handed me asdic contact with the Boche on a plate. I could ask nothing better than to take the field again partnered by this doughty, well-trained warrior. Conditions were good, though the wind was rising and stirring up the sea a bit."

Walker followed quietly behind the U-boat for a while, calculating that she was steaming at about four knots very deep. He decided to carry out a two-ship "Operation Plaster". Line abreast and close, *Sterling* and *Wild Goose* went in to the attack at five knots, dropping in all some sixty-odd depth charges set to explode between 500 feet and 700 feet at five-second intervals. In their wake the depth charges detonated in a continuous crackling roar like an express train tearing through a tunnel. The sea split and heaved under the explosions and even the experienced sailors, accustomed as they were to the weight and ferocity of Walker's methods, were stunned by the non-stop crashing and cracking from below the surface.

Walker was in effect using his depth charges as main armament and firing them in salvoes as though from guns. *Starling's* crew were startled when, while all were gazing astern at the exploding sea, a bang shook them from ahead and a gush of water appeared over the bows. This could hardly be a depth charge. After a few minutes Walker ordered "Cease Fire" and both ships stood by to wait for tangible evidence of a sinking.

It was not long in coming. Oil, clothing, planks of wood, pulped life-jackets, books and mangled remains of bodies provided all the evidence needed of death and destruction far below them. Using the loud-hailer, Walker shouted to Wemyss to follow him and, as the two ships rejoined the carriers, *Starling* flew from her yardarm the eagerly expected signal: "Splice the mainbrace." In this way, the 740-ton underwater raider *U-502* was destroyed.

Five uneventful days later, the sloops refuelled from *Activity* and received orders to support the west-bound convoy S.L.147 which was believed to be heading for trouble. Quick calculations in *Starling* showed to everyone's joy that a large "pack" was gathering and the Group could arrive in time for the impending battle.

The striking force made contact with S.L.147 on 7 February and Walker took overall command of the escort. Leaving the close escort group in their stations, he placed his sloops round the convoy as an outer screen six miles out. *Nairana* and *Activity* were ordered to operate their aircraft in the deep field by day and to enter into the middle of the convoy at night.

During the 7th, Admiralty reports of U-boats heard chattering by wireless in the convoy's vicinity indicated a "pack" of about ten. Next day the pack increased until it became likely that at least fifteen U-boats were converging for the fatal pounce. Tension grew as warning signals poured in during the afternoon. After an exchange with the Commodore, Walker sent a general message ordering all ships to action stations at nightfall.

He stayed happily on his bridge all that day, well wrapped-up in his fading old grey pullover and stained leather waistcoat. With one U-boat already destroyed on this voyage, the 1944 season had opened well for his Group. He would have been just as cheerful had he known that no fewer than twenty-six U-boats were in contact and waiting for the cover of darkness to spring upon their prey—a convoy of eighty-one ships with two aircraft carriers looming high in the centre.

As dusk faded into darkness, the night became eerie; a heavy damp mist settled over the scene, covering ships and men in a white frost-like dew; sea and sky merged in a haze of deep midnight blue gradually blotting out the horizon until the ships seemed to be flying through thin, wispy, low-lying cloud. A hush settled over both sea and ships and the darkness closed in, muffling all sounds other than the swish of bows cutting into green, unfriendly water.

To Walker and the thirteen other warship commanders it was a game of patience, waiting to see from which quarter the enemy would make his first lunge. To the eighty-one Merchant Navy captains it was more like roulette. Whose number would come up first? Which of them would be the first to explode in flames?

Wild Goose was six miles ahead of the convoy on the port quarter and it fell to her port bridge look-out, Able Seaman J. G. Wall, a young reservist sailor, to sound the alarm which rang through the silence to be repeated in dozens of ships spread across miles of the Atlantic. Raking his sector with binoculars on this deathly black night, he beat the radar by sighting a U-boat trimmed down on the surface with only her conning tower showing at a range of nearly a mile and a half.

His report, shouted excitedly to a tense group of officers on the bridge, sparked off the warning and, as the close escort hugged their charges protectively, Walker ordered the convoy to make a drastic alteration of course. The enemy had launched their attack; now his sloops could get down to the earnest business of killing.

Wild Goose turned towards the U-boat, increased to full speed and prepared to ram. The enemy, realizing he had been sighted, crash-dived. When the sloop arrived only a swirl of water marked the spot. But the enemy captain was curious and, instead of diving deep and taking avoiding action, he stayed at periscope depth to keep track of *Wild Goose's* movements in the hope of slipping past her and continuing his swoop on the convoy.

Again it was Able Seaman Wall who succeeded where instruments failed. A shout brought Commander Wemyss to the side of his bridge to gape in astonishment, while Wall pointed to a periscope poking out of the water approximately twenty yards away. Wemyss fumed; he was searching the area with his asdic and going too slow to punish the enemy's impertinence with a shallow-set pattern of depth charges. His machine-gunners had just enough time to pepper the two or three feet of periscope with fire—scoring several hits—before the U-boat commander, anticipating the awful retribution which might follow his impudence, downed periscope and dived away.

Wild Goose obtained asdic contact in time to direct the newly-arrived *Woodpecker* into a creeping attack. When the last depth charge had exploded, Walker raced up, took one look at the surging water and signalled *Woodpecker*: "Look what a mess you have made." After some crackling cross-chat, the three sloops regained contact with the enemy and settled down to the attack formula—convoy, aircraft carriers, close escort and the rest of the Group steaming rapidly out of danger.

Walker directed *Woodpecker* into the first attack while *Wild Goose* prepared to follow. Firing her charges, *Woodpecker* slowly moved over the U-boat, dropping twenty-six set to explode at maximum depth. A few moments of expectant silence fell after the last charge had detonated; then a tremendous explosion came from the depths below and for a fraction of a second the sea was petrified into immobility, before boiling in angry confusion. Another of Doenitz's prized fleet, U-762, was destroyed, blown apart by the depth charging and finally disintegrating under the impact of an internal explosion.

The three sloops fired snowflake rockets to illuminate the scene and, in their bleak flare, pieces of wreckage could be seen floating forlornly on waves blackened and quietened by the weight and flow of the U-boat's oil. *Starling* lowered a boat, and collected a German coat and other evidence of destruction before Walker led the three triumphant ships back to the convoy. It was shortly after midnight and the score was one up and more to come.

★　　　★　　　★

Kapitänleutnant Hartwig Looks, a U-boat officer since 1936 and now captain of *U-264* with 14,000 tons of Allied shipping to his credit, had lost the convoy. He had been in contact since the previous morning, knew there were probably twenty of his brother U-boats in the vicinity with more arriving at regular intervals and decided to launch his attack on S.L.147 at midnight on the night 8-9 February. It was a large convoy and he had hopes of more than usual success. His ship was the first in the U-boat Arm to be fitted with that ingenious extensible Diesel air intake and exhaust device which allowed U-boats to "breathe". Instead of having to surface to charge its batteries, *U-264* could stay submerged at periscope depth with the "Schnorkel" poking up like a periscope. This meant he could submit to a prolonged destroyer hunt without having to surface.

Shortly before midnight, an escort force had come chasing towards him and he had dived thinking they were about to attack. The exploding depth charges had fallen quite near, but far enough away for Looks to be tolerably certain someone else and not *U-264* was under attack. Looks took his boat deep and continued on the same course as the convoy had been steering all day. At a crucial moment his hydrophones broke down and he could no longer hear the convoy's propellers. Taking a gamble, he stayed on course and came up to periscope depth to check his position in relation to the convoy.

His quarry had altered course and Looks saw nothing but darkness as he turned the periscope in a complete circle. Inwardly furious, he brought *U-264* to the surface and headed northwards in the hope of finding other prey.

Soon after *Starling*, *Wild Goose* and *Woodpecker* had resumed their stations, the close escorts to port of the convoy beat back a skirmish with two U-boats creeping in on the surface. The action was too far away and over too quickly for Walker to play any part in the proceedings.

The night was enlivened further by the sudden roar of aircraft

engines, followed by the brilliant glare of flares dropped over the
convoy in an attempt to provide the U-boats with silhouetted
targets. It seemed, however, that the "pack" were not to be
tempted even by their flying brethren. No attack followed and,
somewhat mystified, Walker had to wait until just before
6 a.m. when all ships of the Group and the close escort intercepted by HF/DF[5] a U-boat signalling by wireless on the
surface.

Bearings put the enemy ten miles ahead of the convoy, so he
ordered *Magpie* and *Kite*, the nearest sloops, to investigate.
Fifteen minutes later, while *Magpie* was still some distance astern
of *Kite* and racing to catch up, the U-boat was suddenly sighted
as it came out of a patch of mist steaming fast towards the convoy
and only 800 yards away from *Kite*. Her commanding officer's
instinctive reaction to Walker's long and patient training was
to realize instantly the danger of being attacked by "gnats".[6]
As the U-boat crash-dived, he reduced speed to seven knots and
fired a single depth charge in the hope of counter-mining a
"gnat" torpedo before it could strike home. A second or two
later a violent explosion threw up a column of water twenty
yards on *Kite's* port beam.

Her captain's fears had been well-founded. The U-boat had
fired while diving and the depth-charge explosion had set off
the "gnat" warhead, causing a double explosion. Immediately
Kite increased to full speed and ran over the diving position to
fire a full pattern of ten depth charges. This brought no result
and, after *Magpie* joined, the two ships gained asdic contact and
settled down to a classic Walker hunt.

At the moment *Kite* and the U-boat sighted each other, *Wild
Goose* obtained radar contact with another U-boat little more
than a mile away on the convoy's port bow. Also fearing a
"gnat" torpedo, she reduced speed to seven knots and fired off

[5]High Frequency Direction Finder.
[6]The "gnat" torpedo was a German magnetic weapon, commonly known
as a "Chase Me Charlie".

a starshell. The first salvoes revealed the U-boat about to dive, and a few seconds later a loud explosion was heard astern. A "gnat", having failed to pick up her slow-revving propellers, had missed and exploded at the end of its run.

Wild Goose's first depth-charge attack at shallow settings drove the U-boat deep and by the time Walker came up in *Starling* he was again handed asdic contact "on a plate". By 8.30 a.m. Walker had directed *Wild Goose* on two creeping attacks and carried out another himself during which another "gnat", unable to home itself on to targets moving at slow speeds, detonated at the end of its run, a few hundred yards astern of *Starling*. Although the crews of the three sloops were well aware that slow speeds were the best defence against this deadly weapon, the men could not help showing some anxiety. It was not natural to amble slowly about the ocean while the enemy fired torpedoes; especially worried were the depth-charge crews on the quarter decks who would be the first to suffer should a "gnat" prove hypersensitive and "hear" even the slowest revolutions.

Half an hour later oil came to the surface—but the U-boat was still on its feet, if a little groggy.

At 9 a.m. the convoy, carriers and close escort steamed between the two battle grounds, each about six miles on either side of it. As they cleared the area, the senior officer of the close escort signalled Walker: "Good luck, hope to see you again." The reply came: "We seem to have nabbed a couple of particularly tough babies. Will be rejoining soon."

This was nearly wishful thinking. *Starling* was only just moving when suddenly a chorus of amazed, urgent shouts came from all parts of the ship. Walker spun round and, only a few hundred yards away, the shallow-running torpedo could be seen streaking towards them. There was no time to pick up speed and take avoiding action. The enemy had come up to periscope depth, fired an ordinary torpedo at a sitting target and gone down again. Walker's mind raced: unless he found a way out in the next few seconds, *Starling* would be a blazing, sinking wreck. With eyes fixed on the bubbling track of the deadly missile, he gave orders.

"Hard a'port . . . Stand by depth charges . . . Shallow setting . . . Fire."

The crew, many of whom had already run to the far side away from the expected explosion, while others had thrown themselves flat on the deck, were astounded to hear a command for the charges to fire at shallow setting while their ship was dawdling along. The explosions would blow the stern off.

Suddenly the air was torn by two almost simultaneous, shattering roars. The first came from the depth charges, and the second, by far the more frightening, from the torpedo which had gone off only five yards from *Starling's* quarter deck. A lightning decision, coupled with instant and disciplined obedience, had certainly saved the ship and countless lives—for the depth charges had counter-mined the torpedo a second before it struck home against *Starling's* thinly-plated hull.

A huge wave pyramided vertically high above *Starling's* masthead, the sloop shook and jerked as though being shaken by some gigantic hand; reserve depth charges were thrown overboard by the shock blast, luckily failing to explode; tons of water fell in solid green sheets over the depth-charge crew standing momentarily stunned on the quarter deck but still doing their duty automatically; all electrical switches were thrown open in the power rooms; and worse, every bottle in the wardroom was shattered into fragments.

Starling gathered speed and shook herself clear of the swilling water while depth charges continued to leave the ship in the strict, methodical pattern of the creeping attack. There was not a hitch or a delay in the drill. Remarkably, *Starling* had suffered no damage, and on the bridge Walker murmured: "Interesting. This chap seems to know his job. It's almost a pity to think we shall kill him without ever seeing what he's like."

In the next half-hour, Walker directed *Wild Goose* on two

more creeping attacks and followed up with both ships carrying out an "Operation Plaster". In this last run, he took his revenge and delivered the death blow. A few minutes later a loud underwater explosion cracked to the surface, and soon a huge air bubble boiled up and collapsed, spreading chunks of wood and human remains over hundreds of feet of sea. At 10 a.m. after collecting wreckage and other evidence, *Starling* and *Wild Goose* steamed off to assist *Kite* and *Magpie*. *U-734* had gone the way of so many others, but it had taken nearly 150 depth charges dropped over more than three hours to destroy her. And she had come closer than any U-boat to destroying *Starling*.

On joining *Kite* and *Magpie* at noon Walker found that they had carried out a series of creeping attacks without result. As *Kite* had first made contact with the U-boat, he sent *Wild Goose* and *Magpie* to patrol the area, gained contact himself and directed *Kite* into two more attacks using more than fifty depth charges.

In this last attack, the enemy showed himself as cunning and tough as the one before. As *Kite* steamed in slowly to begin her depth-charge barrage, a "gnat" was fired in self-defence. While it was still twenty yards away, the first depth charges set off immediately counter-mined the torpedo—which *Kite* had not yet seen. There was a thunderous crash and, to *Starling's* crew, it looked as if their sister ship had been hit squarely amidships. For long heart-stopping seconds the wide column of thin green water hovered over the shocked, surprised *Kite*. Cheers rang out from *Starling's* men as first *Kite's* mast appeared, then her bridge, and finally the whole ship—unbelievably, wonderfully intact. She had shuddered and kicked under the impact of the blast, but was still on course and the depth charges were tumbling from her racks and shooting from her throwers in well-drilled precision. There had been no faltering in the continuity of the attack.

But the sloop was badly shaken and several leaks had been sprung in her stern. She had only seventeen depth charges left, so Walker sent her out of the touchline and brought *Magpie* in for the next assault. With *Starling* acting as directing ship, *Magpie* now carried out a twenty-six-charge creeping attack with the same result—nothing.

On *Starling's* bridge, Walker grinned appreciatively. This was an opponent worthy of his best. Twisting, altering his depth constantly, the enemy commander was making every attack fall wide of the mark. Walker worked out a new procedure on the spot. *Magpie* was equipped with "Hedgehog", the multi-barrelled mortar-bomb thrower which could destroy only if one or more bombs scored direct hits. He would direct her in for a "Hedgehog" barrage and follow up with a depth-charge attack himself. When he announced this to *Starling's* officers—there were chuckles all round. Imagine aiming another ship's weapons to fire twenty-four bombs and expect any of them to score direct hits on a target 700 feet blow.

"I was highly tickled by this hedgehoggery," he wrote later. "Complicated instruments are normally deemed essential to score an occasional hit with this weapon. But under my orders over the R/T, *Magpie* steamed in to attack and fired off her bombs when told as if firing depth charges for a creeping attack. The result was an immediate double explosion which shook both ships. To score two bull's-eyes like that first shot with somebody else's "Hedgehog" 1,000 yards away was, of course, a ghastly fluke, but amusing considering no instruments at all were used."

This unorthodox and unscientific attack had without doubt succeeded. To make sure, Walker accepted the risk that the enemy might still be capable of firing "gnats". At 3.30 p.m. *Starling* raced in at full speed for a ten-charge pattern set deep. A few seconds later, when the crashing roar of the last depth charge had died away, the remains of *U*-238 bobbed sadly on the surface. *Magpie* was now a fully-blooded member of the Group.

Walker had been in command of the battle for nearly thirty-six hours without a break. With eighty-one merchant ships depending on him, two aircraft-carriers hoping he would protect them, a close escort screen of six warships feeling unhappily impotent in their role of static defenders, and his own sloops spoiling for trouble in the outfield, he had faced one of the most dangerous "pack" attacks of the war and ripped it apart by killing three of the enemy in relentless thrusts and beating off less-skilled raiders. This had been done without loss in ships, and at least 140 Germans died while the British sailors had not suffered even a slight wound.

Tired, but seemingly fresh, outwardly matter-of-fact yet inwardly tensed and fizzing with excitement at the victory, Walker was outspoken in his criticism of certain parts of his Group's efforts during the night; but in his heart deeply proud and content with every one of them.

The Group stayed with S.L.147 until the following morning, the 10th, but the crippled enemy failed to appear. At dawn, after exchanging signals with the Commodore, the aircraft-carriers and the close escort, *Starling, Wild Goose, Woodpecker, Kite* and *Wren* and *Magpie* formed up in line abreast, hunting formation, and set course for another convoy, H.X.277, which included the Norwegian tanker, *Thorsholm,* fully stocked with depth charges to replenish escorts in the unfortunate position of *Starling* and *Kite.*

Re-ammunitioning with depth charges at sea was a long, tedious and nerve-racking business requiring skill, patience and an even temper. Walker snatched his first two hours of sleep for nearly three days while the Group was *en route,* but the afternoon of the 10th spent steering alongside the *Thorsholm* proved the most gruelling experience of the voyage. Only twenty-five yards apart and rolling heavily in a high swell the two ships steamed together, each of the tanker's rolls threatening to capsize the sloop. The depth charges were hauled over by hand singly, at times sinking below the surface or being carried away to bump dangerously against the ship's side as both sending and receiving ships rose and fell unevenly on the swell.

To avoid the whole Group being immobilized, Walker ordered *Wren* to stand by while *Wild Goose, Woodpecker* and *Magpie* sailed off to support a following convoy, H.X.278. The Group was all keyed to carry the battle to the enemy; any let-down now would accentuate their weariness and Walker was keen on getting *Starling* back into commission with the power to punch hard. At dusk he called a halt to the ammunitioning and headed south at full speed with *Kite* and *Wren* to join the rest sweeping far astern of the convoy.

So many signals of congratulation had been received from Liverpool and the Admiralty—each was read out to the crews of all ships by their commanding officers—that there was an air of carefree omnipotence around. The knowing ones on the mess decks were no longer taking bets on whether the Group would make a "kill" this trip, but on how many and at what time the next would be sighted. . .

The Wooden Horse

by ERIC WILLIAMS

The Wooden Horse *is told in the third person, but it might well have been told in the first; for the "Peter" of the book was, in fact, Eric Williams.*

The Wooden Horse—*a vaulting-horse designed to mask the building of an escape-tunnel—was Williams's second bid for escape; his first (told in* The Tunnel) *failed, but only in so far as he was recaptured in Holland.*

This record is notable, not only for the superlative persistence of the two tunnellers, their ingenuity, their endurance; but it also stresses the solidarity of the prisoners-of-war who, day after day, exhausted their ill-nourished strength by playing strenuous physical games around the horse, to cover their comrades' operations.

BETWEEN them[1] they had built a vaulting-horse. It stood four-feet six inches high, the base covering an area of five feet by three feet. The sides were covered with two feet square plywood sheets from Red Cross packing-cases stolen from the German store. The sides tapered up to the top, which was of solid wood boards padded with their bedding and covered with white linen material taken from the bales in which the cigarettes arrived from England. There were four slots, four inches long by three inches wide, cut in the plywood sides. When pieces of rafter six feet long and three inches by two inches thick had been pushed through these holes the horse could be carried by four men in the manner of a sedan chair.

The horse was kept in the canteen. A canteen in name only—

[1]The prisoners-of-war of Stalag Luft III.

a long, low extension to the camp kitchen containing the barber's shop and a large empty room used as a band practice room. Like all the other buildings in the compound, it was raised above the surface of the ground; but it was built on a brick foundation and more solidly than the living quarters. The entrance was by double doors reached by a short flight of wide wooden steps.

While the horse was being built John had been recruiting prisoners for the vaulting. He had posters made which he stuck up round the camp, advertising gym classes which would be held every afternoon. Special prisoners were detailed to talk to the German guards, remarking on this typical English craze for exercise and tell them, casually, about the vaulting-horse.

Some days later the few afternoon walkers on the circuit were surprised to see the double doors of the canteen open and a team of prisoners dressed only in shorts march down the wooden steps and form up in a line near the trip-wire. They were followed by the four strongest members of the team carrying a box-like object slung on wooden poles. The box was carried to a spot about forty feet inside the trip-wire, where it was carefully placed on the ground and the poles withdrawn.

The team formed up and under the direction of one of the prisoners began to vault over the box. The guards, bored with watching the prisoners walking the endless circuit of the wire, turned towards the unusual spectacle. They did not give their whole attention to the vaulting. A boxing match or faked spontaneous fight was a well-known *Kriegie*[2] method of distracting the attention of the guards while an attempt was being made on the wire. So the guards watched the vaulting but cast an occasional glance along the strip of wire for which they were responsible.

The standard of vaulting was high. The captain of the team led his men in a complicated series of jumps. Only one of the men was not so good. His approach was clumsy and his vaulting not up to the standard of the others. The guards soon singled

[2]Kriegie—slang for prisoner-of-war, from the German *Kriegsgefangener*.

him out as the butt of the party and grinned whenever he failed to clear the horse. The vaulting had drawn a crowd of amused prisoners, who jeered and catcalled whenever he made his run up to the box. Every time he failed to clear the horse he drew a guffaw of laughter from the surrounding prisoners.

Soon the guards in the boxes were leaning on their elbows waiting for him to make his run. It was not often they had the chance to laugh at the British prisoners. The boot was usually on the other foot. The more the spectators laughed, the more determined this man appeared to be to clear the obstacle. He took a final, desperate leap and in missing his footing he lurched into the horse and knocked it over. He knocked it over on to its side so that the interior was in full view of the guards.

The horse was empty. The vaulters righted the box and went on with their sport. Soon they carried the horse back into the canteen, where they left it until the following afternoon.

Before they left the canteen they tied pieces of black cotton across the doorway and from the edge of the horse to the skirting board. The following morning the cotton was broken. The ferrets[3] were taking no chances. During the night the vaulting-horse had been examined.

It was after breakfast, a week after the vaulting had first started. Peter and John were walking round the circuit. The object of their conversation—it had been nothing else for a week—was the vaulting-horse.

"I think we might start digging to-morrow," John said. "The goons have got used to the vaulting now. We've knocked the horse over often enough for them to see there's nothing going on inside. Besides, the chaps who are vaulting want to get some return for their labour. They won't just go on vaulting if nothing happens."

Peter was smoking a pipe. "Did you ever hear the story of the two bulls?"

"No," John said, "what was that?"

[3]Ferrets—security guards in German P-o-W. camps.

"There were two bulls in a field. One was an old bull, the other was a young bull. Suddenly the young bull said to the old bull, 'Look! The farmer left the gate of the field open. There are some cows in the next field. Let's dash down and do a couple of 'em.' 'No,' said the old bull, 'let's *walk* down and do the lot.' "

John laughed. "Very true, very true. If we were the only two I couldn't agree with you more. But it's the vaulters. If they don't see us actually making progress they'll get browned off and want to pack in."

"Yes, I know, I'm rather worried about the vaulters. It's tough going on the little food we get. How long do you think it'll take us to dig the tunnel?"

"Let's see." John hitched his shorts with his elbows. "We've got about forty-five feet to go to the trip-wire, thirty feet across the danger strip. That's seventy-five feet. The wire itself is about eight feet thick, so that makes eighty-three feet. We should break at least thirty feet away from the wire because of the outside sentries. That gives us one hundred and thirteen feet altogether. That's if we go straight. Allow a bit for going round rocks or tree roots, and make it a round figure of one hundred and twenty feet. . . . A hundred and twenty feet. If we do five feet a day it will take us twenty-four days."

"We shan't do five feet a day," Peter said.

"Oh, I don't know. I could dig five feet in a day. Make it three feet if you like, that will make it about six weeks."

"It's not a matter of how much we can dig in a day—it's a matter of how much we can carry away in the horse. Do you realize how much sand weighs?"

"You should know that—you're the construction boss."

"As far as I can remember a yard of sand weighs about ten hundredweight, but I don't know whether that's wet or dry. Ours will be wet, of course. But knowing that wouldn't help us much. What we want to know is how big a pound of sand looks, so that we can figure out how much we can dig in one session. How much do you think they can carry in the horse—with one of us inside as well?"

"What do you weigh?"

"I don't know. I was eleven three when I was shot down. I expect I'm about ten seven or ten ten now."

"Then I'm about ten. Supposing we say we can carry ten stone of sand."

"That's a hundred and forty pounds—let's go and weigh a pound of sand and see how much it looks. I think a foot a day seems more reasonable than three feet."

"What shall we use as a pound weight? I think a gallon of water weighs about ten pounds."

"We'll use an unopened tin of Klim[4]—that weighs exactly a pound net. We'll make some scales with an empty Klim tin on the other end and fill it with damp sand until the scales are even. Then we'll know what a pound of sand looks like."

"Right," John said. "We can't go in yet. They're holding a Latin class in our room."

"I suppose I ought to be going to German classes really."

"Oh, I shouldn't bother. After all, we shan't travel as Germans. A little knowledge is dangerous. If you start learning German now and start talking outside, you'll get us both in the cart. Your best role is dignified silence. We'd better travel as Frenchmen and I'll do the talking. As long as you can say '*Ich bin Auslander—nicht verstehen*' that should get you through."

"O.K.," Peter said. "*Ich bin Auslander—nicht verstehen.* Sounds impressive. What does it mean?"

"It means 'I am a foreigner—I don't understand'."

"That's a damn good line. I suppose I just keep on saying that until you come along."

"You can pretend to be deaf and dumb if you like."

"I know! I'll have a pronounced stutter. Then if they ask me anything I'll stutter like hell and you interrupt and tell them what they want to know."

[4]Powdered milk.

"Yes, I'll do that if they talk French, but if they don't you just stick to the '*nicht verstehen*' business."

"Right," Peter said. "*Ich bin Auslander—nicht verstehen.*" He walked on round the circuit thinking of the escape. *Ich bin Auslander—nicht verstehen.* What a vocabulary to try to cross Germany with. But even if I spoke fluent German, how much better off would I be? It's all a matter of luck, this escaping business. Chaps have got through to England without any German at all. And fluent German speakers have been brought back. And that's looking too far ahead too. We've got to get out of the camp first. Let the morrow look after itself. It would be nice to be back in England, though. Feeling as though you were doing something instead of stewing here waiting for the end of the war. Back on the squadron with the flying, and the fear, and the relief, and the parties in the mess, and the feeling that it could happen to anyone else but not to you. And the feeling of thankfulness the next morning that it hadn't happened to you, and that you could go out that night and you wouldn't have to worry again until the night after. . . .

That evening Peter made the top section of the shoring for the vertical shaft. He made it with four sides of plywood packing case reinforced and slotted so that they could be assembled into a rigid four-sided box without top or bottom. The box would stand a considerable inwards pressure.

John spent the evening in making twelve bags from the bottoms of trouser-legs. Several of the prisoners had made themselves shorts by cutting their trousers off above the knee. When John had sewn the bottoms together, roughly hemmed the tops and inserted string, the trouser-legs had become bags about twelve inches long. He fashioned hooks from strong wire with which he intended to suspend the bags inside the horse.

During the week they had made two sand pits, one at the side and one at the head of where the horse was standing. They had made these ostensibly to soften the shock of landing on their bare feet. Actually they served as a datum mark to ensure that they always replaced the horse on the exact spot.

The next afternoon they took the horse out with John inside it. He took with him a cardboard Red Cross box to hold the surplus sand, the trouser-leg bags and hooks, one side of the vertical shoring and the bricklayer's trowel they had stolen from the unfinished shower baths.

My God, Peter thought, this is worse than going on your first "op"! He was holding one end of the front transverse pole and walking slowly towards the spot where they would place the horse.

John crouched inside the horse. His feet were on the bottom framework, one on each side of the horse. In his arms he held the equipment. The horse creaked and lurched as the bearers staggered under the unaccustomed weight. They got the horse into position and began to vault.

Inside the horse John worked quickly. Scraping up the dark grey surface sand he put it into the cardboard box and started to dig a deep trench for one side of the shoring. He put the bright yellow excavated sand into the trouser-leg bags.

As the trench grew deeper he had difficulty in reaching the bottom. He made it wider and had to bank the extra sand against one end of the horse. It was hot inside the horse and he began to sweat. He finished the trench and put the plywood sheet in position. He replaced the surface sand, ramming it down with the handle of the trowel, packing the shoring tight. The top of the shoring was six inches below the ground.

Standing on the framework of the horse, he carefully spread the sand over the plywood sheet, packing it down hard, finally sprinkling the grey sand over the whole area covered by the horse—obliterating his foot and finger marks.

Calling softly to Peter, he gave the word that he had finished.

The vaulters inserted the carrying poles and staggered back into the canteen with John and the bags of sand.

Once inside the canteen they transferred the sand from the

trouser-leg bags into long, sausage-like sacks made from the arms and legs of woollen underwear. These they carried away slung round their necks and down inside their trouser-legs.

The sand was dispersed in various places around the compound, some of it finding its way by devious routes to the latrines, some of it buried under the huts, some of it carried out in specially-made trouser-pockets and dug into the tomato beds outside the huts.

It took them four days to sink the four sides of the box. Working alternately, they sank the box in the ground and removed the sand inside it. When they reached the bottom of the woodwork they dug deeper still, putting bricks under the four corners of the box to support it. They made a trap of bed-boards and replaced this and the surface sand whenever they left the hole.

Finally they had made a hole five feet deep and two feet six inches square. They had dropped the wooden box twelve inches as they worked. The top of the box was now eighteen inches below the surface of the ground. This eighteen inches of sand above the wooden trap gave them security from the probing-rods of the ferrets and was also deep enough to deaden any hollow sound when the trap was walked on. But it was too much sand to remove each time before reaching the trap. To make this easier they filled bags, made from woollen undervests. These they placed on top of the trap, covering them with nearly six to eight inches of surface sand. The bags were thin enough not to impede the progress of the ferrets' probe and enabled them to uncover and recover the trap more quickly.

The wooden box stood on four brick piles two feet high. On three sides the shaft below the wooden box was shored with pieces of bed-board. The fourth side was left open for the tunnel.

It was possible to stand in the shaft, but it was not possible to kneel. To get into the tunnel they were forced to make a short burrow in the opposite direction. Into this they thrust their feet while kneeling to enter the tunnel.

The first seven feet of the tunnel was shored solid with bed-boards. The shoring was made by Peter, in the evenings, in the security of their room and taken down to the tunnel in sections and reassembled there. The whole of the work was done with a table-knife and a red-hot poker. To assemble the shoring Peter lay on his back in the darkness of the narrow tunnel, scraping away sufficient sand to slide the main bearers into position before inserting the bed-boards. He had to work slowly and carefully, fearful all the time that a sudden fall of sand would bury him. He was alone down there and even a small fall of sand would be enough to pin him, helpless, on his back in the narrowness of the tunnel.

When the ceiling of the tunnel was in position they had to fill the space between the top of the tunnel and the wooden ceiling with sand. If this were not done the sand would fall and the ceiling become higher and higher until a telltale subsidence of the surface would reveal the path of the tunnel.

After the first seven feet of shoring, which they built to take the force of the impact of the vaulters on the surface, the tunnel ran on without any shoring whatever.

The tunnel was very small. They had quickly seen that the progress of the work would be determined by the speed with which they could get the excavated sand away. The smaller they made the tunnel the less sand they would have to dispose of and the faster would go the work.

While one of them supervised the vaulting the other dug in the tunnel. He worked alone down there. Once he got into the tunnel with his hands in front of his head he had to stay like that. He could not get his arms behind him again. Nor could he crawl with them doubled up. It was fingers and toes all the way until he got to the end of the tunnel. Once he got there he scraped some sand from the face with a trowel and crawled backwards down the tunnel, dragging the sand with him. When he got back to the vertical shaft he had brought enough sand to fill half a bag. And there were twelve bags to fill.

There was no light in the tunnel and very little air. He worked entirely naked and spent his spell of work in a bath of perspiration. He worked naked because it was cooler and if he wore even the lightest clothes he scraped a certain amount of sand from the sides of the tunnel as he crawled along. Each bag of sand that was scraped from the sides of the tunnel meant one less bag taken from the face. So he worked entirely naked and as he sweated the sand caked on him. He got sand in his eyes, in his ears, in his nose; and under his foreskin. They grew segs on their elbows and knees and broke their finger-nails. As the tunnel grew longer the work became more difficult and the air more foul. They did not put up air holes for fear of the dogs.

And so they worked until they had dug a tunnel forty feet long. After forty feet they could do no more. They had reached the limit of their endurance. The farther they pushed the tunnel the more difficult the work became. The air was bad; and they were taking two hours to fill the twelve bags.

Not only were the tunnellers exhausted by the twenty-four times repeated crawl up the tunnel, but the vaulters—who had been vaulting every afternoon of the two months it had taken to dig the forty feet—were exhausted too. The tunnellers were given extra food, but the vaulters were not, and they had little energy to spare.

Peter and John had devised games and variations on the theme of vaulting. A dozen men could not vault for two hours without looking unnatural about it. The whole time one of the tunnellers was below ground the other would be in the vaulting team trying to make the two hours that the horse stood there appear as natural as possible. It was not easy, especially when the ferret was standing within earshot of the horse, watching the vaulting.

They organized a medicine-ball and a deck-tennis quoit and stood in a circle round the horse throwing them to one another. They even organized a run round the circuit, leaving the horse vulnerable and alone with the trap open below it.

It was a considerable physical strain working in the tunnel; yet both of them preferred it to organizing the vaulting.

The end came one afternoon while John was in the tunnel. Peter had gone to the main gate to find out how many Germans were in the compound. It was ten minutes before they were due to take the horse in.

As he was working back towards the horse he was met by one of the vaulters, pale-faced and running.

"What's wrong?" Peter asked.

"There's been a fall."

"Where?"

"Near the horse."

"Is John all right?"

"We shouted to him, but we can't get a reply."

Peter ran towards the horse. A fall probably meant that John was trapped. There were no air-holes. He would be caught in the end of the tunnel, suffocating, trapped by the fall of sand.

The vaulters were grouped round a man who was lying on the ground. Peter glanced towards the sentry boxes above the wire. The guards were watching.

"Where's the fall?" he asked.

"Wilde's lying on it. A hole suddenly appeared, so Wilde lay on it to stop the guards seeing it. He's pretending he's hurt his leg."

"How's John?"

"We can't get a reply."

Oh God, Peter thought, John's had it. He wanted to overturn the horse and go down, but the thought of the discovery of the tunnel stopped him. Old John would be furious if he panicked for nothing.

"Send someone for a stretcher," he said. "We must make this look as natural as possible."

Two of the vaulters went for a stretcher. Peter crouched by Nigel's feet, his head near the horse. "John," he called, "John!"

No answer.

"Roll over, Nig," he said.

Nigel rolled over. There was a hole, about as thick as his arm, going down into the darkness of the tunnel.

"John," he called. "John!"

"Hallo, Pete." The answer was weak.

"What happened?"

"There's been a fall, but I can clear it. I've taken some of the shoring from the shaft. I'll have it fixed in a jiffy. Can you fill it in from the top?"

"O.K. Let me know when you've got it fixed." He pretended to attend to Nigel's leg.

"The bloody goons seem interested," Nigel said.

"The chaps with the stretcher will be here in a minute," Peter told him. "They'll carry you to your hut. That'll explain what we've been doing."

Presently he heard John's voice, thinly, from inside the tunnel. "I'm just putting the shoring in. You can fill-in in about five minutes."

What a man, Peter thought. What a man. Good old John. He poked solicitously at Nigel's leg. The two vaulters returned with the stretcher and a first-aid kit. Peter made a great business of bandaging Nigel's leg while the others, shuffling round, kicked the sand towards the hole.

"It'll sink a bit," Peter said. "We'll kick some more over it later on. What's the time?"

"Three-thirty."

"Christ, it's roll-call at four! We must get John up before then."

He banged on the side of the horse. There was no reply.

Ten minutes passed. Still there was no sign from John.

Oh, God, we've had it, Peter thought. If we can't get him up before roll-call we've had it. "Come on, chaps, let's get vaulting," he said. "We can't just stand around here."

They began to vault again. Then he heard John's voice, urgently, from inside the horse. "Hey, Pete, what's the time?"

"You've got five minutes."

"It's a hell of a mess."

At the end of the five minutes they carried him into the canteen. He could hardly stand. "It's a hell of a mess," he said. "There's a bit of tree root there and the vaulting must have shaken it loose. I've jammed it up temporarily but it needs proper shoring."

"I'll take some down with me to-morrow," Peter said.

The next afternoon he went down with some wooden shoring. He found the tunnel choked with sand. Soft shifting sand that continued to fall as he worked. He worked in the dark, entirely by feel, and the air was bad so that he panted as he worked. Sand fell into his eyes and his mouth. He worked furiously, clearing the sand away and fitting the shoring into position.

When the shoring was fitted he managed to pack some of the sand away between the shoring and the sides of the tunnel. The rest of it he spread about the floor, lying flat on his belly and pressing it down with his hands.

When he finally got back into the horse he could hardly find the strength to replace the trap. He put it back, and the sand above it, and gave John the signal that he was ready to be taken in. When he reached the canteen he crawled out from under the horse and fainted.

That evening he was taken to the camp hospital. It was a total collapse. He had taken too much out of himself with the digging, the vaulting and the worry. The British doctor prescribed a week in bed. The matter was out of Peter's hands and he lay in bed wondering what John was doing.

During the week he was in hospital no digging was done; but the horse was taken out every afternoon to avoid the suspicion of the guards.

Service Most Silent

by JOHN FRAYN TURNER

The Royal Navy is, by tradition, the Silent Service; but the most silent cadre in that taciturn arm was the little group of experts who handled the earliest of Hitler's "secret weapons"—the new mines, acoustic, magnetic and the rest—which bade fair to devastate our shipping and bring Britain to the edge of starvation and surrender.

Service Most Silent is devoted to re-creating the perils and excitements, the triumphs and the tragedies of this small band whose armament consisted of no more than a few screw-drivers of non-magnetic brass, a handful of spanners, a sheaf of metal rods—and their own incredible ingenuity, technique and courage.

AT THE Director of Mine-sweeping (D.M.S.) division Ouvry[1] asked for Captain Morse. He was shown into a Georgian-looking office, and saw a strained face. "Good to see you, Ouvry. Sorry I'm not at my best, but it's been a pretty gruelling night. Reports are coming in all the time. If it's not mines dropping it's ships going down. You may like to be working something out. It seems generally agreed from signals received that the mines look like sailors' kitbags suspended from parachutes. If only they were as harmless! As for the losses, the latest is the *Gipsy*. Naturally we suspect magnetics are responsible for the new batch of sinkings this week, but there's still no proof—and nothing conclusive we can do in the way of antidotes till we get the proof. I've sent people down to Southend, Harwich and Grimsby to get all the details they can, to talk to the men who've been wrecked. We'll have to wait for their reports."

[1]Commander J. G. D. Ouvry, D.S.O., R.N.

Ouvry was given a desk in one of the outer offices and found the ordinarily august organization of the Admiralty in the grip of a mounting sense of frustration, which conveyed itself to him in some measure as he sat trying to clear his mind and get his ideas down on paper about the possible appearance of the mine, and the way it worked. He concluded that it might be magnetic or acoustic, and a ground mine. But as it was liable to fire when removed to shallow water—less than fifteen feet, say—the only evident way of dealing with it would be for a driver to unfit and unprime it under water; after which the weapon could be hoisted to the surface. Alternatively, to bore holes in the vicinity of its firing source and flood it. Again, the mine could be retrieved in safety. This was all to some extent conjectural, however, as circumstances would have to be treated on their merits entirely, and theory was liable to complete revision in the cold light of fact.

The day dragged by. Later on Morse sent for Ouvry again.

"We've had further signals from Hull and Grimsby, but they're not much help, I'm afraid, Ouvry. The skipper of the *Yarmouth Trader,* for instance: he's said they sighted a large bundle attached to a 'chute descending fast into seven fathoms. Anderson is up there now. The *Yarmouth Trader* marked the position of the object by a dan[2] in mid-channel. Admiralty permission was then given to offer a thousand pounds to a diver to go down and investigate, but in view of subsequent developments the same day and night at Southend this became unnecessary." At this point a Wren entered the room. "Excuse me, sir; Lieutenant-Commander Lewis[3] has just got back from Admiralty and would like to see you."

"Good. Show him in, will you? I was just going to tell you about him, Ouvry. He's been down to Southend all day trying to find out the facts—and if we can get to any of last night's batch. Ah, Lewis, Ouvry has come up from *Vernon,*[4] and I

[2]Dan: a small buoy.   [3]Lieut.-Cdr. R. C. Lewis, D.S.O., O.B.E., R.N.
[4]H.M.S. *Vernon*: the R.N. mine and torpedo shore-base at Portsmouth.

suggest you two have a chat to settle a plan of campaign in case anything turns up."

"Certainly, sir. We'll leave you for the time being, and report back later if we don't hear from you in the meanwhile."

Ouvry and Lewis made their way through the labyrinth of corridors that is the Admiralty, and eventually found the canteen and a hot meal. Over a rationed rissole Lewis explained how he (under Rear-Admiral Lyster) had been switched to the investigation of mines only a few days earlier.

"Cameron, a Wavy Navy two-ringer, and I got out a nine-point programme, including visits to ships damaged and interviews with survivors. When the *Belfast* was mined on Tuesday Cameron left for Rosyth, and as the latest reports of laying began to come in I motored down to Southend at 0300 this morning. Armitage has gone to the Humber, as Morse may have told you, and Captain Barrett's at Harwich. You've most likely heard from them during the day."

Ouvry told him about the Grimsby episodes.

Lewis went on: "I've managed to fix the approximate position of three or four of the mines from observers, and I've got some information about the Hun's laying methods. I spent most of the day, in fact, talking to masters of merchant-ships lying off Southend who saw the thing dropping last night. It's all too easy for Adolf, Ouvry; there's hardly any effective ack-ack. But we'll do our damnedest to beat 'em somehow."

This man Lewis was certainly a tonic. Ouvry liked him immensely—his cheerfulness, everything about the robust, ruddy, and reliable colleague. But no one could offset the shadow which was cast across the old cobbled forecourt of the Admiralty that night as they strolled back to Morse's office.

"Go off and get some rest, Ouvry," the Captain advised. Both men were aware of the sense of strain; both had had a broken night. Morse wanted to be sure that Ouvry kept fresh in case he was wanted—fresh not only in body, but in mind, for he had to be alert.

As Ouvry picked his way up to Trafalgar Square and turned sharp right into Northumberland Avenue, Lorna[5] switched off the bedroom light at Somerfields and settled into a restless kind of sleep. And at the same moment, too, a German seaplane was steering an unsteady course over the Thames Estuary—it was a moonless night—the pilot peering into the pitch void and driving rain, looking for bearings. Dimly he made out the river-mouth and prepared to run in on course. He came a little lower to be sure. Two hundred feet. One hundred and fifty feet. At that second the machine-gun outpost on the end of Southend Pier which Roger Lewis had organized only hours earlier shattered the night with a staccato series of bursts. Already in a state of nervous tension with the stress of night flying in filthy conditions, the pilot was shaken out of his wits by the guns. He was lower than he thought. He would never get away. Instinctively he pressed the button on his control panel, and his lethal load was released. Two bundles dropped through the night air for a few seconds, and almost before their parachutes had time to open Hitler's secret weapon number one was neatly deposited into the sea off Shoeburyness.

Local observers realized that the unknown objects might well be mines, and that they would most likely be uncovered at low water—0400. They had been dropped at high tide. A call was put through to the Admiralty as soon as it seemed sure that mines were the answer. D.M.S. 'phoned Ouvry. "Pack your bag and come straight over to Admiralty. It's Morse here, and we've got a Jerry mine for you." Ouvry had just dropped off into a first deep sleep at his hotel. For a second the words were meaningless. Then the whole wonder of them rushed round his brain. At last, thank God! The waiting's over! It's up to us!

Over in the D.M.S. office Lewis met him, and wasted no words: "A 'chute[6] mine's been sighted near Southend. I'm organizing transport, and have been in touch with the Navy down there. We've got to get down right away. It'll be dry in

[5]Mrs. Ouvry.   [6]Parachute.

214

two or three hours. The car's coming at 0100. We've just time to peep in and see Admiral Lyster."

"Where is it exactly, Lewis?" the Admiral asked.

"On the mud-flats, more or less, at Shoeburyness, sir. We'll have to hurry—we don't know how long it will be dry for. The tide comes in miles round that coast in a matter of minutes, it seems, so we ought to be there just before low water."

"Right, you two; don't let me keep you. You've got my blessing. Take care of yourself, Ouvry. Leave all the organization to Lewis, and you just concentrate on the mine. That's an overtime job, anyway. I don't have to tell you, I know, but the orders are: recover it at all costs."

A knock at the door. A duty rating ventured in. "Car waiting at the front entrance, sir, for Southend."

"Now, look, Ouvry, you've got the key job, so you go in the back and try and get some sleep. It's not the sort of thing you can tackle if you're tired."

"But I'm perfectly all right," protested Ouvry.

"You're going to sleep—if I have to put you off myself! And, driver, we want you to make Southend as fast as humanly possible without wrecking the whole machine. I know the way, so I'll sit in front with you."

The driver took him at his word and crashed fifteen red lights before getting clear of the London area. They were approaching Shoeburyness faster than the tide was quitting it. The blacked-out traffic signals, with their thin, slit crosses of light barely visible in the rain, became less and less frequent, until nothing could be seen at all. The flat Essex road came at them with dull regularity.

"It's no damned day-trip to Southend, this, is it?" observed Lewis to the driver quietly, whose only response was to grunt and dig his heel into the rubber flooring of the car and press his toe forward on the accelerator.

0300: the Palace Hotel, Southend. Ghostlike. As in some

Priestley play—free of space and time. Fog had come down during the last part of the journey and slowed up what had looked like standing as a record run to the holiday resort. As the car drew into the curved drive Lewis turned back to Ouvry. "How did you sleep, old man?"

"'Fraid I didn't. I remembered that I've left my 'rendering mines safe' notes on the dressing-table at the hotel, so I've had to go through them all again in my mind!"

"Well, I'll be damned!" Lewis exploded.

They parked their baggage, changed cars, picked up Commander Bowles' of N.O.I.C.'s staff, together with a local photographer Bowles had managed to round up, and proceeded along to Shoeburyness. As the car sped past the Kursaal—dark silhouettes of a scenic railway—Bowles told the others that one of the vessels held up out in the tideway, a frozen-meat ship, had swung on the turn of the tide about the time the new batch of mines had been dropped, and just by this gentle action had fired one of them. Whatever device it was firing the mines, taking one to pieces was going to be no ordinary ordeal.

"By the way," went on Bowles, "although your job's hard, there's one bit of luck. Shoeburyness is a military station with an artillery range. They fire their missiles out over the mud and recover them at low water. So all the gear you want will be at hand; and there's a fully equipped workshop, too, you may be glad of before you've finished."

Ouvry thanked him for these encouragements. The sense of expectancy heightened.

At Shoeburyness Commander Maton met them with a party of soldiers. Bowles made the introductions. Ouvry told them: "I doubt if we'll be able to tackle it on this tide. Light is vital—and this rain makes it pretty well out of the question. We'll have to secure it and wait for the next low tide in the afternoon. Incidentally, I suppose you've located it all right? If so, let's get over and see it, shall we?"

'Naval Officer in Command.

"Everything's arranged for you," said Maton. "We've certainly found one and we've got ropes and stakes, and here are some thigh-boots for you. Hope you can find the right size from this selection."

"Wait a second, though," Ouvry answered. "Before we go we'd better unload all the metal we're carrying. Money; cigarette-cases; everything. And what about buttons; they'll have to go, too; we can't chance anything."

So these came off, and the party moved forward.

It was 0400. A vile night. Black—and wet. A private led them, splashing through pools left by the ebbing tide. An Aldis lamp held aloft swayed to and fro crazily with each step, lighting small patches of the rippled sand. The private waded on. He it was who had seen the parachute dropping from Shoeburyness. Another few minutes passed; then he called out excitedly, "There it is ahead, sir."

To the rest of the party it was still out of range. They rushed up. "Don't go any nearer," warned Ouvry. He scanned the few remaining yards to where the soldier was pointing. His heart pounded. Ouvry and Lewis, torches in hand, moved towards it for a better look.

Here it was . . . the unknown quantity . . . inanimate object . . . one touch might animate it . . . blow them to bits. What was it? Magnetic? Acoustic? Cosmic? Could be any or all.

Out of the dark it seemed to edge towards them with each successive step they took. A black, glistening hippopotamus, sinister, shiny, looming into the torchlight. Half embedded in sand five hundred yards below high-water mark. A little pool encircling the end in the mud. Half a mile out to sea in the before-dawn chill of a November night. Excitement intensified on the rain-swept shore.

The winning of the war might depend on these next few hours.

More than the length of a man, it was. Nearly seven feet. And about two feet in diameter. Cylindrical, made of some aluminium alloy. That much they saw at once. Tubular horns on the rounded, embedded nose attracted their attention. Ouvry moved to the other end. Neither he nor Lewis spoke. An acoustic vibrator could respond to a voice—and anything might be inside. Ouvry pointed the tail out to Lewis. It was hollow and open, with a massive phosphor-bronze spring sticking out. Apparently this was where the parachute had been attached. Now no sign of it could be found. But the mine was the vital thing, and specifically two devilish devices near the nose, forward. Prominent on top of the mine, one was brass, one aluminium. The brass fitting Ouvry took to be a hydrostatic valve, which duly encouraged him. But the second was different from anything he had been used to or seen on our own non-contact mines. The aluminium was polished, and secured by a screwed ring sealed with tallow. Another encouragement: attached was what seemed to be a "tear-off" strip, twisted but secure—possibly a safety arrangement.

Somehow, later that day, Ouvry had to find a way into the mine. These two fittings were the only visible means. Once off, it would be up to him to make the thing safe so that the secrets could be unlocked. But he was looking too far ahead. Now the first job was to consider what tools he would need. The mysterious second fitting seemed as if it would harbour the primer and detonator, so this would have to be tackled first. But no tools he had ashore came near to matching the ring securing the fitting. Nor would any of the non-magnetic tools which were coming up from *Vernon* in the morning do the job. A four-pin spanner was wanted, so Ouvry motioned to Lewis to take an impression of the aluminium fitting on a sheet of an Admiralty signal-pad. He placed the paper gently against the fitting, still more softly pressing it to the shape. Lewis handed the sheet to Ouvry, who passed it on to Maton.

Ouvry beckoned the photographers—one official, one the local commercial cameraman, collected earlier. From every angle they took a series of flashlight pictures, the surrounding sand leaping into stippled relief, then becoming once more shrouded. Soldiers passed hemp lines round the mine, and lashed them to the stakes plunged into the soft mud-sand. Ouvry and Lewis jotted down their final notes before stepping back—into the known again.

"Good work, chaps," Maton volunteered to all and sundry. Then to Ouvry: "You'll want a non-magnetic spanner made to unscrew the ring? I'll get the workshop to fix one in brass by noon. That should be in plenty of time for the tide. Some brass rods of all sizes might come in useful, too."

"That'll be fine. You're making it all as easy as it could be."

Making their way back to the beach, they came across the parachute, sodden with sand and sea. It seemed to weigh a ton, but a few good heaves brought it out of reach of the tide.

"I should try and get a bit of rest if I were you," Maton told the two Lieutenant-Commanders. "I tell you what. Come along to my house—Bowles, you as well—and Ouvry and Lewis can have an hour at least before breakfast." Both of them felt too strong a sense of suppressed excitement to do more than doze, and at 0600 the dawn heralded a breakfast of fried eggs as a special treat. Ouvry felt better. He looked out over Southend to the incoming tide. As the two men made out their preliminary report and attached it to the photos of the mine which had just been printed, they realized the responsibility resting on them. It seemed to outweigh the danger—although they were conscious of that, too.

The 'phone rang. Maton took it. "Another one, you say? Three hundred yards away from the first? We'll be down at once." Then, turning to his guests: "No rest for the wicked. They've sighted a second mine near the first."

In a matter of minutes they were at the nearest point to the stretch of beach. Drawing on their waders for the second time in a few hours, they lunged into the deepening water to try to locate it. But the tide was flooding fast. An old man looked out of a still-older hulk moored nearby. "You won't find it now," he called over to them. "It's been covered for some minutes.

But it'll be dry again at low water." They decided to wait for the falling tide for this one, as for the other.

Ouvry took a call from Sayer[8] at *Vernon* during the morning. "We'll be able to tackle it early p.m.," Ouvry told him, "and will let you know the result as soon as we can. There's only one other thing on my mind. Lewis and I are busy preparing the plan of attack, so I wonder if you'd mind giving my wife a ring for me. I'd be very grateful."

"My dear Ouvry, I was going to do so, anyway, the second I had put down the receiver. And it's we who should be grateful —not you. Best of luck again."

Soon afterwards Baldwin[9] and Vearncombe[10] arrived with the rest of the tools, direct from *Vernon*. It was good to see them, Ouvry thought. The Chief, completely and utterly loyal, the epitome of all that was best among non-commissioned officers. No more than medium height, with a weathered face. And young Vearncombe, the tall, good-looking, two-badge A.B.— as reliable as the Chief. Yes, it was certainly good to have these two with him. And Lewis, a tower of strength and support. Lewis responsible for the organization, Ouvry for the technical job of tackling the mine.

"Now that we've settled the best method of attack," Ouvry suggested to Lewis, "I think the only sensible procedure is to split the four of us into groups in case of accidents. That will double our chances, and the second pair may be able to profit from any miscalculations. There's the other mine left for them. That's the deciding factor as I see it."

"If it's really the way you want it," yielded Lewis grudgingly.

"Baldwin and I have got the background for this sort of thing —as far as anyone has—so we'll kick off, and you and Vearncombe can wait on the foreshore. I'll signal each move I make, and you can tick them off on the list, so you'll know how far

[8]Commander G. B. Sayer, D.S.C., R.N., Commander M. (Mining).
[9]The late C.P.O. C. E. Baldwin, D.S.M.
[10]Able Seaman A. L. Vearncombe, D.S.M.

I've got. I'll wave both hands above my head after each episode.
But don't feel left out in the cold, for I've a hunch that we'll all
be needed before the day's out—one way or the other."

There was no hint of drama in his voice. He was just stating
facts.

It was 1300. Neither of them felt like lunch. The tide had
fallen clear of both mines. Maton and some of the soldiers took
up a sheltered position on the foreshore opposite the mine. A
tractor lorry with a crane attached stood by hopefully, for the
time when one of them would be ready for collection. While
the military photographer took a series of daylight pictures,
with long rulers to mark the length and height of the thing,
Ouvry and Lewis strolled over to look at the second specimen.
Like number one, its nose was nuzzled down deep into the sand,
but the whole thing was on a different slew, leaving a large plate
exposed which could not be seen on the first. The horns, they
concluded, were in no way dangerous, merely projections to
bury in the seabed and keep the mine steady, so that it would
not roll with the pressure of the water. That was one item less
to worry about—but plenty remained. Night had passed, but
all was still mystery. A live acoustic mine might kill at the first
touch on its shell. A magnetic mine might equally easily explode.
Both were liable to have some German device to stop their
secrets being shared—a booby-trap.

The time had reached 1330. Ouvry thought of his wife as he
and Baldwin waved to Lewis and Vearncombe.

Sayer had told her of the plan. He did not tell her not to
worry. At 1330 she cleared away the boys' dishes and knew the
operation was on. Pounding from the radio, the wild waves of
a Sibelius symphony broke over her emotions. But in the midst
of their turmoil she sensed a strange calm. She looked out over
the Solent. A destroyer was ploughing over the Stokes Bay
course, where British magnetic mines were being tested. The
Isle of Wight car-ferry plodded slowly from the mainland.

But few ships sailed otherwise. No channel was safe from the air, not even the Solent. John must manage it. . . .

. . . Ouvry and Baldwin walked quickly over to the mine. A few paces off Ouvry saw a little brass ring reclining in the sand. "That looks as if it may be the missing part to that spindle of the top brass fitting, Chief. Yes, it is—look. I feel better already. Now let's forget the brass hat and concentrate on the aluminium one! You can see the shell's aluminium too. The black paint's chipped off still more after last night. Now, how about that fitting?"

1337. Baldwin handed him the four-pin spanner. Ouvry looked closely into the fitting and saw a small plate, jointed with tallow, an oval-shaped groove filled with black wax, a screwed recess, and the copper "tear-off" strip he had seen in the early hours. The strip was masking one of the holes for the spanner. Baldwin went to pull it off. But Ouvry stopped him.

"Don't do that. It may be some safety device. Just turn it back carefully."

The Chief complied.

Ouvry tried the Shoeburyness-made spanner. "It fits," he whispered. His throat was parched. The wind had dried his lips too. A whining, wintry wind. This was it. The moment had come at last. Moving the spanner unbelievably slowly, he unscrewed the ring a fraction of a turn. Nothing happened. They were still alive. Ten degrees . . . twenty . . . ninety . . . one-eighty . . . a whole turn. All was still well. He glanced up at the Chief. Another turn. A few more. And the ring was free.

"A rod, Chief."

Baldwin offered a choice. Ouvry took the smallest, jammed it into the opening. He took what he saw inside to be either a detonator or some sort of magnetic-needle device. Either was dynamite. Again at a crawl, holding the rod delicately, with precision, he lowered it into the opening, angler-like. The hook on the end looped over the fitting, and he withdrew his catch a fraction of an inch at a time. It slid smoothly out. Ouvry was sweating now. Spray in the wind sprinkled his face. His waders stuck in the mud, then squelched free. If this were the detonator he had only to drop it once. There would be no second chance—not for him, anyway. Inch by inch it came. Then it was out. Back in shore, Lewis adjusted his glasses more finely. "He's got something. Look, the Chief has signalled. Thank God for that much."

1349. Ouvry peered down into the dark void the fitting had left. Dimly he saw a pocket containing a tubular disc of explosive and a primer. And under the disc two more solid discs. He fished for these, this time with a brass rod filed to a pointed end. But they would not come free.

"Never mind, Chief. Let's look at what we've caught and leave the one that's got away for the moment."

A cylindrical cup was screwed into the underside of the fitting in his hand, which was evidently the detonator—or, at least, *a* detonator.

"I think this is it, Chief. If it's the detonator the worst is over. But we'll have to take a look at the underneath of the mine. Run ashore and fetch the others to help manhandle it. We couldn't budge it an inch alone."

"Aye, aye, sir."

1404. Ouvry suddenly felt good. He breathed deeply. The strong Southend air reached the lining of his lungs. That *must* be the detonator. And if it is the firing source, what have we got to worry about? Nothing—much.

Looking away south he saw the end of Southend Pier. No one stirred on it, save the naval gun-crew Lewis had organized. A good job I've got someone with some organization. The wind again, coming in short, blustering bursts over the mud-flats. The pools of water left by the tide quivered as it whipped at them. Over on the Southend cliffs he made out momentarily a royal-blue trolley-bus. So life was going on normally. Out here it was if they were marooned on an island of space and time with a sea of mud enveloping them. The Chief had reached the others. The three of them were hurrying out now. Ouvry felt quietly confident. But at the back of his mind stuck obstinately the suggestion that the day's work was not yet over.

"It's too early to be too excited," he told Lewis, who was approaching him warmly, "but, all being well—all will be well. Can you help turn it? We might just manage it between us."

With ropes they nearly did it. As they paused, thinking they would have to enlist the aid of the Army after all, a lone figure, complete with bull-terrier, threaded his way out to them.

"Hello, there!" called Ouvry. "It's Dr. Wood, isn't it?"

"That's right. I was up at Admiralty when your message came through this morning, so I hurried down to see how it's going."

"Right in the thick of it now. Just at this second you've come quite providentially to bend a fifth pair of shoulders—or lend a fifth pair of hands. We've got to turn it as quickly as we can. The tide will be coming in again in an hour or two."

1422. Dr. Wood, chief scientist of the Mine Design Department at *Vernon*, just tilted the scales. The underside rolled clear, coated with damp mud-sand. It was now about 120 degrees round from its former position, so that both top and bottom fittings were accessible. Ouvry could collect the loose primer discs he had not been able to reach at the earlier angle. Just as on mine number two, this one had a plate flush with the shell, diametrically opposed to the brass "hydrostatic valve" on top. This was confidently unscrewed. Beneath it appeared a circular screwed bung with four recesses. No spanner seemed suitable to shift it, so some elementary force had to be applied. This took time.

1457. There seemed to be no end to the gadgets—like forcing a way through an eternal jungle with each bush thicker than the last. So it wasn't going to be as easy as Ouvry had thought.

Another screwed plate met the gaze of the little company. Two terminals mounted neatly on it had two leads winding away out of sight through a hole into the bowels. No-man's-land. Suddenly it occurred to him that *this was the main detonator circuit*—and not the other. It all had to be gone through again, but an air of confidence pervaded the scene now. Still in slow motion, Ouvry twisted both leads round and round in turn till each strand of each wire snapped under the strain. Then he insulated them. Break an electrical circuit—always a good policy. No spanner fitted the screws securing the plate, so a non-magnetic screwdriver filled the bill. As he took the plate out Ouvry saw that it was a detonator carrier with an electric detonator similar to that used on the German horned mines. Out it came—and he felt on top of the world.

1510. He could not see to get at the primer from this side, so the mine was rolled back, the original brass fitting taking up its position on top. This was the continuation of the detonator-primer pocket. Ouvry undid the cover with a spanner , and, as if to echo their elation, the fitting inside leaped out under the force of a strong spring! After a general surge back—and a chorus of relief—the long phosphor-bronze spring followed it, cascading high into the air, before coming to rest in the wash of the incoming tide. The priming charge was easily removed, and there remained only a large hydrostatic arming-clock.

1527. Triumphant, all four of them signalled gaily to the soldiers inshore for the tractor and the crane. The five leads to the clock were cut, and the trophies carted ashore.

By 1600 it was all over. The mine was hoisted into the lorry, and sent away for safe storage overnight under cover. The light was failing, so no attempt was made to get to the second mine, in any case already awash.

Up on the beach they all stretched out in glorious relaxation. Lewis laid the arming-clock down. Straightway it started ticking. All four of them hurtled away from it! They were all too well aware of the chance of booby-traps to risk anything at this stage. "Nothing to worry about," laughed Ouvry. "It's only the spindle." And all was really well at last. At 1630 they took a combined lunch-tea. And by 1700 a report to the Admiralty informed their Lordships at the naval nerve-centre that Hitler's secret weapon number one was lying harmlessly in a Shoebury-ness shed, awaiting transport to *Vernon* the following morning.

Boldness Be My Friend

by RICHARD PAPE

*Richard Pape, a Warrant Officer of the R.A.F., was one of the indefatigable
escapers. His aircraft was so badly damaged over Berlin that it crashed in
Holland. He was on the point of being rescued when he was caught by the
Gestapo and shipped to Silesia. Thrice he escaped, only to be recaptured
and subjected to the brutalities of the Nazi officials. He switched identities
with other prisoners; he devised codes and sent messages back to Britain;
finally, he tricked the German medical services into recommending his
repatriation.* Boldness Be My Friend *is, perhaps, the most savage and
unsympathetically-written of all British books of war memoirs; but as a
record of ingenuity and endurance it must command a permanent place in
the literature of the barbed wire. But despite his sometimes repellent tough-
ness of idiom he was—as is here demonstrated—capable of supreme self-
sacrifice.*

*Richard Pape, a pre-war journalist, suffered appalling disfigurement
and was one of the "Guinea Pig Club"—the men who benefited from the
miraculous plastic surgery of Sir Archibald McIndoe—to which and to
whom he dedicates his book.*

D ESPITE the tragic, muddled and incredibly poverty-stricken
existence of Polish people under the ruthless pressure of
the German Occupation, the Sisters of Mercy treated us nobly.[1]

But as the days trickled by a deep smouldering pain developed
in one of my lungs and my temperature started to dance about
the thermometer. My lungs had not resisted the hardships of our
prolonged flight across the Polish plain. The long forced
marches, completed when we were half-conscious from lack of

[1]In the early sections of his book, Richard Pape shows himself as a bitter
anti-Catholic.

sleep and almost frozen from lack of warmth, had seriously sapped my resistance, and the sodden clothing and the steaming of my heated body had struck at my lungs.

One Sunday morning the pleurisy took a turn for the worse. The pain grew to a torment, and by nightfall I was unconscious. It was thirty-six hours before I was conscious and coherent again, but my physical condition was very weak.

During my illness, a young nun called Maria was my constant companion and devoted nurse. She would whisper to me: "*Ein' feste Burg is unser Gott*" (Our God is a strong tower). I was impressed by her charming and correct manners, her *naïveté* and her sensitiveness. As she sat by my bed like a ministering angel, I confided to her all my thoughts, hopes and ambitions. Quietly and whimsically she would listen, composed and beautiful, a balance of sympathy and understanding.

Maria, in her turn, told me about her family in Posen, and from her vivid descriptions I felt that I had known her father, mother, brothers and sisters for years.

Gradually my health improved and my strength accumulated. The prospect of my weakened lungs jeopardizing further escape decreased as the tugging pain gave way to only an occasional sharp stab. But I realized that for quite a time I would not be capable of standing up to any tests of physical endurance and hardship. Yet with each day that passed our time in Czestochowa was running out. Underground organizers had made arrangements for our journey eastwards and soon we would have to go. It was planned that, in the company of a Sister of Mercy, we would leave our hiding-place, and with forged curfew-papers go down to the station and take the train for Cracow. The Sister of Mercy would escort us on the first leg of the journey, and bid us farewell when we actually boarded the Trans-Polish express which would carry us to the Ukraine. Poles of the Resistance Movement in the East would be informed of our departure, and they would meet us and take us under their wing.

A forged passport was being made out for me in the name of

Henryk Kowalski, a concrete labourer who, according to other papers being prepared, was being directed to the East by the German Military Directorate for duties in road construction. I was instructed to memorize the details surrounding my new name and character. First an Englishman, then a New Zealander, now a Pole.[2] What the devil next?

A few nights later the underground people gave us a strict and final briefing. We were made to swear on oath before the Cross that if we were captured and tortured no word would pass our lips about where we had stayed. If the Gestapo learned of the nunnery the loyal Sisters of Mercy would suffer torture and possibly death.

On the stroke of nine o'clock Mieteck[3] and I, with the nun detailed to escort us, stepped outside the nunnery into the moist darkness. It was snowing. As we passed through the gate I turned to take a final look at the building which had sheltered us, and to express my heartfelt thanks to the kind women within it. The nun squeezed my arm, and said softly: "Come, brace yourself for the journey to the station."

The streets were deserted. The houses we passed looked gaunt and browbeaten, and the big moon seemed puzzled. The swishing reflections it cast on the window appeared to suggest a sulking, downcast shame. It was not wholesome in Czestochowa after curfew, a town simmering with hate, a town suffering the most infamous treatment at the hands of its jackbooted occupiers.

We had covered half the journey to the station when out from the shadows stepped a German military policeman. "Papers," he barked. Quietly and with perfect composure the nun handed him the documents. In the light from a flashlamp they were

[2]Pape exchanged papers and personalities in order to muddle his trail and facilitate his escape.

[3]A Polish fellow-prisoner with whom Pape made one of his several bids for escape.

closely studied. Although Mieteck and I affected nonchalance, our hearts nevertheless pounded and our muscles were tensed.

"*Gut*," said the German as he thrust the papers back into the nun's hand.

Prickling with relief we went on.

The station was crowded with ill-clad and listless men and women, the majority of them *en route* under German orders to join labour corps behind the lines in the East. We mooched among these people, with their pathetic little bundles of belongings, for over three hours, waiting for a long-overdue train, and the freezing night air did not assist our comfort.

The station walls were splashed with big posters screaming a campaign of hate against the Jews. One registered itself vividly on my mind. It portrayed an old Jew with a beaked nose and skullcap busy dropping dead rats into a mincing machine while from the other end sausage was issuing into a bowl. The caption read: "No more Jewish foodshops for Poland. We must exterminate Jewish poison as we would exterminate rats."

A violent pogrom was in swing against all things Jewish in Czestochowa. The Germans had restricted all Jews to the ghettoes, and Jewish property and businesses had been seized and confiscated. The nun told us that it was a common sight in the town to see former Jewish business and professional men, clad in rags, sweeping the streets with German guards, a pistol in one hand, a whip in the other, standing over them.

Public exhibitions were organized by the Gestapo in the market square and the unwilling Poles were compelled to attend. The exhibitions featured the mass shaving of female heads, a punishment meted out by the Germans for what they termed disobedience to German occupational regulations. The "disobedience" was refusal by Polish women to consort and fraternize with the soldiers who sought to gratify themselves. The women were fastened to benches and publicly horse-sheared. Sobbing with shame and fright they were released only when they were close-cropped.

Towards the end of the three hours' wait I felt stirrings of the burning in my lung. I became frightened when I contemplated trouble that might interfere with the second phase of our escape. By the time the train drew in I was soaking wet with perspiration in spite of the coldness of the night air. This was the first time I had ventured outside the nunnery since I had first entered it, and I endeavoured to console myself with the thought that it was a purely natural readjustment to getting about again and being active. But it was a relief when the train finally drew in, and I was able to relax on a wooden seat in the corner.

We chugged out of the station into a blinding snowstorm, and the good nun opposite took out from her bag a flask of hot coffee. Without inquiring about my condition she gave me three tablets and told me to "try and sleep".

The train was due to reach Cracow in the morning, and Mieteck was worried in case some delay caused us to miss the Trans-Polish express to the Ukraine.

"Don't worry," the nun reassured him. "This is a most important feeder train, and the Ukraine express will wait."

The tablets put me to sleep for a while and when I awoke I was oozing perspiration. The pain in my lung was stabbing severely and a sticky heat seemed to be rising from my chest to my brain.

Snorting and slicing through a phantom world, the train breathed heavily across a desert of white towards Cracow.

The high-riding moon, like an imperial spectator, washed the width of the visible world with a luminous glow. The train had acquired greater confidence as the snow had ceased to fall, and at intervals snorted a shriek of defiance.

The rhythmic optimism of the train did not stimulate my own courage to combat the sharpening pains in my shoulder, or help me to dismiss the burning behind my forehead and the prickings behind my eyes. After two-thirds of the distance had been covered, I was struggling to stop myself from writhing with pain. I knew all too well that as far as further travel was concerned, I had had my chips.

The thick atmosphere of the carriage became unbearable. Assisted by Mieteck I was moved into the lavatory, where I was violently sick.

Facing Mieteck I told him what I had decided. "Sorry, Mieteck, I can never get as far as the Ukraine in this condition," I said. "I'm getting worse and I would only jeopardize your chances. In fairness to you the bond of partnership is finished. All I want to do is keep a reasonable state of mind until we get to Cracow, where I am sure to find some place to curl up and rest awhile. You carry on and get back to Britain."

Mieteck was deeply upset. He brought the nun to my side in the small space between the carriages. She told me to hold out with all the determination possible until we got beyond the barriers at Cracow. Once there she would immediately contact people who would look after me until I was fit.

"When you are fit to travel again," she said, "we will all return to Czestochowa, where we will get you properly well so that you can continue your escape. Mieteck refuses to leave you until you are yourself again."

I returned to my seat but during the final stage of the run a compelling voice reminded me that Mieteck's escape must go on. Since he was determined not to leave me it was up to me to leave him.

The train pulled in to the platform and thronging, bustling activity hemmed us in. The fresh, cool air was a relief, and I suggested to Mieteck that we might make a call at the lavatory. The nun waited at a coffee stall and, joining a small queue of men a little distance away inside a large lavatory, we waited our turn, Mieteck behind me.

I stepped forward to a position almost at the far end of the chamber, at least thirty compartments away from Mieteck, divided by wide and lofty slabs of slate. The instant he was out of sight behind the surface of slate I slipped out of the narrow entrance a couple of yards away, and made straight for the waiting nun.

Hurriedly I told her not to attempt to stop me from leaving them, and that she must see that Mieteck caught the train to the Ukraine. I could not go on hindering his chances, and I preferred to leave this way. I told her to tell Mieteck that his progress would be my progress, and that she could trust me never to breathe a word about her and her loyal people.

I fell down the stairway into a busy Cracow thoroughfare. Mingling with pedestrians, I walked quickly and blindly on-wards, my brain throbbing and my senses wavering. My escape was over, everything was finished, and all I wanted was a place where I could sit down and sleep. Up one street and down another I wandered at random until I came to a wide-open space, a public Garden of Rest surrounded by tall, frowning buildings. I fell on a vacant bench and remembered nothing more until I came to my senses some hours later.

Pape was recaptured, broke out again, and was again recaptured.

It was while I was in Stalag Luft VI that I began to work on a new method of smuggling messages out from Germany to England—openly, in rings worn by repatriated prisoners. It was a crazy idea, but it worked. There was no attempt to conceal the rings. If there had been the whole scheme would have failed. But because the prisoners wore them even while they were being stripped naked and searched by the Germans none were ever detected.

I made the rings from the stems of old toothbrushes, collected from dustbins or bought for ten cigarettes each. First I boiled the stems and then bent them round ring-sticks of various sizes. Next came the cutting and polishing. It was essential to make them as small as possible, and I tried to keep them to much the same size as the ordinary signet ring.

In the head (where in a normal ring the jewels are set) I hollowed out a tiny aperture into which I coiled a strip of paper containing the message. Above the message I laid a minute snap-shot of the person who was to carry the ring, or of someone close to him—sister or wife or mother—and sealed the whole affair with a strip of celluloid. Once the celluloid was removed, the snapshot and coiled paper popped out.

The job was not easy. The various parts of the ring had to be cemented with acetone. At first I had great difficulty in obtaining supplies, but eventually I got a German guard under graft and blackmailed him. He had a brother who was a laboratory chemist in a Breslau Military Hospital and once I had the guard properly under my thumb I got as much of the stuff as I needed.

The first ring was taken out by "Wingy" Woodhead, a Yorkshireman who had lost his right hand while doing forced labour for the Germans in a Polish mine. The ring contained my photograph, and I urged him to deliver it to Ernest Osborn, of *The Yorkshire Post.* "Give it to nobody else," I told him, "and guard it with your life. When you hand it over, tell him to take a sharp knife and lever just below my picture."

Afterwards "Wingy" told Osborn that his only anxious moment was during the final searching by the Germans for concealed messages. He was stripped naked and his clothes and body searched minutely. All the time the ring lay on his finger in full view—yet the Germans ignored it.

The first success was followed by many more. One by one the repatriates went out with my rings, some of them to Canada, some to Australia, and some to New Zealand as well as Britain.

The rings proved useful for other things, too. On one occasion it was vital that a diamond, needed for special cutting purposes, be sent from our camp, through the secret chain of bribed guards, to a Russian watchmaker in hospital in Breslau. On another occasion I sent a tiny phial of deadly poison half-way across Germany to Slovakia. It began its journey in the custody of pro-British German guards, was later put in the post and finally delivered to its recipient buried inside a potato.

Each ring took from ten to twenty hours to make, and a South African, H. J. Boking, helped me with the carving and polishing. He never knew that I was slipping messages inside them; he really thought they were genuine mementoes.

There lived in Luft VI more than three hundred Yorkshire airmen whom we organized into a society called "The White Rose Club". We formed our own concert party; organized a fine debating and sports club and, quite unknown to the Germans, produced every three weeks our own newspaper. I was the editor, lay-out artist and printing press.

The paper usually contained not less than 10,000 words, and every letter had to be hand drawn. We called it *The Yorkshire Post,* in acknowledgment of Yorkshire's influential morning newspaper.

The book was a combined effort of literary and artistic talent drawn exclusively from the membership of "The White Rose Club". Drawings and articles were submitted to me and included if they proved of sufficiently high standard. "Tally Ho" procured the necessary paper and ink for its construction, whilst my pen nibs were fashioned from the steel tape which bound Red Cross crates.

We called the book *The Kriegie Edition.* It was completely hand lettered throughout, and possessed a most impressive hand-carved cover in Red Cross plywood. The original of *The Kriegie Edition* excited considerable interest in the Press in Britain, and *The Yorkshire Post* reproduced and printed the volume in facsimile. Copies were presented to all the next-of-kin of the 300 Yorkshiremen in Luft VI. The Prime Minister, Sir (then Mr.) Winston Churchill, the Air Minister, and the Minister of Information, publicly acclaimed our enterprise and ingenuity.

The book took three weeks to produce. I would begin work on it at 7 o'clock in the morning and continue until darkness. Barrack friends took it in turn to remain seated at either end of the barrack block and at the approach of a guard they would yell "Goons up". At the warning I would cork my ink, pack my sheets together, remove three floorboards and conceal the manuscript below the floor under my bed. The entire *Kriegie Edition* was written stretched out on the floor under the bottom bunk of a set of three-tier beds. By the time the investigating German patrol had reached my bed I was stretched out on the straw and snoring in a most healthy and harmless manner. As soon as the guard on the door yelled "Goons gone" I was back at work under the bed.

The Dangerous Skies

by A. E. CLOUSTON, D.S.O., D.F.C., A.F.C. and BAR

Air-Commodore A. E. Clouston is a major figure in the Royal Air Force, but it was as a civilian pilot that he made his name. He tested many strange machines before the war, competed in many races, and hit the headlines when he broke the existing records for the London-to-the-Cape, the London–Australia and the London–New Zealand flights. It was with the greatest difficulty that he got into the R.A.F.—the Service doctors would have none of him; but at the outbreak of the war he was recalled and tested all manner of new devices, good and bad, at the risk of his life.

The Dangerous Skies is a book which gives the reader a real sense of the excitement and the exhaustion of the early record-making days. The passage reproduced here explains what sheer flying ability and sheer courage can do in the face of overwhelming odds.

THE Battle of the Atlantic grew in intensity. Our submarine sightings and sinkings mounted, but so did the toll of our aircraft and the toll of our ships. Unless we could step up the number of sinkings, visiting Naval intelligence officers told us,[1] the country would be starving within weeks.

We had the very latest radar, built in America from British design, but I was not happy about the results it was yielding. An American, Captain Hickman, was attached to us for maintenance supervision and I asked if he could fly with us to test the set under actual operations.

Hickman was willing, so off we went. The great improvement from his expert operation and adjustment of the set was quickly apparent. Our radar picked up everything the sea had

[1]Us: the Royal Air Force.

to offer—whales, broken, half-swamped boats, shoals of tunny-fish off Spain, and enemy aircraft in the sky.

Bad weather forced us to land at Gibraltar at the end of our patrol. On our return patrol to the United Kingdom the following day Hickman, with his eyes concentrating on the radar screen, told me of two rain squalls three miles away on our port bow. I confirmed that I could see the heavy rain under those two black clouds in that otherwise sunny, clear sky.

"Fine," said Hickman. "Behind one of those squalls is a submarine."

I veered cautiously over to the edge of the squall. The sub. was there all right, a German one, running at top speed on the surface about five miles away.

We banked quickly into the cloud and with the crew at action stations began to stalk the sub. Undetected, we gained the cover of another smaller squall cloud ahead. It took us to within half a mile of the submarine, and still she had no idea of our presence.

The routine patter chattered over the intercom. "Depth charges selected . . . bomb doors open . . . O.K., boys, here we go. . . ."

I put the nose down. From 1,000 feet we dived out of cloud and rain into brilliant sunshine. Sea and submarine raced to meet us. We could almost hear the shouts of *Achtung* and the racketing hooter of the sub's internal, action stations, alarm.

Three power-operated turrets swung to meet us, and the multi-gun units lined up in our path of flight. Grapes of flak began to blister the sky around us, jolting and shaking the air-craft. We were looking down the barrels of their guns. It was impossible for them to miss at such point-blank range.

But the stick of depth charges was away, straddling the submarine, and the Liberator was straining and shuddering as I levelled her up at ten feet, and had to bank violently to avoid hitting the periscope with the port wing. Then the blast from our own high-explosives lifted us into the air.

We came round for another attack. The submarine was trying

to crash-dive, sliding under the water with the gunners still firing in their turrets. We could see the tense fear in their faces, but still they kept up the barrage, firing at us to the last as the waves drowned them in their seats.

The sea closed over the conning-tower; and then the tail rose out of the water, standing up almost vertically for moments that seemed minutes, its propellers threshing the air. At last, slowly, lazily almost, she slipped below for the last time, and the sea began to boil with bubbles of air, and oil, and mud, and debris.

It had all happened so quickly that it was almost as if it had never been. The tense thrill and exaltation of the flight were gone, replaced by a quieter sense of satisfaction and contentment at the success of the attack. For the submarine personnel I could feel no pity, only a detached admiration for the gunners.

I checked in turn with each of my own crew. We had been peppered with thirty-one holes, but no one had been hit. And then, as we circled, taking the usual pictures of the evidence of the kill, one of my gunners arrived with his hands stained red.

"Someone has been badly hit," he said. "There's blood running down the floor of the aircraft."

"It's none of us," I said. "We must have a stowaway then. Go and check where the blood is coming from."

He came back laughing. "It's all right. It's not blood, it's port," he said. "Some flak's gone through that case you bought in Gibraltar."

Yet another new device with which we were equipped as the war was stepped up against submarines was the Leigh-Light. After my experience at Farnborough of trailing flares to light up night raiders, I had some misgivings about the idea from the beginning. The Leigh-Light was a powerful narrow searchlight fitted out under the wingtip so that we could illuminate and attack enemy submarines at night.

Wondering whether the fact had occurred to anyone else, apart from myself, that we were also lighting up ourselves as a beacon to enemy fighters, I took the Leigh-Light out on the first patrol.

All the way down to Gibraltar and back we lit up, much against their will, our own ships and neutral ships but never a submarine.

It was four o'clock in the morning when the quiet of the patrol suddenly erupted.

"Weave, skipper," said the rear-gunner. "Enemy aircraft following us. More than one." Next moment our guns started barking as I took the Liberator down in diving turns to the sea.

There were five of them, maintaining by radar and rearward-facing light, a perfect, tight formation. For over half an hour we kept up a running fight, and then the last of our guns ran out of ammunition. We had not a shot to fire in self-defence.

There was nothing to do but keep on running, twisting, turning, evading, hoping against hope, that our S.O.S.s might bring aid in time. The memory of the S.O.S. I had picked up on my first trip, from the Fortress attacked by the nine Ju-88s, the recollection of the oil, and the dinghy, and the pigeon—all that had been left to greet us—came back to me. Now I was almost at the end of my twelve months' operational tour. It was so often the way; an ironic fate that waited right until the very end, until you were starting to think that there might be a future after all, before claiming you.

Still the five enemy fighters hung on, keeping perfect copy-book formation as they attacked, broke off, and circled to the attack again. It was that maintenance of formation that suddenly gave me the idea. If I could keep up a series of steep climbing and diving turns, the Huns on my tail would have to pay more attention to their flying, and that would mean less attention to our Liberator.

My arms and shoulders ached as it was, and I was in a cold sweat, near to exhaustion from the strain of twisting and turning the heavy aircraft. Already my second pilot had had to relieve me for brief intervals. Together we buckled to again, standing and turning the Liberator on her tail, diving and turning her on her nose with one eye kept warily on the sea. For fifteen minutes the enemy fighters kept up with a follow-my-leader pursuit; and then as I waited, tense and ready to act, the warning "Attack from green quarter, here they come," that had sounded over the intercom. at monotonously regular intervals for the past fifty minutes, no longer sounded. The silence grew and grew until there was no doubt about it. We had in truth shaken them off.

It seemed incredible when we got back to St. Eval that we could count only nine bullet holes in the aircraft.

We were back; and soon afterwards my posting arrived. I was to take over command of a new station opening at Langham. It meant ordering small "scrambled eggs"[2] for my cap. I hoped my bank account would be able to stand the cost of the gold braid.

[2]"Scrambled eggs": the gold braid worn by Group-Captains and high-ranking officers.

The Long Walk

by SLAVOMIR RAWICZ

Of all the many stories recorded by the heroic, unhappy Poles—who first sustained the full fury of Nazism at war—The Long Walk is one of the most moving. Slavomir Rawicz, captured after the brief Polish campaign, was sent to a Siberian concentration camp. With six comrades, two compatriots, two Balts, a Yugoslav and "Mr. Smith", an American, he escaped in the early spring of 1941.

The little group marched steadily southward, through Siberia, Mongolia, across the Gobi and Tibet, to India, a journey of some 6,000 miles covered on foot, and carried out with none but the rudest, most home-made of equipment, without stores, without even a map. Near Lake Baikal they fell in with a Polish girl who joined the little band.

Of the eight, only four reached the haven of India; four succumbed to the rigours of near-starvation, lack of water, extremes of heat and cold. At the time of this passage, they are crossing the Gobi Desert.

Two days without water in the hillocky, sand-covered, August furnace of the Gobi and I felt the first flutterings of fear. The early rays of the sun rising over the rim of the world dispersed the sharp chill of the desert night. The light hit the tops of the billowing dunes and threw sharp shadows across the deep-sanded floors of the intervening little valleys. Fear came with small fast-beating wings and was suppressed as we sucked pebbles and dragged our feet on to make maximum distance before the blinding heat of noon. From time to time one or other of us would climb one of the endless knolls and look south to see the same deadly landscape stretching to the horizon. Towards midday we stuck our long clubs in the sand and draped our jackets over them to make a shelter. Alarm about our position must have been general but no one voiced it. My own feeling was that we must not frighten the girl and I am sure the others kept silent for the same reason.

The heat enveloped us, sucking the moisture from our bodies, putting ankle-irons of lethargy about our legs. Each one of us walked with his and her own thoughts and none spoke, dully concentrating on placing one foot ahead of the other interminably. Most often I led the way, Kolemenos and the girl nearest to me and the others bunched together a few yards behind. I was driving them now, making them get to their feet in the mornings, forcing them to cut short the noon rest. As we still walked in the rays of the setting sun the fear hit me again. It was, of course, the fundamental, most oppressive fear of all, that we should die here in the burning wilderness. I struggled against a panicky impulse to urge a return the way we had come, back to water and green things and life. I fought it down.

We flopped out against a tall dune and the cold stars came out to look at us. Our bone-weariness should have ensured the sleep of exhaustion but, tortured with thirst, one after another twisted restlessly, rose, wandered around and came back. Some time after midnight I suggested we start off again to take advantage of the cool conditions. Everybody seemed to be awake. We hauled ourselves upright and began again the trudge south. It was much easier going. We rested a couple of hours after dawn, and still the southerly prospect remained unaltered.

After this one trial there were no more night marches. Makowski stopped it.

"Can you plot your course by the stars?" he asked me. The others turned haggard faces towards me.

I paused before answering. "Not with complete certainty," I confessed.

"Can any of us?" he persisted. No one spoke.

"Then we could have been walking in circles all through the night," he said heavily.

I sensed the awful dismay his words had caused. I protested that I was sure we had not veered off course, that the rising sun had proved us still to be facing south. But in my own mind, even as I argued, I had to admit the possibility that Makowski was right. In any case, the seed of doubt had been sown and we just could not afford to add anything to the already heavy burden of apprehension.

So we went on through the shimmering stillness. Not even a faint zephyr of air came up to disperse the fine dust hanging almost unseen above the desert, the dust that coated our faces and beards, entered into our cracked lips and reddened the rims of eyes already sore tried by the stark brightness of the sun.

The severely-rationed dried fish gave out on about the fifth day and still we faced a lifeless horizon. In all this arid world only eight struggling human specks and an occasional snake were alive. We could have ceased to move quite easily and lain there and died. The temptation to extend the noonday halt, to go on dozing through the hot afternoon until the sun dropped out of sight, invited our dry, aching bodies. Our feet were in a pitiable state as the burning sand struck through the thin soles of our worn moccasins. I found myself croaking at the others to get up and keep going. There is nothing here, I would say. There is nothing for days behind us. Ahead there must be something. There must be *something*. Kristina would stand up and join me, and Kolemenos. Then the others in a bunch. Like automatons we would be under way again, heads bent down, silent, thinking God knows what, but moving one foot ahead of the other hour after desperate hour.

On the sixth day the girl stumbled and, on her knees, looked up at me. "That was foolish of me, Slav. I tripped myself up." She did not wait for my assistance. She rose slowly from the sand and stepped out beside me. That afternoon I found to my faint surprise and irritation I was on my knees. I had not been conscious of the act of falling. One moment I was walking, the next I had stopped. On my knees, I thought . . . like a man at prayer.

I got up. No one had slackened pace for me. They probably hardly noticed my stumble. It seemed to take me a very long time to regain my position at the head again. Others were falling, too, I noticed from time to time. The knees gave and they knelt there a few unbelieving seconds until realization came that they had ceased to be mobile. They came on again. There was no dropping out. These were the signs of growing, strength-sapping weakness, but it would have been fatal to have acknowledged them for what they were. They were the probing fingers of death and we were not ready to die yet.

The sun rose on the seventh day in a symphony of suffused pinks and gold. Already we had been plodding forward for an hour in the pale light of the false dawn and dully I looked at Kristina and the other shambling figures behind me and was struck by the unconquerable spirit of them all. Progress now was a shuffle; the effort to pick up the feet was beyond our strength.

Without much hope we watched Kolemenos climb laboriously to the top of a high mound. One or other of us did this every morning as soon as the light was sufficient to give clear visibility southwards to the horizon. He stood there for quite a minute with his hand over his eyes, and we kept walking, expecting the usual hopeless shrug of the shoulders. But Kolemenos made no move to come down, and because he was staring intently in one direction, a few degrees to the east of our course, I dragged to a stop. I felt Kristina's hand lightly on my arm. She, too, was gazing up at Kolemenos. Everybody halted. We saw him rub his eyes, shake his head slowly and resume his intent peering in the same direction, eyes screwed up. I wanted to shout to him but stayed quiet. Instead I started to climb up to him. Zaro and the girl came with me. Behind came the American and Marchinkovas. The two Poles, Paluchowicz and Makowski, leaned on their clubs and watched us go.

As I reached Kolemenos I was telling myself: "It will be nothing. I must not get excited. It surely can't be anything."

My heart was pounding with the exertion of the slight climb.

Kolemenos made no sound. He flung out his right arm and pointed. My sight blurred over. For some seconds I could not focus. I did what I had seen Kolemenos do. I rubbed my eyes and looked again. There was *something*, a dark patch against the light sand. It might have been five miles distant from us. Through the dancing early morning haze it was shapeless and defied recognition. Excitement grew as we looked. We began to talk, to speculate. Panting and blowing, the two Poles came up to us. They, too, located the thing.

"Could it be an animal?" asked the Sergeant.

"Whatever it is, it is not sand," Mister Smith replied. "Let's go and investigate."

It took us a good two hours to make the intervening distance. Many times we lost sight of the thing we sought as we plunged along in the sandy depressions. We climbed more often than we would otherwise have done because we could not bear the idea that somehow the smudge on the landscape might disappear while we were cut off from view of it. It began to take shape and definition and hope began to well up in us. And hope became certainty. There were *trees*—real, live, growing, healthy trees, in a clump, outlined against the sand like a blob of ink on a fresh-laundered tablecloth.

"Where there are trees there is water," said the American.

"An oasis," somebody shouted, and the word fluttered from mouth to mouth.

Kristina whispered, "It is a miracle. God has saved us."

If we could have run we would have done so. We toiled that last half-mile as fast as we could flog our legs along. I went sprawling a few times. My tongue was dry and swollen in my mouth. The trees loomed larger and I saw they were palms. In their shade was a sunken hollow, roughly oval-shaped, and I knew this must be water. A few hundred yards from the oasis we crossed an east-west caravan track. On the fringe of the trees we passed an incongruous pile of what looked like rusting biscuit tins like some fantastic mid-desert junk yard. In the last twenty yards we quickened our pace and I think we managed a lope that was very near a run.

The trees, a dozen or more of them, were arranged in a crescent on the south side of the pool, and threw their shadow over it for most part of the day. The wonderful cool water lay still and inviting in an elliptical depression hemmed round with big, rough-worked stones. At this time, probably the hottest season, the limits of the water had receded inwards from the stone ring, and we had to climb over to reach it. The whole, green, life-giving spot could have been contained inside half an acre.

Zaro had the mug but we could not wait for him to fill it and hand it round. We lay over the water lapping at it and sucking it in like animals. We allowed it to caress our fevered faces. We dabbed it around our necks. We drank until someone uttered the warning about filling our empty bellies with too much liquid. Then we soaked our food sacks and, sitting on the big stones, gently laved our cracked and lacerated feet. For blissful minutes we sat with the wet sacking draped about our feet. With a mugful of water at a time we rinsed from our heads and upper bodies some of the accumulated sand and dust of the six-and-a-half days of travail. The very feel and presence of water was an ecstasy. Our spirits zoomed. We had walked out of an abyss of fear into life and new hope. We chatted and laughed as though the liquid we had drunk was heady champagne. We wondered what hands had brought these stones and planted these palms to make of this miraculous pool a sign that could be seen from afar by thirst-tortured men.

The full extent of our good fortune was yet to be discovered. Some twenty yards east of the pool, on the opposite side from which we had approached, there were the remains of a still-warm fire and the fresh tracks of camels and many hoof-marks, telling of the recent halt of a big caravan. It had probably departed at sunrise. These men, whoever they were, had cooked and eaten meat, and the bones, as yet quite fresh and untainted, were scattered around the wood ashes. They were the bones of large and one small animal and the meat had been sliced from them with knives, leaving small, succulent pieces still adhering. We shared out the bones and tore at them with our teeth, lauding our luck. Poor toothless Paluchowicz borrowed the knife from me and did as well as anybody. When there was no more meat we cracked each bone with the axe and sucked out the marrow.

Inevitably came the question of when to depart. Two of our problems were insoluble. The oasis had water but no food. We had nothing in which to carry water, except our metal mug. Makowski argued that if we waited here a few days we stood a chance of meeting a caravan and securing ourselves a stock of food for the next stage. But I wanted to go. I said that, as we had just missed one caravan, there might not be another for weeks. We would wait on for days until we were too weak from lack of food to move at all and the next travellers might find us dead from starvation. In the light of what was to come, I hope I may be forgiven for my insistence. Yet I think I may have been right. But there is no way of judging the issue now, nor was there then. There was no acrimony about the debate. We were in desperate straits and we had to decide immediately one way or the other. The thing was decided that evening. We would set out before dawn.

We were on our way when the sun came up and for half a day we could look back and see the trees of the oasis. I was glad when I could no longer see their shape against the skyline. For hours Zaro carried the mug, one hand underneath, the other over the top. He had filled it with water after we had all taken our final drinks and as he walked it slopped warm against his palm and little trickles escaped down the sides. When we halted at midday he had lost nearly half the quantity through spilling and evaporation and was complaining about the cramping of his arms in holding so tightly to the can. So, very carefully, sitting up under the small shade of our jackets slung over our clubs, we handed the water round and disposed of it a sip at a time.

This was the pre-oasis journey all over again, but this time we were deprived of even the scant sustenance of a few dried fish. For the first three days I thought we moved surprisingly well. On the fourth day the inescapable, strength-draining heat began quite suddenly to take its toll. Stumbles and falls became increasingly frequent, the pace slowed, speech dried up into short grunted phrases. I remember Makowski saying, "Hell can't be hotter than this bloody desert."

On the fifth day Kristina went to her knees. I turned slowly round to look at her, expecting her to get to her feet as she had done before. She remained kneeling, her fair head bowed down on her chest. She was very still. I moved towards her and Kolemenos stepped back at the same time. Before we could reach her she swayed from the hips and slumped forward, her face in the sand. We reached her at the same time and turned her on her back. She was unconscious. I opened the neck of her dress and started talking to her, gently shaking her, while Mister Smith set to with sticks and *fufaikas* to make shade for her.

She came to quickly. She looked at our anxious ring of faces, sat up, smiled through split lips and said, "I feel better now. I must have fallen over—I don't know how it happened."

"Don't worry," I consoled her, "We'll rest here a while and then you'll be all right again."

She leaned forward and lightly patted the back of my hand. "I won't fall down again."

We sat there a while. Kristina reached down to scratch her ankle and my eyes idly followed the hand. The ankle was swollen so that the skin pressed outward against the narrow-fitting ends of her padded trousers.

"Has anything bitten you, Kristina?"

"No, Slav. Why?"

"Your leg looks swollen."

She pulled up the trouser-leg and looked, turning her foot about as she did so. "I hadn't noticed it before," she said.

We struggled on for a couple more hours. She seemed to be refreshed. Then she fell again and this time her knees buckled and her face hit the sand in almost one movement without even the action of putting her arms out to break the fall.

We turned her over again and wiped away the sand which had been forced into her nose and mouth. We put up the shelter. She lay with eyes closed, breathing in harsh gasps through her mouth. I looked at her ankles and they were a pitiful sight. Both were badly discoloured and so swollen that it seemed they would burst the restricting bottoms of the trousers. I took out my knife and slit the cloth upwards. The skin appeared to be distended by water right up to the knees. I touched the swelling and the mark of my fingers remained for some seconds.

Kristina was unconscious for an hour while we tried to stifle our gnawing anxiety with banalities like: "It must be just a touch of sunstroke." I had a feeling like lead in the pit of my stomach. I was frightened.

She was quite cheerful when she came round. "I am becoming a nuisance," she said. "What can be the matter with me?" We fussed around her.

Kristina got to her feet. "Come on. We are wasting time."

I walked alongside her. She stopped suddenly and glanced down at her legs, her attention attracted by the flapping of slit trousers about her legs.

"My legs are getting quite thick, Slav."

"Do they hurt you, Kristina?"

"No, not at all. They must be swelling because I have walked so far."

The time was afternoon on the fifth day. She walked on for hours without more than an occasional small stumble and was still keeping up with Kolemenos and me when the sun had gone and we stopped for the night. Sitting there among us she stole frequent looks at her legs. She said nothing and we affected not to notice. It was a disturbed night. All except Kolemenos seemed too weary and worried for sleep. Kristina lay still but I sensed she remained awake. I chewed on the pebble in my mouth. My teeth ached, my gums were enlarged and tender. Thoughts of flowing water constantly invaded my mind. I had clear pictures of the sampans I had seen on those northern rivers. I had little fits of shivering that made me stand up and walk around. My head felt constricted. I ached from head to foot.

For the first two hours of the sixth day the air was cool and walking was as pleasant as ever it can be in the desert. But soon the sun began to blaze at us out of a sky empty of clouds.

I took Kristina's elbow. "Can you keep going in this?"

"Yes, I think so."

Five minutes later she folded up and was out, face down in the sand. Again we ministered to her and waited for her to open her eyes. She appeared to be breathing quite normally, like a tired child.

I stood a few steps away from her and the others came over to me. "She is very swollen," I said. "Do any of you know what this means?" Nobody knew the symptoms. We went back to her and waited. I flapped my cap over her face to make some air.

She smiled at us. "I am being a trouble again." We shook our heads. "I am afraid you had better leave me this time."

We all broke into protest at once. Kolemenos dropped down on his knees beside her. "Don't say that. Don't be a silly little girl. We shall never leave you." She lay there for another half an hour and when she tried to force herself up on her elbows she fell back again.

I spoke to Kolemenos. "We must give her a hand." We lifted her to her feet. "I can walk if you stay near me," she said.

Amazingly she walked, Kolemenos and I lightly holding her elbows. After a quarter of a mile we felt her start to fall forward. We steadied her and she went on again. She pulled herself erect and there was not a sound of distress, not a whimper. The next time she slumped forward we could not hold her. She had played herself utterly out and even the gallant will in that frail body could not produce another torturing effort. We were all in a bunch around her as the sun climbed up over our heads. Kolemenos and I each put an arm about her and, half-carrying, half-dragging her, set off again. A mile or so of that and I had no reserve of strength to give her. We stopped and I bent double fighting for breath.

"Stick beside me, Slav," said Kolemenos. "I am going to carry her." And he lifted her into his arms, swayed for a moment as he adjusted himself to the weight, and staggered off. He carried her for fully two hundred yards and I was there to ease her down when he paused for a rest.

"Please leave me, Anastazi," she begged. "You are wasting your strength." He looked at her but could not bring himself to speak.

We made a shelter there and stayed for perhaps three hours through the worst heat of the day. She lay still—I do not think she could move. The ugly swelling was past the knees and heavy with water. Kolemenos was flat on his back, restoring his strength. He knew what he was going to do.

The sun began to decline. Kolemenos bent down and swung her into his arms and trudged off. I stayed with him and the rest were all about us. He covered fully a quarter of a mile before he put her down that first time. He picked her up again and walked, her head pillowed on his great shoulder. I can never in my life see anything so magnificent as the blond-bearded giant Kolemenos carrying Kristina, hour after hour, towards darkness of that awful sixth day. His ordeal lasted some four hours. Then she touched his cheek.

"Put me on the ground, Anastazi. Just lay me down on the ground."

I took her weight from him and together we eased her down. We gathered round her. A wisp of a smile hovered about the corners of her mouth. She looked very steadily at each one of us in turn and I thought she was going to speak. Her eyes were clear and very blue. There was a great tranquillity about her. She closed her eyes.

"She must be very tired," said Sergeant Paluchowicz. "The poor, tired little girl."

We stood around for several minutes, dispirited and at a loss to know what to do next. The shoulders of Kolemenos were sagging with exhaustion. We exchanged glances but could think of nothing to say. I looked down at Kristina. I looked at the open neck of her dress, and in a second I was down at her side with my ear over her heart. There was no beat. I did not believe it. I turned my head and applied the other ear. I lifted my head and picked up her thin wrist. There was no pulse. They were all looking at me intently. I dropped her hand and it thumped softly into the sand.

The American spoke, hardly above a whisper. I tried to answer but the words would not come. Instead the tears came, the bitter salt tears. And the sobs were torn from me. In that God-forsaken place seven men cried openly because the thing most precious to us in all the world had been taken from us. Kristina was dead.

I think we were half crazy there beside her body in the desert. We accused ourselves of having brought her here to her death. More personally, Makowski, speaking in Polish, blamed me for having insisted on leaving the shelter of the oasis.

The American intervened, his voice cold and flat. "Gentlemen, it is no use blaming ourselves. I think she was happy with us." The talk ceased. He went on, "Let us now give her a decent burial."

We scraped a hole in the sand at the base of a dune. Little pieces of stone that we sifted from the grains as we dug deeper we laid apart. I slit open a food sack and laid the double end gently under her chin. We lowered the body. On her breast lay her little crucifix. We stood around with our caps in our hands. There was no service, but each man spoke a prayer in his own language. Mister Smith spoke in English, the first time I had heard him use it. I opened out the sacking and lifted it over her face and I could not see for tears. We covered her with sand and we dotted the mound round with the little stones.

And Kolemenos took her tall stick and copped a piece off it with his axe and bound the one piece to the other with a leather thong to make a cross.

So we said goodbye to her and went our empty way.

*   *   *

Early next morning we piled our *fufaikas* in a mound, split into two trios and set off in opposite directions along the creek. Kolemenos, the American and I in one party walked a mile or more eastward and found nothing. At times the water-course disappeared entirely, as though it had gone underground. When we found it again it was still only a damp trail. Reluctantly we concluded that if there were flowing water it must be in some spring below ground and inaccessible to us. Two remarkably healthy-looking snakes were the only sign of life we encountered. We turned back and arrived at the meeting point. We had some time to wait for Zaro, Marchinkovas and Paluchowicz and had begun to entertain some hopes that their delayed return might mean good tidings when we saw them approaching. Zaro stretched out his hands palms downwards to indicate that the investigation had produced nothing.

"No luck," said Marchinkovas as they came up to us.

"We found nothing, either," I told them.

We drank some more of the brown, turgid water. We bathed our feet again and watched the sun mounting in the sky.

Kolemenos spoke. "All this bloody desert and only us and a few snakes to enjoy it. They can't eat us and we can't eat them."

"Only half-true, that statement." It was Mister Smith. "It is not unknown for men to eat snakes."

There was an immediate ripple of interest.

Mister Smith stroked his grey beard thoughtfully. "American Indians eat them. I have seen tourists in America tempted into trying them. I never tried to eat snake myself. I suppose it's a natural human revulsion against reptiles."

We sat in silence a while thinking over what he had said.

He broke in on our thoughts. "You know, gentlemen, I think snakes are our only chance. There's hardly anything a starving man can't eat."

The idea fascinated and repelled at the same time. We talked for a while about it but I think we all knew we were going to make the experiment. There was no choice.

"We need a forked stick to catch them," said Marchinkovas, "and we haven't got one." ·

"No difficulty about that," I told him. "We'll split the bottoms of a couple of our sticks and jam a small pebble into the cleft."

Kolemenos got up off his haunches. "Let's make a start with the sticks straight away."

We decided to use Zaro's and Paluchowicz's. The splitting was done by Kolemenos with the axe. The wood was bound with thongs above the split and the small stones rammed home. The result was two efficient-looking instruments.

"How shall we know if the snakes are poisonous? Shall we be able to eat the poisonous kind?" This was Paluchowicz, and he was echoing a doubt that existed in most of our minds.

"There is nothing to worry about," said the American. "The poison is contained in a sac at the back of the head. When you cut off the head you will have removed the poison."

Apart from catching our meal, there remained one problem —fuel for a fire to do the cooking. We turned out our bags for the bits of tinder we always carried. Heaped together the pile was bigger than we had expected. From the bottom of his sack Zaro brought out three or four pats of dried animal dung and solemnly placed them on the collection of hoarded fuel. On another occasion we might have laughed, but smiling through split lips was painful.

"I picked it up at the oasis," said Zaro. "I thought it might be needed for fires some time."

I was sorry that we all had not done as Zaro had done back there. This dried animal waste was excellent fuel which burned slowly and produced fair heat. There had been occasions, too, since the oasis when we had come across little heaps of sun-dried debris deposited by the swirling, dancing whirlwinds which we had seen spiralling across the desert. But we had been too intent on our plodding progress to stop and gather these tiny harvests of the wind. From now on the search for tinder was to be a preoccupation ranking almost in importance with the hunt for snakes.

Smith and I got down to the job of preparing a fire while the others went off with the two forked sticks. We scratched down through the powdery top sand to the layer of bigger grains below and through that to the bed of small stones underneath. We were looking for a thin flat stone on which to cook our snake. It was fully an hour before we found one. Among the surrounding dunes we had glimpses of the others creeping quietly around in their quest for some unsuspecting reptile. In the way of things in this life, they spent a couple of hours without seeing a sign of one. When we cared nothing for them we seemed always to be finding them.

The fire was laid. In the blazing sun the flat stone seemed already hot enough for cooking (certainly I think it would have fried an egg easily). Marchinkovas came back to us drop-shouldered. "The snakes must have heard we had changed our minds about them," he said wryly. The three of us sat around the unlighted fire in silence for about another half an hour. There came suddenly a great yell from Zaro. We could not see him but we saw Kolemenos and Paluchowicz running in the direction of the sound. We got up and ran, too.

About fifty yards away Zaro had his snake. His stick was firmly about the writhing body a couple of inches behind the head and Zaro was sweating with the exertion of holding it there. We could not judge the size of the creature because all but about six inches of it was hidden in a hole in the sand and the wriggling power of the concealed length was slowly inching the stick back towards the hole. We were tired, weak, slow and clumsy and we ran around and got in one another's way in an effort to help Zaro. Then Paluchowicz jabbed his stick a couple inches behind Zaro's. I pulled a thong from about my waist, slipped a loop about the snake against the hole and heaved. But there was too much snake inside and too little outside. It was stalemate.

Kolemenos settled the issue. The bright blade of his axe swished down and separated the snake's head from its body. The still-wriggling length was hauled into the sunlight. The thing was nearly four feet long. It was as thick as a man's wrist, black above, with a creamy-brown belly lightening to a dull cream-white at the throat.

Zaro struck a pose. "There's your dinner, boys."

The thing still twitched as we carried it back to the fire. We laid it on my sack and, under the direction of the American, I started to skin it. The beginning of the operation was tricky. Smith said the skin could be peeled off entire but I could get no grip at the neck. Eventually I slit the skin a few inches down and with difficulty started to part the snake from its tight sheath. I had never seen an unclothed snake before. The flesh was whitish at first, but in the sun it turned a little darker while we waited for the fire to bring the flat stone to the right heat. We cut the body lengthwise and cleaned it out.

There was still a little reflex of life left as we curled the meat up on the stone over the fire. It sizzled pleasantly. Fat trickled down off the stone and made the fire spit. We streamed sweat as we sat around the fire. We could not take our eyes off the snake. With our sticks we lifted the stone off, burned the meat and put it back for the final stage of grilling. When we thought it was ready to eat we lifted it, stone and all, on to the sand to cool a little.

It lay eventually on my sack a yard or two away from the dying fire. We squatted round it but nobody seemed in a hurry to start carving it up. We looked at one another. Kolemenos spoke. "I am bloody hungry." He reached forward. We all went for it at the same time. Paluchowicz, the man without teeth, stretched his hand out to me for the knife. We ate. It was not long before the snake was reduced to a skeleton. The flesh was close-packed and filling. I had thought the taste might be powerful, even noxious. It was in fact mild, almost tasteless. It had no odour. I was faintly reminded of boiled, unseasoned fish.

"I wish I had thought of snakes earlier," said Mister Smith.

We drank some more of the muddy water. We watched the sun drop from its zenith. We knew that soon we must move again, and we were reluctant to go, to leave this precious ribbon of moisture and launch out again into the unknown, heat-baked country ahead. Sprawled out there, my stomach rumbling as it contended with its barbaric new meal, I longed for a smoke. We still had newspaper but the tobacco had long gone.

No one wanted to bring up the subject of when we should leave, so we talked about other things. For the first time we exchanged ideas freely about Kristina and Makowski. Why should death have overtaken them and left the rest of us still with the strength to carry on? There was no answer to this question, but we mulled it over. We talked of them with sadness and affection. It was, I suppose, an act of remembrance for two absent friends. And it took some of the heavy load of their great loss from us.

I found myself looking at the five of them, taking stock of them, trying to assess our chances. We were all sick men. Kolemenos had his moccasins off and I could see the inflamed raw patches where blisters had formed on punctured blisters, and I knew he was no worse off in this respect than any other of us. All our faces were so disfigured that our nearest relatives would have had difficulty in recognizing us. Lips were grotesquely swollen and deeply fissured. Cheeks had sunk in. Brows overhung red-rimmed eyes which seemed to have fallen back in their sockets. We were in an advanced state of scurvy. Only the toothless Paluchowicz escaped the discomfort of teeth rocking loose in sore gums. Already Kolemenos had pulled two aching teeth out between finger and thumb for Marchinkovas and he was to practise his primitive dentistry several times more in the future for others of the party.

Lice, scurvy and the sun had played havoc with our skin. The lice had multiplied with the filthy prolificacy of their kind and swarmed about us. They fed and grew to an obscenely large size. We scratched and scratched at our intolerably irritated bodies until we broke the skin and then our sweat-soaked clothes and untended dirty finger-nails caused the tiny cuts to become septic. This unclean affliction, superficial though it was, was a constant source of depression and misery. I killed the lice when I caught them with savage joy. They were pre-eminently the symbol of our fugitive degradation.

In the end no one took the initiative over our departure. There came a time when Kolemenos and Zaro stood up together. We all rose. We adjusted the wire loops about our necks, picked up our sacks. Into my sack went the flat cooking stone. The American carefully stowed away the little pile of fuel. Grimacing, Kolemenos pulled on his moccasins. We drank a little more water. And in the later afternoon we started off.

Many miles we walked that day, until the light of day faded out and until the stars came out in a purple-black sky. We slept huddled close together and were awake before dawn to start again.

Half an hour later Paluchowicz stopped with a groan, clutching his belly, doubled up. In the next hour we were all seized with the most violent, gripping pains. All of us were assailed with diarrhoea of an intensity that left us weak and groaning. With the frequent stops we could not have covered more than five miles by late afternoon, when the attacks began to subside.

What had caused it—the snake-meat or the water? We asked one another this question.

Said Mister Smith, "It might well have been the dirty water. But most probably it arises simply from the fact that our empty stomachs are reacting against the sudden load of food and water."

"There's one good way to find out," Kolemenos said. "We'll eat some more snake. I am still hungry."

Marchinkovas shrugged his shoulders. "It will be snakes or nothing."

Paluchowicz gasped with another spasm of stomach-ache.

"May God help us," he said fervently.

The Little Ships

by GORDON HOLMAN

The Little Ships, *by Gordon Holman, a distinguished war-correspondent,
who wrote himself on to the front pages of the world with his despatches
from the raid on St. Nazaire, deals with the successors in the Second World
War of the Q-ships of the First World War. Although Q-ships were
appreciably bigger, the fire, the dash, the excitement makes them, if not the
lineal, at the least the spiritual, heirs of the earliest anti-submarine vessels.*

*The "little ships"—motor gun-boats, motor torpedo-boats, motor-
launches—were essentially coastal craft, but it was the enemy coast they
harried, far more than their own which they defended.*

Some of them were made of wood: the wooden walls come again.

IT IS noteworthy that, at this early stage,[1] the battle honours
were shared by Royal Navy, Royal Naval Reserve, Royal
Naval Volunteer Reserve, Royal Canadian Navy Volunteer
Reserve and Royal Norwegian Navy personnel.

The action took place in the Channel when a small force of
our light craft on patrol intercepted two large enemy supply
ships with an escort of armed trawlers and E-boats. The enemy
were considerably stronger than our patrol. The British craft
shadowed the enemy for some time and then carried out the
first attack just before midnight. A torpedo crashed into one of
the supply ships of about 3,500 tons. The ship was badly damaged and, according to the subsequent Admiralty communiqué,
probably sunk.

[1] In 1940-41. "Motor gun-boats" were first mentioned in an official Admiralty
communiqué early in 1942, but they were operating long before that date.

The Germans opened a heavy fire on our little ships but the attack was pressed home although the enemy coast was less than three miles away. A pitched battle took place between our craft and the strong escort forces of the convoy. As a result one E-boat was sunk and an armed trawler set on fire. Meanwhile the convoy was still being shadowed, although additional German E-boats had come out to the aid of the hard-pressed escort. The enemy were blazing away with their 37-mm. guns, but they did no damage to the British force, except to wound slightly two gunners.

A second attack was carried out on the convoy with even more satisfying results than the first. The second supply ship, a vessel of about 4,000 tons, was torpedoed and blew up. Air reconnaissance the following morning confirmed that the ship was sunk, the masts of a new wreck being seen, with much wreckage around on the sea.

In the latter part of the action one of our boats was hit and set on fire in the engine-room. The engineers, half suffocated, were dragged out on deck and then, although the engines were stopped and the boat was under heavy fire, one of the crew got down on the deck and, leaning over the side of the boat, thrust the nozzle of an extinguisher through the hole in the side of the vessel made by the exploding shell and put out the fire. Still the boat remained a fine target for the enemy, but the engineers went back and worked on their engines until they got them going again. The boat got back to England.

*　　*　　*

The Polish people had taken a keen interest in the fast little ships and from public contributions started before the war it was planned to build four vessels.

The most notable of all the actions in which Polish light craft have taken part was one of the many fought in the summer of 1942. It earned for the Commanding Officer of the boat concerned the title of "the little Nelson". It was on a night when British light forces were engaging the enemy in the Channel. The Polish M.G.B. was carrying out a reconnaissance to the eastward of the British patrols when she sighted six German E-boats. Earlier there had been another Polish gun-boat with the S.2, the hero of the party. This other vessel, the S.3, had had engine trouble and returned to harbour.

A signal got through to the S.2 at about 1 a.m. instructing her to return to her base, or join up with our other forces, as a strong enemy force was in the vicinity. It was then that the Polish Commanding Officer earned his title. He turned a "blind eye" to the signal, with the pretence that it had not been properly understood. It was shortly after that that the E-boats were sighted. Although support could have been obtained the Polish M.G.B. attacked single-handed and with such fierceness that the vastly superior enemy force was scattered. Some of the E-boats were damaged by the gunfire of the gallant little Polish ship.

The Germans then realized their own overwhelming superiority and endeavoured to encircle the S.2. But the Polish crew fought with such desperate courage that the Germans, again in confusion, fired on each other. At least one E-boat was set on fire and two badly damaged. The S.2, satisfied with a good night's work, broke off the action and headed for home, having suffered only superficial damage and no casualties.

As she made for England the Polish gun-boat met British M.G.B.s racing to her aid, followed, a little later, by the S.3, who, despite her engine trouble, was determined to fight with her sister ship if she could possibly get to the scene of action in time.

It is said that a very senior officer, congratulating the Polish Commanding Officer on his success and magnificent fighting spirit, remarked dryly that "the Nelson touch was not always guaranteed to produce such happy results". They were happy results, however, for the Commander, because he received, in due course, the award of the D.S.C. and the Polish Virtuti Militari.

★   ★   ★

Richards,[2] Sidebottom[3] and Lloyd[4] marked up further successes during August, 1942. Richards and Sidebottom met five or six R-boats in the Straits of Dover. Richards set one of them on fire and, when she sank, picked up fifteen ratings as prisoners-of-war. The Commander of the German boat was killed. Sidebottom went in and rammed one of the R-boats. Although the enemy vessel was not seen to sink, she was so badly damaged that it was thought unlikely that she got back to her base.

Lloyd, still nosing around off the Dutch coast, met up with four German flak ships off Flushing. With his remarkable capacity for seeing at night, he got a torpedo into one of the flak-ships, which was probably sunk. The other flak-ships were shot up and then Lloyd returned to his base to report, and say, as he had often said before, "No casualties".

Around this time there happened an incident which typifies the audaciousness of these light forces. One moonlight night the Germans, keeping a keen look-out from the French coast, sighted a little vessel cruising along quietly about three miles off shore. It followed such a steady and unworried course, although well within range of the shore batteries, that they could not believe that it was an enemy craft. On the other hand, they had no notification that any of their own forces were to pass that way at that time. This ship was so small that it was possible they had forgotten to send the usual notice about her movements. A signal lamp flicked out an inquiry.

The little vessel at once acknowledged the challenger. Her signal lamp spoke in return. As they deciphered the dots and dashes the astonished Huns read, "H-E-I-L C-H-U-R-C-H-I-L-L!"

[2] The late Lieut. G. D. K. Richards.

[3] Lieut. Sidebottom.

[4] Lieut. H. L. ("Harpy") Lloyd.

By the time the searchlights had switched on and the guns had started to train, the British M.L., for so it was, was "hopping it" out to sea.

A vessel of the Fifth M.L. Flotilla was responsible for this escapade and it is understandable why they received the name of the "Fighting Fifth". The young R.N.R. officer who was in command of the boat which so coolly affronted the Nazis was the only one at that time in this flotilla who was not R.N.V.R. Every boat had seen some action and one had a record of twelve engagements with aircraft and several other fights with surface craft in less than six months.

★　　　★　　　★

German E-boats were out in force and another of our patrols, led by Lieut. J. B. R. Horne, R.N., met four of them and severely handled one before they got away in the darkness. Then Lieut. Thorpe ran into an even larger mixed force of E- and R-boats. Although there were eight or nine of the enemy craft, the British vessels hit them with all the weight they could muster and at least three were seriously damaged.

One of our gun-boats was set on fire. When it was seen that there was no chance of saving her, Lieut .Thorpe skilfully ran his boat alongside the blazing ship and took off survivors. He also stopped to make sure that she would be a total loss and would not fall into the hands of the enemy, although it was broad daylight by this time and the Dutch coast was only 25 miles away.

Reference has already been made to the long and excellent record of Lieut. Thorpe, but, in addition, he should be mentioned as one of those who worked unceasingly during the days when the B.E.F. were falling back on the coast of northern France. He was then in command of a motor anti-submarine boat. Horne, too, has had more than three years in Coastal craft, after pre-war service in several ships including the cruisers *Sussex, Berwick* and *Sheffield.* His D.S.C., gazetted in May, 1942, was "for courage, skill and seamanship in action against the enemy in H.M. motor gun-boats".

As October arrived, Dickens[5] was at it again in an action fought with powerful escort forces off Terschelling. The first interception was made by Lieut. J. E. Dyer's patrol who attacked and torpedoed a medium-sized supply ship which blew up. Dickens' part was to close with one of our gun-boats which had been hit and stopped and which was being engaged by four enemy craft. The action was fought very close to the coast and it would have been suicidal to try to take the damaged boat in tow. But before the crew jumped aboard Dickens' boat they set their craft on fire and she was last seen burning fiercely.

Another of our boats was lost a few nights later in a fiercely-fought contest with enemy torpedo-boats and E-boats off the Belgian coast. One of the E-boats was hit and blew up.

About the middle of the month there was a fine instance of R.A.F. and naval co-operation. Coastal Command aircraft, out on an evening reconnaissance flight, sighted an enemy supply ship with a powerful escort of torpedo-boats and minesweepers. Coastal Forces were at once put on the scent and they came up with the enemy off Cap de la Hague. They went straight in with the determination of so many bull-terriers, damaged the supply ship with gunfire and set two of the escorting vessels on fire. The blaze could be seen from the English coast. The Germans were so shaken by the force of the attack that the remainder of the escort scattered and retired. Then one of our torpedo-boats hit the supply ship with two torpedoes. There was a big explosion and the enemy ship blew up. Our casualties were confined to two ratings wounded.

★　　★　　★

Two of the officers who were together in this attack were also together in the M.T.B.s that went out to give battle to the

[5]Lieut. P. G. C. Dickens, son of Admiral Sir Gerald Dickens, grandson of the novelist.

Scharnhorst and *Gneisenau*—Lieuts. Richard Saunders, D.S.C., R.A.N.V.R., and Arnold-Forster. The latter, at 22,[6] is a veteran of Coastal Forces, having won the D.S.C. and been twice mentioned in despatches. He lives at Zennor in Cornwall and, before the war, was an apprentice in an ocean-going merchant ship. Saunders was skipper of a schooner sailing from Sydney, Australia.

Explosions which practically lifted the attacking craft out of the water were described after another March success which accounted for two more supply ships. The Commanding Officer in this case was Lieut. D. G. H. Wright, D.S.C., R.N.V.R., of Northwood, Middlesex, who told this graphic story afterwards: "We had trailed the convoy for more than an hour before drawing level and turning to attack. To get the full advantage of the moon and prevent our own position being betrayed, we were forced to pick an attacking position between the convoy and the enemy coast. I picked out the three largest of the merchant ships as our targets, but before we got into position we were sighted. We were about a mile to starboard of the convoy when they threw up a tremendous barrage of flak, and the destroyer let go with all her heavy stuff. The scene was brilliantly illuminated by star-shells and tracer, augmented by flares dropped by enemy aircraft. But we pressed on to closer range and then let go our torpedoes. As we disengaged there was an unmistakable explosion which indicated a hit on one of the merchant vessels. We retreated under a tremendous shower of fire, and although the fire was pretty good and uncomfortably close, we escaped without so much as a bullet hole. The whole thing was over in a few minutes."

Lieut. J. Perkins carried out the attack on the second merchant ship alone. He found himself shut out of the first attack, so decided to shadow the other vessel until an opportunity arrived to fire off his torpedoes. They got a hit and Lieut. Perkins' comment was: "We were perhaps taking a bit of a chance by

[6] Lieut. M. Arnold-Forster, at the time of writing.

running the gauntlet alone, but perhaps the bunch of heather brought on board by my navigating officer, Lieut. Hugh Drummond, of Stirling, had something to do with our luck."

Before the end of the month Lieut.-Commander H. McL. Duff Still, R.N.V.R., Lieut. Donald G. Bradford, R.N.R., and other commanders had taken toll of the enemy. It should be made clear that although the names of commanders are mentioned here in order to identify the various actions, they would be the first to say that the credit every time is shared with every officer and rating in the flotillas they command.

Lieut. Bradford, for instance, has said of his crew: "They share with me the ambition to board an E-boat and have a hand-to-hand showdown before bringing it home." He firmly believes that he has the toughest crew in Coastal Forces. When, in company with the M.G.B. commanded by Lieut. Philip Stobo, R.N.V.R., of Rickmansworth, his craft fought a superior force of E-boats which was found lurking in our convoy lanes, Lieut. Bradford's boat rammed one of the enemy vessels. Going at full speed the British gunboat cut into the German craft about twenty feet from the stern. She heeled over at an angle of about fifty degrees and then the gunboat went right over her. By the time it had circled round again there was nothing to be seen but some floating wreckage.

Two of the crew who went through this hectic action with Bradford were having their baptism of fire—Ordinary Seaman H. Wood, of Nottingham, and Ordinary Signalman James Blair, from Roxburghshire. The Coxswain, who was at the wheel for five hours altogether, was Leading Seaman J. Phillips, of Bristol, and among the gunners were Able Seaman George Jennings, of Ilford, Essex, Able Seaman James Fleming, of Liverpool, and Able Seaman Harry Tonkin, from Cornwall. The First Lieutenant, Sub-Lieut. Frank Hewitt, of Hadley Wood, Herts, interspersed his plotting duties in the wheelhouse with dashes to the bridge to fire off pans of Lewis-gun ammunition at close range.

The only man who was not too happy about the action was Able Seaman Metcalfe, who, carrying out duties as ship's cook, had a joint of beef roasting when the fight started. He manned a gun and, when he next remembered the beef, it had been cooked to a cinder.

We Die Alone

by DAVID HOWARTH

*Jan Baalsrud, a Norwegian who escaped to Britain, undertook to go back
to the islands used by the Germans as an air-base; he was to undertake a
sabotage operation.*

*But the plans went agley; Baalsrud was left entirely on his own and con-
ducted a single-handed odyssey for weeks on end: hiding, fighting, and—
interminably—walking. He was caught in a blizzard and suffered frost-bite,
snow-blindness, pneumonia.*

*His own fortitude is beyond praise, but his story throws into high relief
the courage of those who put their own lives and their families' lives to the
hazard to succour him. They kept him hidden in their homes; then they
carried him to a hide-out in the mountains, making perilous journeys to take
him supplies, and scouring the neighbourhood for those who could help him
further.*

*This passage deals with his last ordeal—just before he was rescued and
taken across the border into neutral Sweden.*

HE[1] LAY between the snow wall and the rock for nearly three
weeks. In some ways it was better than the grave:[2] he could
see rather more of the sky, although he could not see round him
beyond the wall; and there was enough room to move about so
far as he was able. But in other ways it was worse: it was more
exposed to the wind and weather, and it was much more affected
by the change in temperature between night and day. In the
grave, it had always been a bit below freezing point. In the open,
whenever the sun broke through the clouds it melted his sleeping-
bag and the snow around him till he was soaked; and when the

[1]Baalsrud.
[2]He had been hidden in a pit only just before.

sun dipped down at night towards the north horizon, his blankets and clothes froze solid. But although this was extremely uncomfortable it never made him ill. In conditions which were more than enough to give a man pneumonia, he never even caught a cold, because there are no germs of such human diseases on the plateau.

He was well stocked with food when they left him there, and different parties of men came up from the valley every three or four days to keep him supplied. None of it struck him as very nice to eat, especially after it had been thawed and frozen several times, and he had nothing to cook with. But still, one can live without such refinements as cookery and he was very grateful for it. There was dried fish, and cod liver oil, and bread. It was a question whether the bread was worse to eat when it was wet or when it was frozen. There was also some powdered milk which had to be mixed with water. It occupied him for long hours to melt the snow between his hands so that it dripped into the cup he had been given, and then to stir the powder into it.

Later on, when the thaw began in earnest, an icicle on the rock beside him began to drip. At the full stretch of his arm, he could just reach out to put the cup under the drip, and then he would lie and watch it, counting the slow drops as they fell, and waiting in suspense as each trembled glistening on the tip. Sometimes when the cup had a little water in the bottom, the drops splashed out and half of each one was lost. When he was feeling weak, this seemed a disaster, and he would swear feebly to himself in vexation. But in the end he invented the idea of putting a lump of snow on top of the cup, so that the drops fell through it without splashing. It took hours to fill the cup. The end result, with the milk powder mixed in it cold, was a horrible drink, but it helped to keep his strength up, and he drank it as a duty.

Sometimes in those solitary days, between the chores which always kept him busy, he still had the strength of mind to laugh at the contrast between himself as he used to be and his present state of elementary existence. Looking back, his life before the war, and even in the army, seemed prim and over-fastidious. There was a certain kind of humour in the thought that he had once taken some pride in his appearance, chosen ties as if they were important, pressed his trousers, kept his hair cut, and even manicured his nails. Grubbing about in the snow for a crust of bread reminded him of a time he had had to complain in an Oslo restaurant because there was a coffee stain on the table-cloth, and of how apologetic the waiter had been when he changed it for a clean one.

It had seemed important; in fact, it had been important to him as he was in those days. If the man he had then been could have seen the man he was now, the sight would have made him sick. He had not washed or shaved or combed his hair for weeks, or taken off his clothes. He had reached that stage of filth when one's clothes seem to be part of one's body, and he smelt. But, luckily, what had happened to him in the last few weeks had changed him, and he did not mind his dirt. It had changed him more fundamentally than merely by making him dirty and ill and emaciated and crippling his legs. It had changed him so that it was quite difficult for him to recognize the spark of life which still lingered inside that feeble disgusting body as himself. He knew already that if he lived through it all he would never be the same person again. He would have lost his feet, he supposed, but he would have grown in experience. He felt he would never dare to be impatient again, that he would always be placid and tolerant, and that none of the irritations of civilized life would have the power to annoy him any more. Travel broadens the mind, he thought, and laughed out loud because the plateau was so damnably silent.

When he fell into a doze during those days, he often dreamed of wolves. This was a fear he had been spared during his first week on the plateau, because nobody had told him there were wolves up there; but there are. They sometimes attack the rein-deer herds, and the Lapps on skis fight running battles with them. They seldom, if ever, attack a man, even if he is alone, but nobody could say for certain whether they would attack a help-less man if they were hungry, as they often are in the time of the early spring. The Mandal[3] men had taken the danger seriously enough to warn Jan about it and give him a stick to defend himself. Later, when they realized that a stick was no good because he had not enough strength to beat off a rabbit with it, they brought up brushwood and paraffin so that he could fire it if the wolves closed in on him. Of course, he had a pistol, but it only had three rounds left in it, and he said he wanted to keep them for bigger game than wolves. Jan felt it was silly to be afraid of an animal, or even a pack of them, which had never actually been known to kill a man, so far as anyone could tell him. Yet the thought of it worked on his nerves. Until he was told of the wolves, he had only the inanimate forces of the plateau to contend with. He had relied on his solitude, feeling as safe from a sudden intrusion as he would in a house with the doors and windows locked. With all the dangers that surrounded him, at least he had not had to keep alert for any sudden crisis. But now, as he lay behind his wall of snow, unable to see what was happening on the snowfield around him, helplessly wrapped in his sleeping-bag, he knew he might see the sharp teeth and the pointed muzzle at any moment within a yard of him, or feel the hot breath on his face when he was sleeping, or hear the bay-ing and know they were watching him and waiting. This, more than anything, made him feel his loneliness.

In the comparatively roomy space behind the snow wall, he could wriggle one leg at a time out of the sleeping-bag and look carefully at his feet, which he had never been able to do inside the grave. They were a very disgusting sight. His toes were still worse than anything else, but the whole of each foot was so bad that it was frost-bitten right through from one side to the other between the Achilles tendon and the bone. All the way up to his knees there were patches of black and grey. He had quite given up thinking of ever being able to walk on them again. As soon

[3]The town from which he was succoured.

as he got to a hospital, he supposed, somebody would put him straight on an operating table and cut off his feet without thinking twice about it. He was resigned to that, but he still very much wanted not to lose his legs. Apart from the problems of keeping himself alive, he had thought more about his legs than anything else, wondering whether there was anything he could do to help to save them. He had made up his mind some time before about one drastic course of action, but in the grave there had not been enough room to put it into effect. He was still under the impression, rightly or wrongly, that gangrene would go on spreading, unless one got rid of it, like dry rot in a house. The source of it all was his toes. They were not part of him any more, although they were still attached to him, and it seemed only common sense that he would be better without them. There was nobody he could expect to help him; but now the time and the chance had come, and he made his preparations to cut off his toes himself.

He still had his pocket-knife, and he still had some brandy. With the brandy as anaesthetic, and the knife as a scalpel, lying curled up on his side in the snow with his leg drawn up so that he could reach it, he began carefully to dissect them one by one.

It would have been best to get it all over quickly, but apart from the pain and the sickening repulsion, it was difficult to cut them; more difficult than he had expected. He had to find the joints. His hands were rather clumsy and very weak, because there had been some frostbite in his fingers, too, and the knife was not so sharp as it had been. He grimly persevered, and slowly succeeded. As each one was finally severed, he laid it on a small ledge of rock above him where he could not see it, because he no longer had strength to throw it far away. After each one he had to stop, to get over the nausea and dope himself with brandy. Someone had brought him some cod liver oil ointment, and he smeared a thick slab of it on each wound and tied it in place with a strip of blanket.

This grisly operation was spread out over nearly three days.

At the end of it, there were nine toes on the ledge. The little toe on his left foot did not seem so bad as the others, so he kept it. When he had finished, he felt very much better in his mind. Of course, there was no immediate improvement in his legs, but it gave him some satisfaction to have done something which he hoped would help to save them; it was better to know that the rotten revolting things were gone and could not poison him any more. It made him feel cleaner.

After it was all done, he went back with relief to the simple routine of his daily life: feeding himself, collecting ice-water, mixing milk, trying to clean his pistol; once in a while as seldom as he could, rolling a cigarette with infinite care and finding the box of matches which he kept inside his underclothes next to his skin; trying to put ointment on the sores on his back without getting too cold; sometimes treating himself to a sip of brandy; and always keeping on the watch for new attacks of frost-bite. It was terribly difficult not to lie there listening, imagining the sound of skis or the distant snarl of wolves. Sometimes he stopped up his ears to keep out the ghastly silence, and sometimes he talked to himself so that there was something to listen to. When people did come from Mandal, shouting "Hallo, gentleman" from far off, the sudden disturbance of the silence was a shock, and often it took him some time to find his voice.

They paid him faithful visits all those weeks, toiling up the long climb every third or fourth night. When they came, they always brought fresh food, and usually some dry wood to make a fire to heat a drink for him; but lighting fires always made them uneasy in case the smoke or the light was seen. Whenever he heard them coming, he pulled himself together and tried to look as alive as he could, because he had a fear at the back of his mind that they might get depressed and give him up as a bad job and stop coming any more. On their side, they felt they had to cheer him up, so that the meetings were usually happy, although the happiness was forced. Sometimes there was even something to laugh at, like the time when one man forgot the password. The story of how Jan had shot the Gestapo officer had got around, and he had the reputation in Mandal of being trigger-conscious and a deadly shot. So when this man found that the words "Hallo, gentleman" had quite escaped his mind at the critical moment, he hurriedly dropped on his hands and knees and crawled up to Jan on his stomach, keeping well under cover till he was close enough to talk to him and make perfectly certain that there would not be any unfortunate misunderstanding.

On one of their visits, Jan asked them for something to read. What he really wanted was an English thriller or a French one, because during the last couple of years he had got more used to reading foreign languages than his own.[4] But nobody knew of anything like that in Mandal, and the man he happened to ask could only offer him religious works in Norwegian. He declined that offer, but afterwards the man remembered an annual edition of a weekly magazine which he could borrow. Jan thanked him, and the heavy volume was carried up the mountain. But as a matter of fact, Jan did not read very much of it. He never seemed to have time.

Somebody had the brilliant idea, when Jan had been up there for some time, of bringing up a roll of the kind of thick paper which is used for insulating buildings. They bent this over Jan in an arch, like a miniature Nissen hut, and covered it over with snow, and blocked up one end with a snow wall. It was just big enough for Jan to lie in, and it protected him quite well. In fact, it sometimes seemed warm inside. But it had its drawbacks: whenever it seemed to be going to get tolerably warm, the snow on top of it melted and dripped through on him mercilessly, and made him even wetter than before.

Sometimes his visitors came with high hopes, but more often the news they brought him from the valley was disappointing. On one night soon after they left him there, two men came up full of excitement to say that a Lapp had arrived in Kaafjord and promised to take him to the frontier straight away. They

[4]Baalsrud had lived in England for most of the war.

expected him either that night or the next, and they waited all night to help Jan when he came. But the morning came without any sign of him. For the next three successive nights men came from the valley to wait with Jan for the Lapp's arrival, and to make sure he did not miss the place. They kept watch for him hour by hour; but no movement broke the skylines of the plateau. On the fourth day they heard that the Lapp had changed his mind because of a rumour that the Germans had sent out ski patrols on the frontier.

During the next few days this rumour was confirmed from a good many different sources. Recently, everyone had been so completely absorbed by the problems of Jan's health, and the weather, and the journey across the plateau, that they were well on the way to forgetting about the Germans. It was a long time since the garrison had come to Mandal, and that had been the last German move, so far as anyone knew, which had seemed at the time to be part of a deliberate search. The Mandal men had got used to the garrison and begun to despise it. But now it began to look as if the Germans were still on the hunt for Jan and even had a rough idea of where he was. When Jan was told about it, he reflected that the Germans had got a jump ahead of him for the first time in his flight. In the early days, when he was on the move, they had never done more than bark at his heels; but now, it seemed, they had thrown out a patrol line right on the part of the frontier which one day he would have to cross; and unless he crossed it within a few days, he would have to do it in daylight. If only he had been fit, both he and the Mandal men would have treated the patrol as a joke, because like all Norwegians they had a profound contempt, which may not have been justified, for the Germans' skill on skis. Even as things were, nobody except the Lapp was deterred by this extra danger. If they could only get to the frontier, they were sure they would get across somehow.

But soon after this rumour started there was an extraordinary event on the plateau which really did make them take the danger of Germans more seriously. The most remarkable thing about life on the plateau had always been that nothing happened whatever. Day after day could pass without any event, even of the most trivial kind; and Jan discovered that most of the events which he seemed to remember were really things he had dreamed or imagined. His commonest dream or hallucination was that he heard someone coming. One day, when he was dozing, he heard voices approaching. It had often happened before; but this time, as they came near him, he realized that they were speaking German. He could not understand what they were saying, and they soon faded away again; and when he was fully awake, he thought no more of what seemed a slight variation of his old familiar dream. But the next night, when a party from Mandal came up to see him, they arrived in consternation, because there were two sets of ski tracks which passed thirty yards from the place where Jan was lying, and none of the Mandal men had made them.

It was one of those utterly mysterious things which start endless speculation. Up till then, they had always regarded the plateau as a sanctuary from the Germans, partly because they had never thought the Germans would venture to go up there, and partly because the job of looking for one man in all those hundreds of miles of snow was so hopeless that they had been sure the Germans would not waste time in trying it. Nobody could imagine where the small party of men who had made the tracks could have come from, or where they had been going, or what they had meant to do. They were not from the Mandal garrison, because that was always kept under observation, and the place was more than a day's journey from any other German post. They could not have been part of a frontier patrol, because it was much too far from the frontier. Yet if they were searching for Jan, it seemed an incredible coincidence that they should have passed so near him, unless there were hundreds of patrols all over the plateau, or unless they had a very good idea of where he was. Besides, to search in that secretive way was un-German.

If they did know where he was, they would know he could not be living up there unless Mandal was looking after him, and their reaction to that would certainly be to use threats and arrests in Mandal in the hope of finding someone who would give him away and save them losing face by having to scour the mountains.

They argued round and round the mystery for a long time on the plateau that night, with a new feeling of insecurity and apprehension. It had been pure luck that the Germans, whatever they were doing, had not seen Jan when they passed him. There had been a snowfall earlier in the day which had covered the trampled snow around his lair and all the old ski tracks which led up to it from Mandal. But if they came back again, they would find the new tracks and follow them straight to the spot. Altogether, it was alarming, and the only comforting suggestion that anybody thought of was that the tracks might possibly have been made by German deserters trying to get to Sweden. Nobody ever found out the truth of it. Those voices in the night remained a vague menace in the background ever after.

When the Lapp lost courage and changed his mind, it was only the first of a series of disappointments. Hopeful stories of reindeer sledges expected at any moment kept coming in from Kaafjord and other valleys in the district, but every time the hope was doomed to die. After a fortnight in which all their plans were frustrated and came to nothing, the Mandal men got desperate. Every time they went up to look at Jan they found him a little weaker. He seemed to be dying by very slow degrees. Besides that, the spring thaw was beginning in earnest, and with every day the crossing of the plateau and even the climb out of the valley was getting more difficult. The snow was rotten and sticky already on the southern slopes, and the next week or two would see the last chance of a sledge journey before the following winter. During the thaw every year the plateau becomes a bog, criss-crossed by swollen streams, and nobody can cross it; and after the thaw, when the snow is all gone, the

WE DIE ALONE

only way to move a helpless man would be to carry him, which
would be even slower and more laborious than dragging him on
a sledge.

So they decided to make a final attempt to man haul the
sledge to Sweden while there was still time, using a larger party
which could work in relays. Accordingly, six men went up on
the night of the ninth of May, and dragged Jan out of the paper
tent and started off again to the southward. But this attempt
achieved nothing except to raise false hopes once more. They
had only covered a mile or two when clouds came down so
thickly that they could only see a few feet ahead of them. They
could not steer a course in those conditions, so they turnedround
and followed their own tracks back to where they had started,
and put Jan into the paper tent again.

After this failure, Jan really began to get despondent. He never
lost faith in the Mandal men, and still believed they would get
him to Sweden somehow if they went on trying long enough;
but he began to doubt if it was worth it. Nobody had told him
much about what was going on, but he could see for himself
what an enormous effort Mandal and the surrounding district
was making on his behalf. So many different men had come up
from the valley by then that he had lost count of them, and he
had some vague idea of the organization which must lie behind
such frequent visits. As time went on, it seemed more and more
fantastic that the German garrison could go on living down there
in the valley, in the midst of all this hectic activity, and remain
in happy ignorance of what was happening. Every new man
who came to help him meant a new family more or less involved
in his affairs, so that the longer Mandal had to go on looking
after him the more awful would be the disaster in the valley if
the Germans did find out about it. Jan knew, and so did the
Mandal men, the results of the uncontrolled anger of Germans
when they found out that a whole community had deceived
them. It had happened on the west coast, and villages had been
systematically burnt, all the men in them shipped to Germany

279

and the women and children herded into concentration camps in Norway. There was no doubt this might happen to Mandal, now that so many people were involved, and Jan had to ask himself what the reward of running this risk would be. To save his life was the only objective. When he looked at it coolly, it seemed a very bad bargain. There was no patriotic motive in it any more, no idea of saving a trained soldier to fight again; looking at his legs, and the wasted remains of what had once been such a healthy body, he did not think he would be any use as a soldier any more. If he died, he thought, it would be no more loss to the army; he was a dead loss anyway. And it was not as if he were married, or even engaged. Nobody depended entirely on him for their happiness or livelihood. His father had another son and daughter: his brother Nils would be quite grown up by now: and even Bitten, his young sister whom he had loved so much, must have learned, he supposed, to get on without him, and perhaps would never depend on him again as much as he had always imagined. He wondered whether they had all given him up for dead already, and whether he would ever see them again even if he did live on. As for his war-time friends of the last two years in England, he knew they would all have assumed he was dead if they knew where he was at all.

This idea only came to him slowly, in the course of about ten lonely days after the last abortive journey. It took him a long time to come to a firm conclusion, because by nature he had such a very strong instinct to live. But inevitably the time came, in the end, when he unwillingly saw one duty left to him. His own life was not of any overriding value to anyone but himself; and to himself, life only meant a few more weeks of suffering and a hideous death, or at best, he believed, a future as a more or less useless cripple. The life of any one of his many helpers, healthy and perhaps the focus and support of a family, out-weighed it in the balance. He saw quite clearly that he ought not to let them run any more risks for him, and he knew there was only one way he could possibly stop them. His last duty was to die.

To decide to commit suicide when one's instinct is utterly against it argues great strength of mind. Jan's mind was still active and clear, but his decision had come too late. By the time he reached it, his body was too weak to carry it out. He still had his loaded pistol. Lying alone in his sleeping-bag among the wastes of snow, he dragged it out of his holster and held it in his hands. He had used it to save his life already, and he meant to use it again to end it. Until the last week he had always looked after it with the love he had always had for fine mechanism, but lately he had begun to neglect it, and it grieved him to find it was rusty. He held it in the old familiar grip, to cock it for a final shot, but it was stiff and his fingers were very weak. He struggled feebly with the simple action he had been trained to do in a fraction of a second, but it was not the slightest use. He no longer had the strength in his hands to pull back against the spring. He felt a friend had failed him.

Afterwards he tried to think of other ways of doing away with himself. If he could have got out of the sleeping-bag and crawled away into the snow, he could have let the frost finish the work it had begun. But it was a long time then, over a week, since he had had enough strength to disentangle himself from the blankets or move his body more than an inch or two. He thought of his knife, too, and tried its edge, but it had not been sharp when he had cut off his toes, and now it was rustier and blunter, and the thought of trying to saw at his own throat or the arteries of his wrist was so horrible that his resolution wavered, and he feebly relaxed and tried to make up his mind anew.

It was absurd really. He felt he had made a fool of himself. He had struggled so long to preserve his own life that now he had not enough strength in his fingers to kill himself. If he had not felt ashamed, he would have laughed.

The Frogmen

by T. J. WALDRON and JAMES GLEESON

"And with his augur sharp in her side he bored holes three
And he sank her in the Lowland Sea."
That ancient exploit, recorded in the traditional song of "The Golden
Vanitie", was the origin of underwater warfare, which came to its climax
in the submarine. But it is the oldest device which strikes novelty—and in
our super-mechanized, hyper-scientific Second World War, one of the
most startling innovations in secret destruction was that of the tiny team of
individualists who attacked the greatest ships of war.

The idea was first put into operation by the Italians; but the Admiralty,
with great speed, adopted and improved on the technique. Teams of midget
submarines and "chariots"—a torpedo actually ridden under the water by
two men—assaulted Tirpitz in her Norwegian fjord; others operated in
the Far East; still others, with poetic justice, carried the Frogman's war
into the waters of "Mare Nostrum"—as Mussolini once, with such foolish
braggadocio, styled the Middle Sea.

THERE was operation "Principle" at Palermo, where a
chariot,[1] piloted by Lieut. Greenland[2] with Leading-
Signaller Ferrier,[3] ran in unseen and made a perfect attack on a
cruiser which sank. Lieut. Cook[4] and A. N. Worthy[5] ran into
trouble—the war-head came adrift, but was re-secured. Lieut.
Cook unhappily lost his life, and Worthy drove the chariot
ashore and blew it up. Sub-Lieut. Dove[6] and Leading-Seaman
Freel[7] made an excellent attack and placed the war-head on the

---

[1] A two-man torpedo.
[2] Lieut. R. T. G. Greenland.
[3] A. Ferrier, C.G.M.
[4] Lieut. H. F. Cook.

[5] H. V. Worthy (Despatches).
[6] Sub-Lieut. R. G. Dove.
[7] J. Freel.

stern of the S.S. *Vimina*. She was seriously damaged and later torpedoed when she was being towed from Palermo. Prior to that attack, the Italians had no idea that we were using chariots, and thought it unlikely that we should be, at that stage of the war.

So the underwater offensive in the Mediterranean mounted, culminating in the attack, perhaps the cheekiest of all, in the harbour of La Spezia, right in the birthplace of the Italian two-man torpedoes. In February, 1944, three crews of charioteers established a secret base at San Vito, at the entrance to Taranto harbour. One of the crews, consisting of Lieut. M. R. Causer[8] and Seaman Harry Smith,[9] was chosen to attack the Italian 10,000-ton cruiser *Bolzano* which was lying in the heavily defended anchorage of La Spezia. The *Bolzano* was the last of the eight-inch gun cruisers with which Italy had entered the war, and she was at that time German-controlled.

Causer and Smith made contact with the captain of an Italian Motor Torpedo Boat which had been based on La Spezia before coming over to the Allies when Italy surrendered. The plan was for the M.T.B. to drop them within two miles of the harbour entrance. The entrance to the harbour consisted of a mile-long channel with a breakwater and boom defences stretched across at the mouth of the harbour. Causer and Smith were to attack the cruiser—get ashore—lie low all day—and then make their way about a mile up the coast where they were told they would find a large rock about two hundred yards out to sea. They were to swim to the rock, and during the night a fast motor-boat would come in and take them off. That, however, is not the way things worked out.

The two-man torpedo was placed aboard the M.T.B., together with the diving equipment, and from Naples they headed for Corsica, which was held at that time by Allied troops. On 22 June[10] they sailed from Corsica in an Italian destroyer with the M.T.B. in attendance, and about twenty

[8]Lieut. M. R. Causer, D.S.O.   [9]Harry Smith, C.G.M.   [10]1943.

miles from the Italian coast they transferred to the M.T.B. for the last leg of the journey to La Spezia.

Shortly afterwards the M.T.B. stopped and the captain said that that was as far as he could possibly go. He had let them down; he promised to go within two miles of the harbour, but he evidently got frightened, and he dropped them at least seven miles from the harbour—which didn't help the original plan much. The torpedo was lowered over the side and Causer and Smith got aboard, and with a final wave to the crew of the M.T.B. headed for La Spezia at 22.30 hours.

They travelled on the surface until they sighted the harbour entrance, when they took a bearing and dived to twenty feet and proceeded at that depth for about thirty minutes. When they surfaced again they were well within the harbour approaches, and heading for the breakwater and boom defences. Searchlights swept the sky and tracers from two shore-based guns were firing out to sea. They dived quickly and carried on towards the breakwater. They had not been going long before they heard the sound of an approaching engine. They slowed down and held their breath while a motor launch passed directly over them. After a while they gently broke surface again, and sighted the harbour entrance to the right of the breakwater, they dived once more and nosed their way towards the entrance.

Here they met their first obstacle, an anti-submarine net, stretched across the entrance, and down to the sea-bed. They dived to thirty feet and started cutting their way through the net. Unfortunately that was not the only net. Altogether they encountered at least half a dozen more, set at different angles, but they hacked and struggled and wormed their way through one net after another until finally they had penetrated the harbour boom defences. They were inside La Spezia.

Slowly they surfaced, and there was the target lying in the centre of the harbour. Lieut. Causer turned round in his seat, and he and Smith solemnly shook hands. Cutting through the nets must have taken several hours and they were well behind schedule; in fact, it was almost daylight. The Italian captain had certainly let them down very badly by dropping them so far out to sea; it had taken much longer than they had anticipated to reach the harbour.

However, there was no turning back now, so they dived to twenty feet and slowly approached the ship until they could see her dark outline on the surface. Quietly they came up beneath her great propellers and pulled themselves along until they were just forward of 'midships, underneath the bridge. They placed four magnets on the bottom of the ship, then released the warhead of the torpedo and lashed it to the magnets. Lieut. Causer then set the time fuse for two hours to give them time to get clear; they mounted the torpedo and dropped down to thirty . feet.

It was at this point that they discovered that the batteries that operated the torpedo were very low indeed, and that they would not be able to make the shore. The plan had been to sink the machine in deep water, get ashore, hide the diving gear and then lie low for a time. This latest discovery, however, caused a complete change of plan. They managed to get to the breakwater, where they scuttled the torpedo. They then surfaced near some rocks, climbed out of the water and took off their diving gear. They had been in the water seven and a half hours. They were both all in, so they slept for about an hour and a half on the rocks. Then at 06.30 hours the explosion occurred. Two large water spouts shot up well above the level of the bridge, she shuddered, started to settle, and then rolled over on to her starboard side. She sank in a quarter of an hour, leaving her port side showing above the water. Thus the wheel had turned full circle—as this ship of war was destroyed in the centre of the very harbour from which this form of warfare had started.

Meanwhile, Causer and Smith were still quite literally on the rocks. It was about half a mile to the shore, but it would have been impossible to swim it because of the activity in the harbour following the explosion, so they stayed where they were and hoped for the best. Later in the day they were spotted by an Italian fisherman and his small son. After some parleying the fisherman agreed to get another boat for them. They had no option but to trust him, and sure enough he returned later with another rowing boat in tow. They got into the boat and mingled with the Italian fishermen in the harbour all day, and at night set out with the intention of rowing to Corsica, ninety miles away. They kept going all night, and the next day they made a landfall, which they thought was Corsica. After they beached the boat they asked a small boy if this was Corsica—only to learn that they were still in Italy. They had in fact travelled some twenty miles farther down the coast.

After wandering and hiding, with the notion of making vaguely in the direction of the Allied lines, they met a woman who put them in touch with some Italian guerrillas. The two Britishers joined the guerrillas and fought with them for about six weeks. The band that they had been fighting with was practically wiped out in a skirmish, so they decided to try and make our own lines and set out in civilian clothes with this intention. They carried their battledress in a sack as an additional precaution because they had both been warned that if they were picked up in civilian clothes they would be shot as spies. They carried on daily getting nearer and nearer to the front line, when by the greatest stroke of bad luck they were picked up by a German patrol in forbidden territory and taken in for interrogation. They were suspected of having been involved in the sinking of the *Bolzano,* but they both stoutly maintained that they were survivors of a big submarine. Eventually Smith was sent to a prison camp in Bremen and later to Lubeck, where he was put in solitary confinement, and otherwise badly used in an endeavour to get him to admit complicity in the *Bolzano* affair, but he stuck to his story until his ultimate release by the 11th Hussars.

Jump For It

by GERALD BOWMAN

"The Caterpillar Club"—the unofficial body consisting of men who have baled out by parachute—forms the sub-title of Gerald Bowman's book Jump For It.

The mere fact of trusting to an "umbrella" of thin silk to drop thousands (or, worse, hundreds) of feet from the sky to earth is frightening enough: will it open, has there been some slip-up in packing, will one pull the rip-cord in time—these are questions which appal those who are not members of the "Club" (and hope never to join it).

But of all the records in the annals of the Caterpillar Club, I give Flying Officer Baker's exploit pride of place, for his parachute opened not too late, but too soon.

THE SKY over Hamburg in January, 1942, was apt to be a lively place. On the night of the 16th of that month the crew of a Stirling aircraft of No. 3 Group, Bomber Command, met with a very hot reception indeed from the powerful ground defences. Every available piece of local scrap iron which could be propelled by explosive means, together with an assortment of highly inflammable chemicals, was industriously being pumped up from the ground all around them.

The Stirling crew returned the compliment according to the highest traditions of the Royal Air Force by dropping their bomb load as squarely on the target as the bomb-aimer and the pilot could contrive. Then the big aircraft shuddered as a direct hit carried away the starboard inner propeller.

Shortly afterwards the behaviour of the dashboard gauges showed that more than one of the fuel tanks had been holed, so that the petrol was pouring out fast. As the aircraft turned on its homeward course heavy cloud stretched as far as could be seen ahead. Every man on board wondered how far they would get before the inevitable happened.

Would it be a case of jumping before they got clear of enemy-occupied territory, or would they have to ditch the machine in the winter wastes of the North Sea? The night was freezing cold; there was no telling whether the cloud mass reached right down to the earth's surface; so that neither prospect was inviting.

As the long trip dragged on everybody realized that the skipper was doing a nice job. Although he had only three good engines, he nursed the aircraft along carefully, using the fuel from the leaking tanks first and running his remaining engines at the best economical settings. At the same time he shrewdly allowed the big machine a small but constant loss of height in order to get every last yard out of the power available.

At last they knew they had crossed the continental coast and were over the North Sea. To the crew of any aircraft suffering "trouble" this part of the journey home always seemed an eternity. The men were all grimly tensed bundles of nerves. They said little. They listened to the engines' beat, tried to think of other things and went on waiting for the faltering note that would mean that the worst had happened.

At last, through a small break in the cloud, they saw that they had passed over the English coast, some miles off course, but still going fairly strong. With nervous tension relaxed, a wave of cheerfulness seemed to pass down the machine. The crew eased themselves in their positions and there was talk and some laughter. "Do you reckon we can make it?" asked the co-pilot, Flying-Officer Baker.

The skipper shrugged. "See that everyone's got a pack on and get them forward," he said. "However far we manage to go, we dare not try and scrape down through ten-tenths cloud. You heard the engineer? We're nearly dry, and the engines may cut at any moment."

As he spoke he was turning the aircraft on the correct course for base, although Baker knew he could never reach it. During the next five minutes, which Baker admits felt nearer five years, the crew got ready and lined up. Then the first engine cut. Almost immediately the remaining two ceased running and the propeller blades became visible, spun for a short time, and then jerkily came to a standstill.

Briefly the skipper gave the order to bale out, his voice sounding unnaturally clear in the sudden silence. This became even more noticeable by reason of the whispering whine of the air outside as he put the big aircraft into a controlled dive.

Baker, as was his duty, stood by and watched the five members of his crew drop away through the escape hatch and instantly disappear in the clear moonlight above the vast carpet of cloud. Then he climbed back up beside the skipper and made his report.

"Everybody away," he said. "Are you all right? Shall I go now?"

The skipper nodded briefly. "Hoppit," he said, "and don't waste time."

The order of abandoning aircraft is one of the strongest regulations in the "Book" of the Royal Air Force. Only after his entire crew has gone does the skipper finally relinquish control and take to his parachute. Baker therefore obediently jumped down between the two pilots' seats to get clear as soon as possible in order to give his captain every chance. But as he did so the rip-cord of his parachute caught in some projection. What it was he never knew, but the immediate result was that his parachute pack opened, and in the fierce draught from the escape hatch the silken folds of the canopy bellied out behind him and blew *inside* the aircraft.

In giving me his report later, Baker admitted he was more terrified at that moment than he had ever been in the whole of his Air Force career. He knew at that moment that the parachute was probably tearing and ripping itself against the mass of awkward angles, handles and objects with which the interior of any aircraft fuselage is crowded. His hopes of using it as a support in the air, even if he managed to get it clear, could be counted as practically nil. Yet his duty was plain and he acted promptly.

Grabbing the shroud lines in his hands, he wrenched himself up between the seats again and shouted out what had happened.

"Don't wait until I've got the damned thing clear," he yelled. "You can get past these lines. Come on, get away!"

The skipper, however, showed himself to be precisely and exactly what the captain of a Royal Air Force machine should be. His reply was typical.

"Don't be a bloody fool," he said. "Get down and get that thing untangled. Shove it out of the escape hatch. You've still got a chance. If you can't go, I can't. . . ."

Baker scrambled down again. What sort of time was left he couldn't tell. When the engine had first cut and the crew had gone away he had marked the altimeter height at 6,000 feet. How long had passed since then he did not know, but he realized that the aircraft had been rapidly losing height.

Meanwhile the problem before him was complicated. If he dived straight out of the escape hatch the chances were about a million to one that his parachute would not follow him. If it did, it would merely be a few wisps of ripped and torn silk which would be less support of his journey towards the earth that a girl-friend's sunshade. On the other hand, if he sat on the hatch laboriously gathering up the billowing folds of the canopy from inside the machine, and pushed them out, it was a thousand to one that they would merely entangle themselves around the tail of the aircraft. Nevertheless, the second alternative was obviously the better. Baker therefore scrambled down to the hatch, sat on the edge with his legs dangling over, and gathered his rigging lines, hand over hand, as quickly as he dared, wondering how many tears had developed. As he worked he could feel the whole fabric of the parachute thrashing on the bottom of the fuselage in the incoming draught. Then, as he paid out bunches of the fabric, the force of the wind outside made it jerk violently in its grasp.

Soon he found he could hardly hold against this wrenching pull. The part of the parachute outside the aircraft was pulling itself out of his hands, with part still inside the aircraft. He wondered wildly what he could do. The question was answered before he had time to work it out.

The answer came in the form of a thudding crack over the head dealt him by the edge of the escape hatch. The outside part of the parachute had completely "taken charge" and dragged him bodily out of the machine. He was three parts dazed, but when his senses cleared he realized he was floating in cloud with the parachute somewhere up above his head in the blackness. Perhaps it is natural that Baker's first instinct was a surge of thankfulness that he was still alive. From the comforting feel of his weight in the web harness, he knew that he was not falling freely. The parachute was sufficiently intact to be giving him support although he had no means of knowing just how much. His second thoughts were for the aircraft he had left, and for his skipper. But although he listened carefully he could hear nothing which was not surprising since the aircraft was without motive power. Otherwise, as most people who have tried it know, parachuting through cloud at night restricts your range of vision pretty well to the end of your nose.

Quite soon, however, there was a difference in the weaving void below him which was difficult to make out in detail, but he knew it meant that he was approaching the ground. He gripped the rigging lines, tensed himself, and strained his eyes fiercely. Still nothing showed. Then suddenly he saw a tree, and landed with heavy force, smashing through the thin ice of a shallow, frozen pond.

Awkwardly, in the manner of a hooked fish, he rolled and plunged while his parachute dragged him about twenty yards clear of the pond before it lodged in a bush and collapsed. He staggered very shakily to his feet, released his harness and tried to get his bearings. He found the darkness almost as intense as it had been during his journey down through the cloud. He set out to try to take a straight path—in what direction he had no idea—and for the next hour stumbled in vague circles until at last a cottage loomed up in front of him. Subsequently he found that it was less than a hundred yards from the point at which he had landed.

Not unnaturally, Baker was almost royally entertained by the good folk who lived in the cottage, directly he had knocked at the door and made his presence known. The nearest Royal Air Force Station was contacted by telephone and he was given the glad news that all the rest of his crew had landed safely and were being cared for. Of the aircraft and the captain, however, he got no word until he had a night's sleep, when he was given the best and most amusing news of all.

The captain, by a mixture of miraculous good luck and first-class skill, had managed to land the aircraft in the darkness. The landing, as might be expected, had been spectacular. The big aircraft dug its nose into the ground, reared tail-up and then almost disintegrated upside-down. After which, when he could think clearly, the skipper found himself hanging head downwards in his harness. All who have tried it know there is one little difficulty about getting out of a safety harness when in an inverted position. This is to avoid dropping several feet on to one's head, thereby breaking one's neck, directly the release is effected. Nevertheless, the skipper managed it. After which, like Baker, he wandered in circles around the crash shouting and whistling but unable to find any form of human habitation in the darkness. Therefore, with commendable good sense, he returned to the crash, climbed into what was left of the fuselage, collected seat cushions and anything else he could find, and calmly settled himself to sleep. The crew of a roving tender from the nearest Air Force station found him in the clear light of day, woke him up, and carried him off to a good breakfast, no worse for his night's adventure.

A little over seven months later, on 24 August, 1942, Baker made his second parachute descent of the war. On this occasion he himself was captain of the aircraft and the upshot of the whole incident was that he walked the best part of the way home. It was rather a long walk—but of that more later.

The main point of interest about that summer night was its beauty. The sky was absolutely clear as Baker's bomber aircraft, having completed a mission, crossed the border between Germany and Belgium on its course back to base. High above, the full moon hung like a great silver ball spreading its soft radiance over the sleeping world . . . and the crew hated every square inch of it. This was because a full moon in a clear sky is just about the most dangerous thing that any bomber crew can encounter. It makes their aircraft a silhouetted dead-duck target for any fighters approaching from below. Moreover, it is almost impossible for the aircraft gunners to pick out the small shape of a fighter rising from the green-grey expanse of the ground below until it has got perilously close. Baker therefore was taking his crew home with "the wicks turned fully up", with everybody tense, and the gunners alert for trouble.

When trouble came none of them actually saw the aircraft which launched it. With a nice, clear target in his sights the pilot of a Me.110 must have enjoyed himself as he came up for his first attack from below and dead behind. Even so, he seems to have been a little over-confident, for his first burst did no more than put the rear gun-turret out of action, produce a small fire, and an equally warm stream of remarks from the flight engineer, who jumped violently and winced over a wounded arm.

Baker, at the controls, immediately flung the aircraft into evasive action, but within his heart of hearts he knew that he hadn't a hope. Once again the Messerschmitt came into the attack, and once again the big bomber shuddered as a burst of cannon shells smashed into the starboard wing-tanks, setting up a blaze of fuel which whipped back into the slip-stream.

As captain, Baker now had to make a decision. It was obvious they would have to abandon aircraft, but it would be best for all concerned if they could get as near home as possible before doing so. Meanwhile, the fire was gaining, so he had to decide how long the wing structure would stand up to the terrific heat before it finally collapsed and put the aircraft into a spin from which it might be impossible for anybody to get clear. However, the only thing to be thankful for was that the Messerschmitt pilot had sheered off, obviously satisfied now that his "kill" was burning.

For about five minutes Baker kept on course until he felt that the wing could not possibly stand up to the strain much longer. He gave the order to abandon ship but, to his horror, discovered that the intercom. had failed, and it was therefore impossible to communicate with his crew. In that moment of helplessness Baker sat rigid . . . and sweated. The fire was gaining and he knew that at any minute the wing might collapse. The lives of his comrades hung upon his ordering them away, but there was no way of passing the order. He wondered wildly what the hell to do and then—with the miraculous inconsequence which is part and parcel of aircraft in war—the intercom. suddenly "came on" again. Baker gasped and shouted his order.

"Bale out, chaps," he yelled. "Jump, everybody. Make it snappy. Get away as fast as you can."

Those who believe in fate or providence will place their own interpretation on the fact that the intercom. remained "live" just long enough for that order to be given. As he spoke the last word, Baker realized that the thing had crackled and gone dead again. He had no time, however, to relax even in this moment of relief. He put "George", his automatic pilot, into action, and as his crew came tumbling forward to go out through the escape hatch he unbuckled his safety harness and heaved himself out of his seat. Then he went aft along the fuselage to make a final check and satisfy himself that all of them had got away.

By this time the fire was just starting to eat its way into the fuselage, so Baker hurried back forward again and took a brief glance at the altimeter, which registered 12,000 feet, before he went to the escape hatch, and rolled himself headlong into the night. For the next few moments he rolled over and over, the sky gyrating about him before he was jerked upright by the opening of his parachute canopy. In his own words: "At some moment unknown to me I had pulled the rip-cord, but what I had done with it I never afterwards knew. When I found myself swinging safely on the open parachute the ring was no longer in my hand. I think at that moment all I felt was regret that this souvenir was lost.

"Above me was my parachute billowing gently, and singing softly in the still night air. Below was the silvery landscape, trees, rivers, fields and houses, everything I had seen so often from the aircraft, but now its beauty enhanced by the utter stillness. As I seemed to hang unmoving above it all I tried to turn myself this way and that to see what had happened to the others who had left the aircraft. But I only spotted one parachute far away below me and I could only hope that the rest of the chaps had landed safely. Then the thought suddenly came to me that very soon my parents would receive that grim telegram: "The Air Ministry regrets . . ." I knew what a multitude of fears that terse announcement of "missing" could carry to parents and what unpleasant visions it might cause. Yet there was I, enjoying the incomparable beauty of an August night over Belgium, and, in one sense, thoroughly enjoying it."

Baker's descent took a long time since he had baled out at considerable height. He saw the abandoned aircraft crash and realized that he was going to land quite close to it. Indeed he actually landed so close that he could make out the figures of the local inhabitants around the wreck and heard their excited voices as they talked and called out to each other. Apparently, however, they did not think of looking up above them and it seems certain that none of them saw him as he drifted down not far away and settled into the trees of a pine wood.

He tried to spill his parachute in order to avoid the wood, but could not manage it. Therefore he held his feet tight together and shut his eyes just before he felt himself breaking the smaller outer branches. With a fairly heavy thud, he found himself rolling over on the pine-needle floor in the middle of the trees, and staggered to his feet, virtually unhurt.

Baker scraped a hole for his parachute in the pine needles and made sure that it was well hidden. Subsequently, he found that the spot he had landed on was about twenty miles south-west of Brussels. Meanwhile, since it was his object to evade capture, he set off at a brisk pace to put as much distance between himself and the crashed aircraft as possible.

In an earlier part of this story I mentioned that he went for rather a long walk. The distance, in actual fact, was from that spot near Brussels to Gibraltar. He managed it in less than eight weeks, and then got himself aboard a boat for home.

It is typical of him that when I checked the details of his story he said, "I say, old boy, must you use my name? After all, it's the least important part . . . and all that happened to me might have happened to anybody!"

The Green Beret

by HILARY ST. GEORGE SAUNDERS

The Commandos wear "The Green Beret", and Hilary St. George Saunders took their badge as the title of his history of that supremely hardy body which derived its name from the swift-moving, dazzlingly evasive units of Smuts and de Wet in the Boer War. From 1942 onwards the Commandos were in the forefront of every amphibian and land action: Lofoten, Dieppe, Anzio, Jugoslavia, Walcheren are but a few of the names blazoned on their banners.

The assault on St. Nazaire is ranked by the Commandos' historian as "The Greatest Raid of All".

O NE SUNDAY in February, 1942, Lieutenant-Colonel A. C. Newman (The Essex Regiment), commanding No. 2 Commando, was summoned by Brigadier Haydon to attend a conference at Irvine near Ayr. The colonel arrived, as he says, full of hope but a trifle wary. His Commando had not yet been employed as a unit, though two troops of it had taken part in the Vaagso raid, and many of its men had fought in the short-lived Norwegian campaign of 1940. For months its existence had been an unending round of training, and to his imperfectly concealed chagrin, Newman had to listen at the conference "to the brigadier's orders for summer training". Another dismal period of "waiting for a job" loomed ahead; but as the members of the conference were leaving the room, Haydon drew Newman aside and told him what was in the wind. That night Newman left for London with orders to report to the headquarters of Combined Operations, leaving his second-in-command to choose one hundred picked men from his

Commando. The enterprise in which they were to take part was of great pith and moment.

On the west coast of France where the River Loire joins the sea, stands the port of St. Nazaire. During the war the fact that it possessed the only dry dock on the Atlantic seaboard capable of holding the German battleship *Tirpitz*, made it of very great importance in the long-drawn-out battle of the Atlantic. The dock, which has two names, the Forme Ecluse or the Forme Louis Joubert, is 1,148 feet long and 164 feet wide. It was to this haven that the *Bismarck* was undoubtedly making when she was sunk on the 27 May, 1941. But her sister ship, the *Tirpitz*, was still afloat, and as spring began to oust winter in 1942 it was learned through various intelligence sources that this great vessel, then in Norwegian waters, was preparing to enter the Atlantic. Once there, the damage she might do to shipping might well be incalculable. The chance that she would put to sea and risk the fate of the *Bismarck* would be much smaller—if the Forme Ecluse could be shut against her. Whether regarded in cold or hot blood, the enterprise was truly formidable, and when the intention was first voiced, one of the planners was heard to observe that anyone who even "thought of doing such a thing deserved the D.S.O.". . .

The raid had two main objects, of which the first—to put out of action the Forme Ecluse by the destruction of the great gates giving access to it—was the more important. The second was to do as much damage as possible to the U-boat bunkers and the docks. It was decided that eighty men drawn from all the Commandos in England should be trained in the technique of demolition, and that the covering force, about one hundred men, should be supplied by No. 2 Commando. The dock gates were to be rammed by a destroyer which, together with light surface craft, was to transport the Commando. To create a diversion the Royal Air Force was to bomb the port.

There were two reasons why light craft were chosen to transport the troops. The approach to the docks at St. Nazaire is by a deep-water channel running under the lee of the north bank of the Loire, and at that time defended by a considerable number of heavy coast defence batteries. South of the channel is a wide expanse of mud flats, covered only at high tide. The high spring tides of the end of March would give just enough water for motor launches to pass over, and also for the destroyer provided she were not too heavily laden. For motor launches to operate at that extreme range extra petrol tanks had to be fitted. This greatly increased the risks they ran from fire and in the event proved fatal to many of their number.

Arrived in London, Newman began work in a room containing an accurate scale model of St. Nazaire and a large number of aerial photographs. Here he was joined by the naval commander of the expedition, Commander R. E. D. Ryder, R.N. The two men—both of them were to win the Victoria Cross—took an immediate liking to each other, and together worked out the plan in detail. At the outset the expedition was nearly abandoned because the Admiralty were at first unable to furnish a destroyer, and suggested instead a large submarine. Such a vessel, however, would have proved quite unsuitable, for men could never have been landed from it with sufficient dispatch, nor would their fighting qualities after three days' confinement in her bowels have been at the required pitch. Fortunately the Admiralty relented and detailed an elderly American destroyer, the *Buchanan*, renamed H.M.S. *Campbeltown*. . . .

In the afternoon of 26 March the force sailed in three columns, the port and starboard consisting of motor launches, and the midships column of two Hunt class destroyers, H.M.S. *Atherstone* and H.M.S. *Tynedale*, with the *Campbeltown* and Motor Gun Boat 314. The weather looked promising, but was somewhat rough for the motor launches. The wind eased, however, and the expedition "steered on through a calm, hazy, moonlit night". . . .

★   ★   ★

So they sailed on "in a nice, tidy formation" until at a position one and three-quarter miles from the target, after the dangerous mud flats had been safely crossed, searchlights were switched on from both banks. The time was then 01.22 hours. The force was flying German colours and the funnels of the *Campbeltown* had been cut to resemble those of a torpedo boat of the Möwe class. The expedition was immediately challenged from the shore, and Leading Signalman Pike, wearing the uniform of a German petty officer, signalled back, calling on the shore batteries to wait, and giving the call sign, which was known, of one of the German torpedo boats. Warming to his work, Pike then sent a signal in plain language with an urgent prefix, stating that two craft, damaged by enemy action, requested permission to proceed to harbour without delay. On the despatch of this false message, a few guns, which had opened fire when the searchlights were turned on, became silent. For a moment it seemed that these *ruses de guerre*—all perfectly permissible by the rules of war—would be successful. Firing opened again, however, from the north bank, but was still somewhat hesitant. Using her brightest lamp, the leading craft, Motor Gun Boat 314, made the international sign for ships being fired on by friendly forces. The firing once more died away; "another six minutes and the *Campbeltown* would be home".

By then she had passed the heaviest batteries, and nothing but a lucky hit on the bridge or steering-gear would cause her to miss her mark. The seconds slipped by. Then at 01.27 hours the Germans opened fire in earnest. At once *Campbeltown* hauled down the German colours, hoisted the White Ensign and replied. The air was immediately full of tracer, not sailing skywards, as it had a short while before when the bombers of the Royal Air Force had come over in accordance with the plan to bomb the port, but "firing horizontally and at close range". A guard ship anchored in the river was hit repeatedly both by the raiders and her own side, and presently went down. Still the *Campbeltown* forged ahead, and after three or four minutes the

fire of the enemy began to slacken. "This was a triumph",
Ryder, with great truth, remarks, "for the many gun-layers in
the coastal craft and in the *Campbeltown*". The old destroyer had
now increased speed to nineteen knots, and at 01.34 hours, only
four minutes after the time laid down in the plan, she struck the
caisson of the lock gates with a crash. The most important part
of the programme had been achieved at the very outset. . . .

Lieutenant T. A. M. Collier, R.N.V.R., put Motor Launch
457 alongside, and from its decks the party led by Captain
W. H. Pritchard, the chief demolition officer, gained the Mole.
He had with him Lieutenant P. Walton, Second-Lieutenant
W. H. Watson, and five men. Pritchard and Walton were both
killed in circumstances which are not known, but before they
died they seem to have sunk two vessels at the north end of the
lock to the south entrance. Watson and his five men, out-
numbered by the enemy and under fierce fire, fought with vain
gallantry to clear the area of the Old Mole, round which Major
Copland, in accordance with the plan, had succeeded in forming
his perimeter.

By now the situation was very grave, if not desperate. About
fifty men were at headquarters, many of them slightly wounded.
They were protected to a certain degree by a number of railway
trucks from behind which they maintained a brisk fire while
waiting for the arrival of the motor launches. "We were still
feeling quite good," reported Corporal Wheeler, one of them.
"Our attitude towards the whole show was that there was a big
chance it would be a sticky one but that we were quite prepared
for it." Newman is of the same opinion: "Everyone," he said
when he returned from captivity, "was behaving magnificently
and coolly returning the fire with ever-decreasing ammunition."

Seeing that all hope of return by sea was out of the question,
Newman determined to regain England through France and
Spain. He ordered the survivors to split up into small groups,

"not to surrender until all our ammunition had been used, and not to surrender at all if we could help it". He told his men that their best chance was to find their way through the town into the open country, and remarked as he finished: "It's a lovely moonlight night for it". His one anxiety was lest the party should be still near the Old Mole when the five tons of explosive in the bows of the *Campbeltown* went off. The men moved off towards the town, and eventually reached it by crossing an iron bridge with the bullets ricocheting off the girders. . . .

But behind the retreating remnants of this gallant force and of the survivors of No. 2 Commando penned in their *café* at La Baule, there remained, when dawn broke on 29 March, the aged *Campbeltown,* stuck "fast in the dock gates". From dawn onwards she was visited by a number of German officers, of whom about forty presently collected upon her decks. Some four hundred other ranks assembled on the dockside and passed the time pleasantly enough in gazing at the destroyer and debating the reasons which had induced the English to ram her into the gates. Towards noon they received an abrupt and lethal answer to their speculations. The five tons of explosive in her bows went up. All on board and the onlookers on the quayside were killed and, according to the delighted inhabitants of St. Nazaire, their tripes festooned the neighbouring houses for two days.

At that explosion panic seized the German troops, and had hardly quietened down when at 16.30 hours on the next day another heavy explosion shook the neighbourhood of the dock. This was caused by a delayed-action torpedo fired by Sub-Lieutenant R. C. M. V. Wynn, R.N.V.R., who, in command of Motor Torpedo Boat 74, had been ordered to put his torpedoes into the U-boat pens if he could. He had been able to fire them through the Old Entrance, and it was one of these which exploded sixty hours later. A second torpedo went off about 17.30, and this final explosion completed the demoralization of the German troops, who for some hours lost all control of themselves. The workers in the dock area were leaving from their day's toil by the only bridge left—that across the northern lock gates of the Forme Ecluse. Sentries sought to bar their way, but the workmen, most of whom were French, forced a passage and reached the bridge which crosses the lock joining the Bassin St. Nazaire with the Bassin Penhouet. Here they encountered another barrier, and here the German guards opened fire upon them. The shooting, which endured for some time, was indiscriminate, and nearly three hundred French workers lost their lives. To these must be added a number of gallant French civilians shot for attacking Germans in the mistaken view that the raid was the prelude to invasion. Among them, however, was not included the old lady aged eighty who, it is related, dropped a flower-pot on the head of a passing German soldier. It was impossible to convey a warning to the inhabitants, or during the raid to make it clear to them that the operation was but a raid and nothing more. The Frenchmen who died that day died as much for their country and for the Allied cause as any who perished in battle. German casualties were still heavier, for by then so great was the panic among the troops that they saw Commando soldiers everywhere, and mistaking workmen of the Todt organization in khaki denims for their late aggressors, shot them down ruthlessly. The panic spread farther inland, and at Nantes the wives and mistresses of German officers ran wildly into the streets screaming that the invasion of Europe had begun.

The cost of the raid was thirty-four officers and one hundred and fifty-one ratings of the Royal Navy killed or missing; and thirty-four officers and one hundred and seventy-eight other ranks from Nos. 2, 3, 5, 6, 9 and 12 Commandos, but mostly from No. 2 Commando. "Taking into consideration the extreme vulnerability of the coastal craft," wrote Admiral Sir Charles Forbes, G.C.B., D.S.O., who was in general command of the operation, "neither the losses in men nor material can be considered excessive for the results achieved." Of those left behind, five—Corporal Wheeler, Lance-Corporals Douglas, Howarth, and Sims, and Private Harding—reached England through France and Spain. The story of the journey made by Wheeler and Sims well illustrates the hardihood and resource of men trained in the Commandos, and the gallantry of the French civilian population, who risked their lives to save them.

Wheeler belonged to a demolition party, and, with Sims, broke away on the orders of Colonel Newman. Presently they found themselves alone in the middle of a street. They entered a house and, summoning all his French, Wheeler said with emphasis to one of its inhabitants: "*La porte arrière; nous voulons escaper!*" The back door was indicated. They went through it and it was shut behind them. They then found themselves confronted by a wall about ten feet high, which they climbed with the help of a pile of logs, and jumped down into a public garden. As it was now getting light and they could see Germans moving up and down, they beat a retreat, and after climbing a succession of walls, dividing private gardens one from the other, reached a newly-built house with an opening about eighteen inches high in one of the walls at ground level. They crawled in and lay there throughout the day, hearing sporadic bursts of small arms fire and the great explosion of the *Campbeltown*. While lying there they made plans in whispers for their long march. "About midnight," reported Wheeler after his return to England, "we crawled out of the hole into bright moonlight. It looked like daylight. We thought we had a pretty fair chance of not being spotted. We climbed over the wall into a street, guiding ourselves roughly by means of the stars and the moon. We made our way along various side streets, keeping close in to the houses. We heard some Jerries singing in a house and wanted to go in and empty our pistols into the party, but thought we had better not. Soon afterwards we struck the main road out of St. Nazaire. We walked along the side, taking it in turns to lead. We went some two and a half miles along the road, and presently got well out of the town. During this time we did not meet a soul."

Presently they found a partly-used haystack and crept into a hole in it. Here they were discovered by a French farmer who took them to a nearby hamlet where they were fitted out with civilian clothes: short black coats and ready striped trousers, "in which," said Corporal Wheeler, "we looked like disreputable bank clerks". Money was collected for them, the village miser being compelled by public opinion to contribute two hundred francs, and they were told to walk in a south-easterly direction, to wait every day until dusk and then to approach any farmhouse they could see, provided it was isolated. They were assured that the farmers who dwelt in them would help them. This prophecy proved entirely accurate. For thirteen days they crossed France, put up each night at a different farmhouse, where after the first shock of surprise they were most hospitably received. "In many of them," recounted Wheeler, "the farmer and his wife would give up their great double bed for us to sleep in, and would regale us on roast chicken and good bottled wine".

They found their way by means of the maps hanging in each farmhouse and forming part of a yearly calendar distributed by a well-known firm manufacturing farm implements. On the fourteenth day they reached the River Loire, which at that time formed the boundary between occupied and unoccupied France. This they swam precisely at noon, while the farmer with whom they had stayed the night before furnished a diversion to distract the German guard on the bridge. He sent his two daughters on bicycles across it at the precise moment when the guard was being changed, and the two girls, entering into the spirit of the game, were careful to display as much of their comely legs they could. So distracted were the guards by this unexpected vision and by the business of marching and countermarching as the sentries were changed, that they had no eyes for the two naked Commando soldiers swimming the stream a hundred yards away. Once on the farther bank they hid among some alders, to which the French girls came bearing their clothes. They pushed forward to their next adventure, an encounter with a gendarme of Vichy France. He demanded identity papers which they could not produce, and Wheeler confessed that he was an English soldier from St. Nazaire. At this the gendarme became very angry and took them to the nearest police post where they met several of his comrades. "He had a very villainous face," reported Wheeler, "and I thought we were for it, especially when they locked the door. So we were, I suppose," he added, "for each in turn wrung us warmly by the hand and kissed us on both cheeks before helping us on our way."

In due course, with the aid of an old French count whom they discovered digging his garden "in order to forget the state of the world," they reached Toulouse, where they fell into the expert hands of Mademoiselle Dissard, the famous "Françoise", who saw them safely across the Pyrenees to Spain, and thence by Gibraltar to England.

The results achieved by the raid on St. Nazaire were very considerable. The great dry dock was put out of action for the rest of the war, and the Germans were compelled to build a sand barrier at its mouth to prevent the waters of the Loire from entering it. The *Tirpitz* remained in Norwegian waters and found her end there when, in September, 1944, the 12,000-lb. bombs dropped by Lancasters of No. 617 and No. 9 Squadrons capsized her near Tromsöe.

By common consent, among those who served in the Commandos, the raid on St. Nazaire was the most gallant of all. Victoria Crosses were awarded to five who took part in it. They went to Commander Ryder, Lieutenant-Commander Beattie, and, posthumously, to Able Seaman Savage of the Royal Navy; and to Colonel Newman and, posthumously, to Sergeant Durrant, the first of No. 2 Commando, the second of No. 1.

"The outstanding gallantry and devotion to duty of this fearless officer," runs a passage of the citation referring to Newman, "his brilliant leadership and initiative were largely responsible for the success of this operation." These words might with equal truth be applied to any and every man who took part in it. In the annals of the Royal Navy and of the Army, indeed in the annals of war itself, there is to be found no braver action than the battle fought that moonlit night among the wide docks and tall warehouses of the port of St. Nazaire.

The Red Beret

by HILARY ST. GEORGE SAUNDERS

"The Red Beret" is the emblem of the Parachute Regiment, whose history between 1940 and 1945 covers fields from Samos and Sicily to Normandy and the Rhine. It was at Arnhem—that superb failure which, like Dunkirk, almost glows with the glory of victory—that the unit touched its peak of bravery.

The late Hilary St. George Saunders, once Librarian to the House of Commons, had great talent for literary tension. He wrote (in collaboration as "Francis Beeding") a whole series of "thrillers"; but with the outbreak of war, his pen joined up. Pamphlet after Government pamphlet—The Battle of Britain was the first and, perhaps, the greatest of them—poured out; and, towards the end of his life, he wrote two regimental histories which may stand as models of their kind.

A T 09.30 on 17 September, a Sunday, the 1st Battalion[1] left Grimsthorpe Castle in lorries bound for Grantham airfield. Mile after mile went by, and no dispatch riders appeared to cancel the operation. Parachutes had been drawn an hour before—a member of "T" Company resolutely refusing one marked "Dummy"—and harness fitted, and the men were in the highest spirits. "It was a perfect summer day. All the planes were lined up in the bright sunshine . . . the men lay on the ground beside them, resting on their parachutes, eating haversack rations." With the order to put on parachutes appeared the battalion joker, "Guv." Beech, the physical training sergeant, who walked down to the line of men wearing "his well-known opera

[1] Of the Parachute Regiment.

hat which he kept taking off *à la* Winston Churchill", and bowing to left and right.

The 2nd Battalion boarded its aircraft in similar conditions at Salthy, and so did the 3rd Battalion.

The journey was uneventful. "Once in the air," writes one who dropped with the 1st Battalion that day, "one could see an endless line of Dakotas behind. One could catch glimpses of fighters diving about round the convoy." They came from the 8th U.S. Army Air Force, which provided continuous and most efficient protection, and which, together with the 9th American Army Air Force, attacked anti-aircraft guns which opened up upon the main stream of Dakotas when it reached the Dutch coast. In the van were twelve Stirlings carrying six officers and a hundred and eighty men of the 21st Independent Parachute Company under the command of Major B. A. Wilson. They constituted the pathfinder force, whose duty it was to lay out the various aids and indications on the dropping zone. "I shall always remember," says Wilson, a man then in his forties, "that first flight on that lovely Sunday morning. I sat with the pilot as we flew in over the Dutch coast. Everything looked so peaceful. There were cows feeding quietly in the fields and peasants going about their work. Not a sign of fighting or war. Not a glimpse of the enemy. I had just said to the pilot, 'This seems a pretty quiet area. Suppose we get out here', when, before he could answer, a number of shells burst round the aircraft. . . . A few minutes later he wished me good luck as I sailed down to the glorious uncertainty of the welcome I should receive as one of the first parachute troops to enter German-occupied Holland. . . . The ensuing half-hour while we waited for the main force to drop was, to say the least of it, interesting."

The interest for Wilson and his men lay in accepting the surrender of some fifteen frightened Germans. During the drop two men were hit, one in his ammunition pouches, the other in his haversack. Neither was hurt. Punctually on time came the Dakotas and a moment later the members of the pathfinder force could see "the blue field of the sky suddenly blossom with the white flowers of the parachutes". The drop of the 1st Brigade was more successful than anything which had so far been achieved by the airborne forces of either side in the war, even during an exercise. Nearly 100 per cent. arrived at the right time and place. By 15.00 hours the units were ready and prepared to move. All had prospered marvellously, but now came the first check. The Air Landing Reconnaissance Squadron could not attempt the planned *coup de main* against the bridge, for the few gliders that failed to arrive were unfortunately those carrying the transport. It fell, therefore, to the 2nd Battalion under Frost,[2] that veteran of Bruneval, North Africa and Sicily, to seize the bridge. His simple plan was for "A" Company in the van to move straight to the main bridge, while "C" Company, following in its rear, was to seize the railway bridge if it was still intact, pass over it and attack the main bridge from the south. To "B" Company, coming last of all, was allotted the capture of the pontoon bridge, if it existed, and, if it did not, the seizure of some high ground called Den Brink, which controlled the entrance to Arnhem from the west. . . .

The force at the bridge under Frost's command now amounted to between three and four hundred men. With dawn came German patrols, including a latrine squad. The latrine lorry was knocked out and the others moved "somewhat aimlessly up and down the road in front of us. Presently the drivers seemed to hesitate. They had seen our ugly eyes looking at them from the windows." Bombs and machine-gun fire killed them all save two, who were captured badly wounded. Hardly had these bewildered Germans been dealt with when the look-outs on the bridge reported that a German convoy had assembled on the farther end and seemed about to rush Frost's position. There ensued, he said afterwards, "the most lovely battle you have ever seen. Sixteen half-track vehicles and armoured cars

[2]Lieut.-Col. J. D. Frost, D.S.O., M.C.

advanced. There they were, these awful Boches, with their pot helmets sticking out. When we dealt with them they smoked and burned in front of us almost to the end of the battle. I believe they belonged to the 9th Reconnaissance Squadron." They were destroyed by Hawkins grenades, an anti-tank gun and Piats. Some reached the school, where Lieutenant D. R. Simpson, M.C., Royal Engineers, with his sappers, provided them with a warm welcome. The school was in shape a square horseshoe, the ends of the two arms being about ten yards from the road. As the German vehicles went by "Corporal Simpson and Sapper Perry, whose conduct that day was outstanding, stood up and fired straight into the half-tracks". The driver of one half-track, seeing what had happened to those who had preceded him, pulled out to the right along the asphalt path running beneath the windows of the school. "His vehicle did not get far before it was hit; its crew climbed out and sought the cover of bushes, but were killed before reaching them."

Much heartened by this small but not insignificant victory, Frost and his men continued to hold their positions under a shower of light shells and mortar bombs, which grew slowly but steadily heavier and began to cause casualties. They were treated by Captain James Logan, D.S.O., Royal Army Medical Corps, of the 16th Parachute Field Ambulance, whose labours were as skilful as they were indefatigable. This fire came mostly from the north and east, from somewhere, that is, in Arnhem. Frost's main fear at that time was that the Germans would obtain a foothold on the southern end of the bridge, and to prevent this he strengthened the number of light and medium machine-guns established in the upper stories of the houses he had occupied during the night. Their fire was returned by 20-mm. and 40-mm. guns, effective weapons which presently set several buildings on fire and knocked down others. Unfortunately the houses which gave the best field of fire over the bridge were made of wood, and these began to burn. . . .

By the end of the first twenty-four hours' fighting the position was this: Frost, with a mixed force, including the 2nd Battalion, was holding the northern end of the bridge and had successfully repelled all attacks; his casualties, however, were increasing, and he was in urgent need of reinforcements. These the 1st and 3rd Battalions were trying to supply and in so doing had been fought almost to a standstill. The strength of the 1st had fallen to about a hundred men, that of the 3rd was little better. . . .

The drops and the glider landings of the second lift were as successful as those of the day before. Once more the R.A.F. and American crews had performed their task with skill. On this occasion one of them showed that type of resolution which makes a man faithful unto death. Over the dropping zone a Dakota with sixteen parachutists on board was hit and set on fire. "Suddenly a little orange flame appeared on the port wing," notes witness. "I watched the plane gradually lose height and counted the bodies baling out. They all came out, although the last two were too low for comfort. But the crew stayed in the plane and flew straight, the flames getting larger and larger, till eventually it flew into the ground". . . .

As the autumn day waned the 10th Battalion found itself unable to hold on any longer and began slowly to withdraw. Queripel,[3] cut off with a small party of men, took cover in a ditch. In addition to the wound in his face, he had now been wounded in both arms. He and his men lined the ditch to cover the withdrawal of the remainder of the battalion. By then they were short both of weapons and ammunition, having but a few Mills bombs, rifles and their personal pistols. German infantry were very near and more than once their stick bombs landed in the ditch, only to be flung back in their faces by the vigilant Queripel. The position became more and more untenable, but he waited until the last moment before he ordered those of his

[3]The late Captain L. E. Queripel, V.C.

men still alive to leave while he covered their withdrawal with the aid of such grenades as remained. "That was the last occasion on which he was seen." His gallantry earned him a posthumous Victoria Cross. . . .

In this heavy fighting the brigadier and those with him took their full share. "My brigade headquarters," wrote Hackett[4] months later when he had returned from Holland, "with its clerks, signallers, Intelligence section and batmen, was holding the centre of our line as a unit. They were a splendid lot. The signallers were mostly Cheshire yeomen, the clerks were also 'foundation members' for the most part and in the close-quarter fighting in the woods on 19 and particularly 20 September did brilliantly under Staff-Sergeant Pearson, the chief clerk, one of the bravest men at really hand-to-hand fighting and one of the soundest in the brigade. . . . I found myself on 20 September as 'a broken-down cavalryman' (Urquhart's[5] phrase) leading little bayonet rushes in the very dirty stuff the brigade had to contend with before we made contact with the division, and I was impressed with the stout hearts and accurate grenade throwing of the brigade Intelligence section, particularly after the Intelligence officer (Captain Blundell) was shot and killed at about twenty yards range on the same morning."

Before recounting the last stand at Oosterbeek, what happened to Frost and the 2nd Battalion must first be recorded. That Monday night, the 18th, which began in flame and smoke from the burning houses, gradually grew quieter, until soon after midnight "there was absolute silence, or so it seemed to me," said Frost, "for some hours". The commander of the defence was able at last to snatch some sleep. Up till then he had had but half an hour, and had sustained himself with cups of tea

[4]Brig. J. W. Hackett.
[5]Major-General R. E. Urquhart, Commanding British 1st Airborne Division.

and an occasional nip of whisky. Before dawn he had had to issue an order bringing sniping to an end, for ammunition was running low and would have to be kept for warding off the attacks which the enemy was bound soon to launch with increasing severity. The bridge was still covered by the guns of the 1st Air Landing Light Regiment under Lieutenant-Colonel W. F. K. Thompson, Royal Artillery, but these were their only support. "It became more and more difficult to move," recounts Frost, "for the Boche were tightening their grip, though they made no effort to close with us. By then the number of wounded was very great, but the number of killed small."

The men at the bridge held on throughout that day, buoyed up by rumours, first that the 1st and 3rd Battalions were at hand, and then in the later afternoon by the news that the South Staffordshires and the 11th Battalion were fighting their way towards them. It was a day of heavy mortaring and shelling by tanks which had crept up to a position close to the river bank. Towards noon Captain A. Franks went out against them, and scored three hits with the last three Piat bombs. The German tanks clattered away out of range and did not return. At dusk, however, a Tiger tank appeared and shelled in turn each house still held by the parachutists. Among the casualties caused by this fire was Father Egan, M.C., who had served with the brigade from the outset, and Major A. D. Tatham-Warter. They were both hit, but both remained with those still fighting and refused to go below to the cellars.

During this day the conduct of Trooper Bolton of the 1st Air Landing Reconnaissance Squadron was particularly noteworthy for the calmness with which he manned his Bren gun and refused to be parted from it. "He hated the thought of anyone using it but himself," says Captain Bernard Briggs, the staff captain at brigade headquarters, who had been at the bridge from the beginning, "and would wake from a cat-nap at any moment and leap to it ready to fire". Lieutenant P. J. Burnett, of the brigade headquarters defence platoon, showed much courage and ingenuity when he succeeded in destroying "a troublesome tank single-handed with grenades". He was to earn the Medaille Militaire Willemswoorde, the Dutch Victoria Cross.

Night fell and it seemed to Frost, looking uneasily over his shoulder, that the whole town of Arnhem was on fire, including two large churches. "I never saw anything more beautiful than those burning buildings."

By now the defenders of the bridge were being driven from the houses as they caught fire. Their method of moving from one to another was, whenever possible, to "mousehole" their way from house to house in conditions which grew steadily worse. During this tedious dusty method of moving from one position to another Lieutenant Simpson succeeded in disabling a tank close to the house in which he was posted. Its crew got out and "crept along the wall till they came to a halt beneath the window where I was crouching. I dropped a grenade on them and that was that. I held it for two seconds before I let it drop."

Two things were of particular concern: the lack of water, and the breakdown of the wireless sets, which made it impossible to keep in touch with the rest of the division except by means of the civilian telephone lines. These, manned by the Dutch Resistance, continued to play a part to the end, the operators paying for their fortitude with their lives. Frost had no continuous means of communicating with the battalions who he still hoped were on their way to his relief, but could sometimes speak with divisional headquarters. Perhaps the reinforcements were not very distant. They might even be within earshot. "During a lull we yelled 'Waho Mahommed'," says Briggs, "hoping there would be some reply. But none came. Then we tore down wallpaper to make a megaphone six feet long, through which we shouted words and epithets that could only be British." But there was still no reply.

Dawn on Wednesday, the 20th, shone on Frost, still clinging with difficulty to the north-west end of the bridge, but able to prevent the Germans crossing it. But now his personal good fortune was to desert him. During the morning he was badly wounded in the leg, and Major C. H. F. Gough, M.C., Reconnaissance Squadron, assumed command, but still referred major decisions to Frost, while Tatham-Warter, "whose conduct was exemplary even amid so much gallantry", took over what remained of the 2nd Battalion. In reporting these changes to the divisional commander at Hartestein, Gough referred to himself as "the man who goes in for funny weapons", so that no German or collaborator listening-in on the town exchange which he was using would be able to identify him.

The area occupied by the parachute troops grew smaller and smaller, though they continued to control the approaches to the bridge. Conspicuous among them at this stage was Lieutenant Grayburn[6] of "A" Company. Early in the action, in leading the unsuccessful attack on the south end of the bridge, he had been hit in the shoulder, but continued to lead his men and was the last to withdraw. He then established his platoon in a very exposed house whose position was vital to the defence. In this he held out until 19 September, when it was set on fire, having repelled all attacks, including those made by tanks and self-propelled guns. Re-forming his depleted force, he was still able to maintain the defence and on 20 September led a series of fighting patrols, whose activities so galled the enemy that tanks were brought up again. Only then did Grayburn retreat and, even so, was still able to strike back. At the head of another patrol he drove off the enemy, thus allowing others to remove the fuses from the demolition charges which the Germans had succeeded in placing under the bridge. In so doing he was again wounded, but still would not leave the fight. Eventually, that evening he was killed by the fire of a tank. In his conduct "he showed an example of devotion to duty which can seldom have been equalled", and was awarded a posthumous Victoria Cross.

[6] Lieut. J. H. Grayburn, V.C.

By the evening of that day all the buildings near the bridge had been burnt down except the U-shaped school. This now caught fire and all attempts to put it out failed. Captain J. Logan, D.S.O., the medical officer, who, with Captain D. Wright, M.C., had been tireless in tending the wounded, therefore informed Gough that he must surrender them if he wished to save them from being burnt or roasted alive in the cellars. Just after dark, under a flag of truce, the enemy picked up many of the wounded, including Frost, who had been expecting his fate and had thrown away his badges. A moment before, Wicks, his batman, had taken leave of him and gone back to the fight. He, too, was soon afterwards badly wounded.

Gough and those still unwounded continued to resist. Though ammunition was practically at an end, they nevertheless succeeded in delivering an attack at dawn on 21 September in an attempt to retake some of the houses. It failed and what remained of the 2nd Battalion scattered in small parties in an endeavour to find their way to the XXX Corps, which they had awaited so long and so vainly. At last the bridge was once more in German hands.

In this action the 2nd Battalion had been wiped out; but seldom can a fighting unit of any army in any age have had so glorious an end. For thrice the length of time laid down in its orders it had held a bridge against odds which were overwhelming from the beginning. Buoyed up by hope and by frequent messages that relief or support was on the way, either at the hands of the rest of the 1st Parachute Brigade and later the 4th Brigade, or from XXX Corps moving up from Nijmegen, when that hope was deferred, the hearts of its officers and men were not sick. They continued to fight, and only ceased to fire when their ammunition was gone and their wounded, now the great majority, faced with a fearful and unnecessary death. The conduct of the 2nd Battalion at the Bridge at Arnhem is more than an inspiration or an example; it was the quintessence of all those qualities which the parachute soldier must possess and display if he is to justify his training and the trust reposed in him. So great a spirit in evidence every moment of those three September days and nights can be overcome only by weight of numbers. That, and that alone, was the cause of their glorious defeat.